The Word in Real Time

AN INTERACTIVE DAILY DEVOTIONAL BOOK

Scripture references taken from the NIV Bible.

To my ~~friends~~ —
God bless you richly.
Kathy Slamp
II Cor. 4:7

By KATHY SLAMP

Dedication...

to David

Forty years...
my husband, my friend,
and my companion.

Truly a man after God's heart.

Other Books by Kathy Slamp...

Walking Through Life Without
Stumbling Over Yourself

Little House in the Arctic

You Might Be a Pastor's Wife If...

Reflection Profiles (A Bible Study Series)

Mastering Women's Ministries (A Manual)

Table of Contents...

Forward...

The Word in Real Time is a daily devotional book. As devotional books go, it is unique. I have followed the International Bible Society systematic Bible reading plan. Each day there is a suggested reading from the Old Testament, the New Testament, and the Psalms or Proverbs. The devotional for the day is taken from the readings for that specific day.

The Word in Real Time becomes, then, a companion for your daily Bible reading and/or a devotional insight for the day. You can begin on any calendar day and follow the readings through for a year, or you can just pick up the book at any given time for an inspirational or devotional thought. At the end of that period, you will have read the entire Bible, and you have a devotional that accompanies your reading for each day as well.

The Old Testament books have been rearranged somewhat to make the reading more interesting and avoid endless genealogies. The New Testament readings continue from Matthew to Revelation, and the Psalms and Proverbs each go from the first to the last chapters. All Scripture references are from the New International Version translation of the Bible.

To the Reader...

I have been captivated again and again about the concept of *real time*. The Word of God is as current as today's newspaper. Like the events of our lives are new each day, so the events of the Word were "real" in the lives of the patriarchs and apostles. Moses, for instance, had no idea what God was doing at the Red Sea. He just believed and followed God. It was *real time*—the present—for Moses when he stepped up to the Red Sea, held out his rod, and God parted the waters. He had no more idea that day how God was working than you and I have for each new day. It was definitely a "real time" experience for the Apostle Paul on the road to Damascus. The relevance of "real time" is what keeps the Bible alive and vital in daily living.

Being consistent in reading the Bible is a struggle. Like many others, over the years I have tried various ways to stay "in the Word." The concept for this book awakened me many nights. As overwhelming as it was, the thought would not leave my mind. After several days of struggling with this monumental task, I knew the idea was from the Lord. The awareness that this book is His kept me going through countless hours of reading, writing, rewriting, and editing. My prayer is that *The Word in Real Time* will be an instrument that will encourage consistent Bible reading as well as being a daily inspiration for your life. God bless you richly as you read *The Word in Real Time*.

Kathy Slamp, author

January

Genesis and Job 1-18
Matthew 1-21
Psalm 1-18 and Proverbs 1-3

My Prayer Time for January...

T hanksgiving _____
_____
_____
_____

I ntercession _____
_____
_____

M inistry _____
_____
_____
_____

E ncouragement _____
_____
_____
_____

Everything New

Recently, we held our brand new grandson. What a thrill! Everything about him is new. His body and looks are new; his life is new; his personality is new; his future is new. He has no past, and he has no scars. He's perfect. We have no expectations of him except that he will grow. Is a baby a blessing? I should say. Everyone talks about *who* the new baby looks like. The overwhelming consensus with this baby is that he looks like his father—our son.

When God created our world, it was all brand new; it reflected the Father. Nothing was messed up; it was perfect. Oops! And then He put man in charge. We must admit it. Man messed up God's brand new world. No one would think about marring a new baby. No, we take special care of him or her. But, we have a way of taking this life and world God gives us and messing them up—just like Adam and Eve did.

A new year always reminds us that there's hope for the future. The first Psalm promises that the Lord *watches over the way of the righteous.* We never know about a new day—much less a new year. As we stay close to Him, He keeps us safe, each day is brand new, and grace for that day is sufficient. The Father expects one thing of you and me this year, and that is that we will grow in Him and grow closer to Him. All year long you and I can reflect the resemblance of the heavenly Father. That's all the world really needs from us.

My resolution: Grow closer to Him this year.

Jesus is an "Event"

One of my first tasks in a new year is putting away the nativity scene. Actually, I have two of them, and they're lovely and sentimental. They portray a sweet story of the little Lord Jesus' arrival as a helpless baby who was really the Savior of the world. These scenes are beautiful, but not totally historically accurate.

Two years after the taxation that forced Joseph to take Mary miles from home in her ninth month, and two years after the angels and the innkeeper and the shepherds and the farm animals, here came the "wise men." These men were *important:* They were rich; they were educated; and they were widely traveled. Their arrival in Jerusalem created such an event that Herod himself invited them to visit his palace.

The Magi complete the story of Jesus' birth. They remind us that Christ is for the humble, but He is also the Lord of all. Herod didn't invite the shepherds or the innkeeper to his palace. It was his selfish, paranoid heart that prompted him to invite the Magi to visit him. Herod knew that if *these* men of means and knowledge would travel hundreds of miles for over two years to meet a baby, that this baby and the super nova Israel witnessed two years earlier were a pretty bit deal.

Jesus is still an event, and He still stirs the hearts of good and evil men. When Jesus truly comes into a life, He makes a difference. There are lights and bells and whistles. People know. People sit up and listen. Allow each day to be an event as Jesus lives through your life.

Don't Miss the Event.

The "Invisible" Shield

An old ad talked about an "invisible" shield that was guaranteed to protect teeth against decay, root damage, or even tartar. If we only used this brand, our dental woes would be over forever. If that were only true. God is big on guarantees; He calls them covenants. Man is big on making messes. Enter Noah. Way back then, man messed up. God had had enough when He saw that *every inclination of the thoughts of his heart was only evil all the time* (Gen. 6:5b). But, He promised Noah's family that they would be spared the pending disaster.

You know the story. God instructed Noah to build an ark, giving him exact dimensions and types of wood. Nothing was left to speculation. Nothing, that is, except "what was a flood?" Until that time, the earth was watered by dew; there had never been rain. Noah didn't understand God's instructions, but he did what God told him just the same. Building the ark took several years—certainly enough time for Noah's neighbors to laugh, scoff, and tease.

God always has the final word, and He always prevails. While Noah's smart aleck neighbors taunted him with jabs like: "How long can you tread water?" Noah and the boys kept on building. Despite the taunting, they remained consistent. At last the rains came, and now Noah's neighbors wanted to be his "new best friend." It was too late. Like God kept Noah and his sons during the difficult days of ark construction, He can keep you in any situation. He is indeed *a shield around us.* He is our protection, our defender, our advocate, and our salvation.

Allow Him to be your shield.

On Being Swamped

I am swamped! We say it all the time, and it computes. In today's world this colloquialism is a no-brainer. Everyone has been there, and often. We all understand the concept of "swamped." We're under life; we're suffocating; we have just too much to do; we're going down for the last time; our family responsibilities are overwhelming. The beat goes on.

Perhaps no one in history understood the concept of "swamped" as much as Noah. Talk about floundering and being afloat with no land in sight. He was overwhelmed with the care of animals and families all cooped up together day after endless day. Just when Noah thought he couldn't take it any longer, God showed up with a rainbow and a promise. He's like clockwork; He never fails. God doesn't "just show up" at the last minute to remind us He's God. He's there all the time. We are just too "swamped" to recognize His omnipresence.

When Jesus was tempted, He answered Satan: *Don't put the Lord your God to the test* (Matt. 4:7). Noah might have said the same thing to his family. After a few months, I imagine they were getting a little testy and began telling old Dad that maybe they would have been better to perish with all the others.

Three events remind us of God's covenant: The raven and the dove who returned with the olive branches, and the rainbow. In the middle of your "swampedness" God has a dove, a rainbow, and a promise. Claim your promise regardless of today's circumstances.

God has a rainbow and a promise.

A City on a Hill

There is a high mesa near Nazareth that at first glance appears insignificant. The first time I saw this inconsequential piece of real estate, our guide said, "Do you see that bluff?" In deference to her, we all gawked. "At the time of Christ," she continued, "there was a village there; Jesus referred to it:" *let your light shine before men, that they may see your good deeds and give you credit and recognition and maybe put it in the newspaper or on radio or TV."*

Woops. That's not what Jesus said. But many of us act like He might have said that. After all, we're human. We need strokes and recognition and credit. Woops again. The entirety of the beatitudes goes cross-grain to human nature. Jesus is teaching us the core of the surrendered life. We are blessed when we mourn; we are blessed when we respond meekly; we are blessed when we show mercy to those who don't deserve mercy. That's just not human.

The world is looking for someone and something that responds differently. That's what Jesus is teaching. We really aren't of this world. Our responses and reactions come from a different world. When something "bad" happens to us, the world watches to see if we are handling it differently. They're checking us out to see if what we say works in the day to day pressures of this world. Jesus said it like this: *...so that they may see your good deeds, and praise your Father in heaven.* It's simply not about us. It's all about Him. You are indeed a "city on a hill." Let that phrase permeate your consciousness and your heart. People are watching. You are...

A City on a Hill! A City on a Hill!

You Have Heard it Said...

When I was a girl, my dad reminded me often that the *letter* of the law wasn't the most essential thing; it was the *spirit* of the law. It's easy to obey the letter of the law. Not particularly fun, but easy. Do this. Do that. Don't do this. Don't do that. It's all so very black and white. It's so simple to dictate what others should do.

When you are living by the letter of the law, it's easy to judge. Many of us who were "raised in the church" have this down pat. In theory, we know how a Christian is *supposed* to look, how he is *supposed* to talk, where he's *supposed* to go, and what he's *supposed* to do. Let's face it. Some of us are terrific Pharisees. But we can't see others' hearts.

Jesus loathes this type of thought process. It goes counter-balance to all His teachings. We cling to our laundry list of offenses: don't murder, don't commit adultery, don't divorce, don't break an oath, take an "eye for an eye." Jesus doesn't throw these out; they still are sins, but that is the "letter of the law."

Jesus law, His ruling, His commandment, His edict—whatever you choose to call it—goes deeper than words recorded in the Bible or written in law books. He gently reminds us that it is the attitude of the heart that ultimately matters. Each law has a core—an essence—a "spirit" as my dad called it. When we get that, it takes the harshness and cruelty out of our attitudes toward others' sins. Jesus forgave. He forgives each of us. His example is clear. And difficult.

Is it the "letter" or the "Spirit" that you follow?

Righteous Credit

Credit can be a bane or a blessing. We need it to purchase a house, a car, college tuition, virtually everything. But credit can eat us alive. It's all in *how* we use it. Abram understood the concept of forgiveness and fairness, and God honored him for it. He was a peaceable, melancholy sole who seemingly allowed Lot to "walk all over him" when Lot chose the better land at their separation.

When Lot was in trouble, Abram wasn't compelled or even required to rescue him from the wickedness of Sodom and Gomorrah, yet Abram went the second mile: *He recovered all the goods and brought back his relative Lot and his possessions* (Gen. 14:16). Abram could have worried about his personal danger, but he chose a different route: *he believed God and it was credited to him as righteousness* (Gen. 15:6).

Jesus understood credit and debt when He taught the disciple to pray: if we want to be forgiven, we must forgive. Generations before the Lord's Prayer, Abram grasped Jesus' concept of forgiveness. Abram could have easily dismissed Lot's plea for help with a cursory comment: "When you had the chance, Lot, you took the better land. Now you've botched it up, and you're in trouble. This isn't my problem. Get yourself out of it."

Abram's character wouldn't let him say that. He got it: *For if you forgive men when they sin against you, your heavenly Father will also forgive you. But if you do not forgive men their sins, your Father will not forgive your sins* (Matt. 5:14-15). Do you want to be credited as a righteous person? Practice forgiveness.

What's your credit rating?

Is Anything Too Hard?

There's something about our human nature that automatically sends us down the easy road. Children whine, "It's too hard!" But adults do, too. We're just a little more sophisticated about it. Given time, we become quite adept and skilled with our "reasons" why we didn't accomplish such and such or why a certain life goal was left by the side of the way.

Sarah and Abraham remind us of ourselves. They were old when God promised them a baby. It hurts when someone makes a promise we *know* they can't possibly keep. Abraham and Sarah both laughed at God; who was He kidding? Giving birth was out of the question. Sarah's biological clock was run down. Her ticker was broken! Perhaps a few years earlier this could have happened, but God simply waited a little too long to pull this one off.

God wasn't kidding, and He never is. When He makes us a promise, He can't or won't break it. God knew they laughed and asked them why. And then God Himself proposed this awesome question: *Is anything too hard for the Lord?* (Gen. 18:14a) Abraham and Sarah, you're nailed!

Jesus visited this subject: "Why do you worry?" he queried. "Birds don't worry; flowers don't worry, yet I take care of them I know what you need and when you need it." God was asking Abraham the same thing Jesus is asking us: "If I can create this whole deal—the world and all that's in it. If I can keep it spinning year in and year out, can't I take care of you? Don't worry: *seek first his kingdom and his righteousness, and all these things will be given to you as well* (Matt. 6:33).

Nothing is impossible when you trust Him.

He is Always Willing

We have wicked cities in the world today, but that's not news. I've visited a few of the notorious ones, but the truth is that wickedness can be found in any hamlet, village, town, or city. It's not the city; it's the attitude of the heart that generates wickedness.

Way back when, Sodom and Gomorrah were a mess; immorality was rampant. When angels visited Lot in His home, the Sodomites tried to sleep with them. Can you imagine? Early the next morning, the angels grabbed Lot and his family and literally jerked them out of danger. God was merciful to them because the instant they ran from the city, it was destroyed by fire. God was willing to spare them.

God is always willing to rescue a sincere person. It's faith that sets us free. The New Testament leper spoke for us all, "Lord, if you are willing..." Jesus was touched by the leper's humility, and in turn He touched the leper. His words were short, but poignant: "I am willing!" Of course, He's willing to respond to a broken, contrite heart.

Surprisingly, it's the Roman centurion—the alien—who speaks our language. He saw the crowds; he witnessed the healings; he heard the messages; and he had a need in his home as well. Surely, this Jewish rabbi wouldn't help him, a Roman employee. Gingerly and humbly, the centurion broached the subject of his sick servant to Jesus. Jesus was so touched by his sincere faith and belief that He healed the man's servant. Lot and the centurion and you and I have a lot in common. When He senses a sincere heart, He's always willing to come to our aid.

He knows your sincerity.

Itty-Bitty Faith

We love to read and talk about Abraham and Moses and Elijah and Isaac and Peter and ... These guys were great! Abraham was a giant of faith. Who today would hike up a mountain with his teenage son, bind him, and lay him on a stack of firewood just because God told him to? That's irresponsible. But Abraham did it; we've read the story over and over. Preachers have worn it out with messages about faith. Wonder of all wonders, God did exactly what He said He would do with Isaac. We know the drill.

That was then; this is now. Surely, God doesn't expect us to do "dumb" things like Abraham. The disciples must have felt that way when Jesus fell asleep in their boat. Jesus was there. They weren't reading about Him. They were eating and walking and working with him daily. Suddenly, the disciples found themselves in the middle of a huge storm on the Sea of Galilee. Goody, goody! Here's an opportunity for Jesus to rescue them. Wishful thinking.

These guys were just like us. They knew the stories; they knew Jesus! But, when they got in the middle of a storm, they forgot that He was in their boat. So, they woke Him. When Jesus rubbed the sleep from his eyes, stretched a bit, and got His orientation, He was perturbed. "You woke me over *this*? This storm is nothing. I've been in the back of the boat all along. When I'm in your boat, you're not going down. Don't you get it, O, ye of itty bitty faith?"

He's in your boat.

11

An Angel for the Journey

People are fascinated by angels and the supernatural. Thanks to Clarence from *It's a Wonderful Life*, we know that when a bell rings, "an angel gets his wings." There *really* are angels. The Bible mentions them again and again. They were present at creation; they were there at Christ's birth; and they were in the life of the patriarchs and the saints.

When Abraham was old, he recruited a trusted servant to journey to Mesopotamia and find a wife for Isaac. It was a long and arduous journey, but Abraham made his servant this promise: *He will send his angel before you so that you can get a wife for my son from there* (Gen. 24:7b). What a promise: an angel before you. What a companion for this journey called life.

God kept his promise. We're familiar with the scene by the well when Rebecca came to draw water. We know that God moved on the heart of Abraham's servant and said "this is the girl for Isaac." When Abraham's servant met Rebecca's brother, Laban, he told him about God's promise. *The Lord... will send his angel with you and make your journey a success...* (Gen. 24:41).

Laban's heart was moved by the conviction of Abraham's servant. *This is from the Lord; we can say nothing to you one way or the other.* (Gen. 24: 50). There is nothing else you can say when the angel of the Lord goes before you. God keeps His word and "good stuff" happens. You're not alone on your journey. Angels weren't just for the servants of patriarchs. They are for the servants of God. He will send his angel before you, and you never make the journey alone.

You're never alone—there's an angel nearby.

It's a No-Brainer

Some people honestly think that the Christian life is going to be a "life of ease." Where does this perception come from? It's a myth, and certainly not Biblical. When Jesus called His disciples, He made the conditions for "followership" painfully clear. It's not an easy way. He gives us authority to "drive out evil spirits and heal the sick." That's neat! What a rush of power. Authority! Power! With authority come criticism, hardships, persecution, and responsibility.

Jesus warned that we would be kicked out of people's homes or maybe even out of town. He said people will hand us over to the local authorities for persecution. There will be betrayal at the highest level—family member against family member. And on and on. So, who would want to follow Jesus?

But the rewards! Jesus' injunction to "freely give because we have freely received" is a "no-brainer." *He who stands firm to the end will be saved* (Matt. 10:22b). Saved from what? I'm glad you asked. We don't like to think, talk, or read about it, but whether we recognize it or not, the Bible is clear that there is coming a day of reckoning. There's where the rewards enter. Repeatedly, Jesus tells us to "Fear not." Now, He tells us what we should solemnly fear. *Do not be afraid of those who kill the body but cannot kill the soul. Rather, be afraid of the One who can destroy the soul...* (Matt. 10:28).

It's a "no brainer." Let's stop the complaining and whining about our circumstances in life and focus on the real fear—the fear of not being ready when our time comes.

I want to be ready. It's a No-Brainer!

Cups of Cold Water

We lived in the desert Southwest for five years. On a dry, hot, blistering day when the mercury tips 110 degrees, nothing satisfies like a cup of cold water. It's sweet; it's rejuvenating; it's essential to life. In fact, water is as necessary to life as air. It's vital.

Jesus taught in parables; and often His talk is so paradoxical that we must mull it over just to fathom what He is *really* teaching. What does He mean that if we love our father and mother more than Him, we aren't worthy? What does He mean when He says in losing life, we actually find it? What does He mean when He teaches that when we receive Him, we also receive the Father? And what is He talking about when He mentions a prophet's reward? The answer to any one of these questions could rightfully generate an entire semester of college teaching.

We do, though, understand the concept of giving a cup of cold water. That easily computes. It's not the deep theological questions that cause most of us to struggle. It's the little and simple things. It's the interruptions of life. But what does He teach about the seeming insignificant things like giving a cup of cold water to a fellow pilgrim? He rewards us for the little things. He takes notice when you say a kind word or encourage a lonely person or help a child or someone elderly. The little things are the essence of His character—the root of Christianity.

Little things always matter.

JANUARY

14

Genesis 29-30
Matthew 11:16-30
Psalm 9:7-23

The Baby War

It's an indisputable fact that a baby is a blessing. Whether it's the first or the tenth, a brand new life and what it brings to the family is always something special. There's an inborn sense of pride and desire to protect that flows through us at the sight of this helpless little potentiality. Rich or poor, educated or uneducated, provincial or traveled, babies are blessings.

Jacob had a house full of warring wives. Leah was fruitful, but Rachel—the woman he loved—was barren. After Leah bore Jacob four sons, Rachel manipulated Jacob into sleeping with her servant, Bilhah. Boom. Jacob was now the dad of Dan. Dan's birth only made Leah mad, but now she couldn't get pregnant. No problem. She had a servant as well, and the next thing you know, here came Gad and Asher, sons of Zilpah. Still the war in Jacob's house continued. Leah had two more sons and a daughter. At last! Rachel had a baby— Joseph. Don't you know that Jacob was relieved? Maybe at last there would be peace under his roof.

We shake our heads and chuckle at the seeming childish and ludicrous behavior of the wives of Jacob. But are we really so unlike them? God says clearly, "it is unwise to compare ourselves among ourselves," but we do it anyway. We look around and see someone who we think God has blessed more than us, and it makes us mad. So we try to manipulate the situation, but we only complicate it. God has blessings for us all. It may not be exactly when we think it should happen. Wait. God has special blessings just for you. His time is right. Look to Him—not to the blessings He give others. He has enough for everyone.

There could be a "Joseph" in your future.

The Word in Real Time

Sabbath Day Miracles

What good thing can be said for the Pharisees? Perhaps this: They were consistent: consistent in their cruelty to Jesus, consistent in their efforts to show Him up, and consistent in their disgusting piety.

It was the Sabbath. Everyone knew the laws, the "don'ts," of the Sabbath. The day of rest had become a day of ritualistic drudgery. Any good Jew never worked on the Sabbath, and work could be defined as *anything*. Enter Jesus. He and His disciples were hungry, so they picked some grain to eat. They weren't shopping for groceries; they were just having lunch. The Pharisees wagged their crooked, sacrilegious fingers at Him with a sneer and a "Naughty, naughty" attitude.

Cut Jesus some slack. But no break was forthcoming. Jesus' answer should have stopped them. But, no. They just went looking for new material. When you look for bad, you find it. Right away, they caught Jesus "healing a man." Again, they shook their fingers at him, and again Jesus came back with scripture. He had to be weary of their pettiness, their worship of the law, and their lack of compassion. *How much more valuable is a man than a sheep!* Jesus responded (Matt. 12:12a).

It's easy for our walk to become an endless list of "don'ts," and thus a ritualistic drudgery. How attractive is that? Sure, the laws of God are essential. But that's just it—the laws of God, not the ritualistic interpretations of men. My father taught me that it is the "spirit" of the law that has value, not the "letter" of the law. Thanks, Dad! God's the judge. Let Him deal with people's hearts and their motives. It sure takes a lot off our shoulders, and it makes the journey so much more enjoyable.

He's the final judge. Aren't you glad?

The "Vocabulary" Patrol

A recent Homeland Security directive shocked us all. We are going to be rated *red, yellow, or green* before we are allowed to fly. *Red* just "flat out" doesn't get to fly; *yellow* gets screened, and *green* sails through. What *new* thing will they concoct next?

Whatever you think about this directive, the concept of accountability is NOT new. It's been around since God held Adam and Eve accountable for their disobedience in the garden. Accountability goes back to basics—back to man's beginnings and his relationships with his brothers.

When Jesus healed the demon-possessed man, the Pharisees scoffed when the crowds called Him the *Son of David*. "He's only the prince of demons," they sneered behind their hands as they spoke to one another in hushed stage whispers. But Jesus "knew their thoughts." To paraphrase, Jesus was saying "You can't hide. Your words and your actions reveal the true you." I can imagine that Jesus' words were searing to these self-righteous hypocrites as He literally let loose on them in front of their constituents.

And Jesus' injunction rings in our ears today as well: *Men will have to give an account on the Day of Judgment for every careless word they have spoken. For by your words you will be acquitted, and by your words you will be condemned.* Whether we admit it or not doesn't alter the fact that there will be an accounting. What about today? Will your "vocabulary and action" rating be *red, yellow, or green*?

I want to be allowed to board the plane.

The Pretty Chicken

O*nce there was a pretty chicken...* My brothers and I are going to put these words on Mom's tombstone. When she said them, we all knew immediately what Mother meant. Everyone loves a story. The four little words *once upon a time* kept us out of bed, gave us quality time with an adult, softened the blows of life's lessons, and captivated our attention and imagination. They are magical words.

Jesus was a master storyteller; He recognized the power of a story. But the disciples didn't get it, "Why do you speak to the people in parables?" they asked. Jesus was well-acquainted with the Pharisees' evil hearts. If He were alive today, Jesus would be slapped with a defamation of character law suit by those guys. His amazing stories protected Him while they bore straight through to the issues of man's heart.

Mother's chicken is from a McGuffey Reader ballad about a young chicken that strutted through a farm yard trying to find a playmate. No animal would indulge his whimsies, so in desperation he approached a hen. She explained that she was setting on eggs and couldn't leave. "It won't matter" said the chick, "It's just an egg. What's an egg to me or you?" If we failed to get the message right away, Mother would finish the hen's words: "What's an egg," said old Aunt Dark Hen. "Can it be you do not know that you yourself were in an eggshell just a few short weeks ago? If kind wings had not warmed you, you would not be out today telling hens and geese and turkeys what they ought to do and say." We got the message, and we remembered it. It was powerful, terse, and to the point. Jesus' parables are still some of our best tools in witnessing and living.

Be a story teller.

Mom Always Liked You Best

Tommy and Dickey Smothers made us laugh with that line, but favoritism of one child over the other isn't funny. The Bible is clear that old Jacob loved Joseph more than his other ten sons. Joseph was the first son he had with Rachel, but the other boys were his as well. The first ten were the sons of his youth, but Joseph was the son of his old age. Whatever the "explanation" for favoritism, the results are nearly always catastrophic.

When old dad sent Joseph to his brothers all dressed up in his new coat while they were in their grubbies working, they just couldn't deal with the inequities of it all. They saw his visit as an unbelievable serendipity to put the issue of Joseph to rest once and for all. Dad wouldn't have to know the "true story;" this was a chance to kill the dreamer.

We know the story in its entirety. Everyone erred: Jacob loved one child more than the others (Gen. 37:3); Joseph displayed great immaturity and insensitivity when he bragged about his dreams (Gen. 37:5-7); and the older brothers simply couldn't get past their jealousy (Gen 37:11). Altogether, this was a volatile mix. Something was bound to erupt. Things weren't going to rock along with the *status quo* forever.

We can choose to be hard on any one of the participants in this saga, but the fact remains: "if the shoe fits, wear it!" This story had a good ending, but it was a long time in the making, and a lot of water flowed under the bridge before reconciliation. What a lesson! Whether you're Jacob, or Joseph, or an older brother, there is a lesson here.

If the shoe fits...

19

The Hometown Blues

My husband is from a small town in Southwest Washington. His boyhood home was a dilapidated, rundown house at the end of a dead end street. It wasn't the best part of town in the least. Nothing good could come from that little dirty street. When you turned the corner to David's street, there was another tiny humble home—not more than three or four rooms. On the mail box hung a swinging sign that simply read, *Honeycomb.* This humble home was the boyhood home of Jimmy Rogers. Jimmy recorded *Honeycomb* in the 50s and this popular hit sold over a million records.

Here's my unbiased opinion: That little town needs a sign of its own: "Boyhood home of Jimmy Rogers and David Slamp." Here, two of *my* heroes lived on the very same block! But human nature is unyieldingly inequitable. We fail to recognize the good that is right in our own front yard. If someone is successful, they must be from some place else. After all, we knew "so and so" when we were kids; we goofed around together; we knew their parents' indiscretions; we simply know too much about them.

Jesus faced this dilemma. His evangelistic campaigns were successful. His following was growing. People loved His storytelling; they were amazed by the healings; and they probably were enjoying His continual word war with the Pharisees. In Nazareth, Jesus taught and preached just like He did everywhere else. But the state of affairs was different there. Nazareth was offended by Jesus (Matt. 13:55-57).

Special people are all around us. They may not record a platinum record, or they may not be "famous" as the world sees it. But they're still special. Cut your family and your neighbors and co-workers some slack. It's just possible that they are from Nazareth.

Ordinary people are "important" people.

High Profile Scandals

Daily we read or hear about a professional ball player who gets trapped by his own lust and sense of invincibility; or the politician who thought He was above the law; or an evangelist who thought he was an exception—that *he* would never fall. All these things sadden and disillusion us. There is a quality about others' failings, however, that vindicates us in a twisted kind of way. We sort of line our lives up by their messed up ones and compare: "Look at me. I'm not rich or famous or beautiful or powerful, and yet my life is better than theirs." That's dangerous territory, because the unadulterated truth is that all of us have feet of clay.

What should sadden us more is when good, pure lives are smeared, maligned, devastated, and destroyed. Such was the case with Joseph. His brothers sold him. They actually got money for their own brother. How humiliating could that be? Despite this, he became successful in an alien land—until he refused favors to his boss's wife. What can I say? There is still no fury like that of a woman scorned! Poor Joseph found himself in jail. His leadership was revealed wherever he went, and soon he was interpreting dreams of his incarcerated companions. But, they forget him as well. Joseph had disappeared into a dungeon in a foreign country. Then, Pharaoh had a dream, and someone finally remembered Joseph. At last, Joseph was promoted from jail to a place of high prominence, power, authority, and prestige.

Our best defense is no defense. Our best defense is our lives. Are you a Joseph? Has life been unfair? Did others succeed when you should have? Were half truths and scandalous gossip spread about you? It's not over. Take heart. You're in good company.

God is still in the business of developing Josephs.

21

Risk Takers are Winners

We dismiss excessive people. "They just went overboard over," we say. We warn our teenager: "Don't go overboard with this relationship." Something about speaking these warnings makes us feel controlled and right. But *overboard* isn't always a bad thing. We can learn from risk takers. In truth, once someone succeeds in "overboardness," we admire and herald their exploits. We would never do that, but it's fun to vicariously enjoy others' risk taking.

When the disciples were frightened by the aberration they saw on the water, Peter recognized Jesus' voice: "Lord, if it's you, tell me to come to you on the water." Risk takers see possibilities before they see risks. Peter recognized Jesus; he didn't see or think about the water. When Jesus told him to come, Peter calmly stepped over the edge of the boat and began walking toward the Master.

He was doing pretty well with this "water walking" until a gust of wind burst across his face. "What in the wide world am I doing?" Peter thought. "This is about the dumbest thing I've ever tried; I'm out of the boat, standing on water. This is impossible." And he began to sink. I'll bet the guys in the boat enjoyed the fact that Peter's rush of adrenalin didn't last long. Sensible people like them wouldn't allow themselves to get into such a humiliating situation.

Sensible people don't walk on water. When Jesus climbed into the boat *with* Peter, the disciples recognized the significance of what just occurred in front of them. Do you get it? When God calls you; He'll be there for you. Don't look down and around at the circumstances that could cause you to sink; look up to the One who is enabling you to succeed. Get out of the boat. As long as you stay in the boat, you're only an observer. Be a participant. Be a risk taker.

Go overboard for the Lord.

Blind Guides

Anyone in authority knows that it's prudent not to mess with influential people. Never do or say anything that might stir up a controlling family, or (for heaven's sake) never say a word about those who give most of the money. Don't even go there. This is a basic principle of sane leadership: Don't upset the *status quo;* don't rock the boat; don't upset the apple cart. There could be hell to pay. "Keep it calm, and keep it safe" is the mantra of the day.

Jesus hadn't read the trendy leadership books of His time. He told it like it was. The disciples read all the books, and they feared that He was too frank. "Do you know," they asked Him, "that you offend the Pharisees when you teach that their words make them unclean?" The disciples were protecting Him, but He didn't need protection. The Pharisees strutted and bragged about keeping all the laws of cleanliness. Yet, they shot off their mouths about anything anytime they chose. Harsh and insensitive to others, Jesus hurt *their* feelings.

The disciples' warnings failed to slow Jesus down. "The Pharisees are blind guides" He responded. This made the Pharisees downright mad. How could this Galilean dare to insult their high standing, their education, and their influence? I have a friend who is blind, and he is always joking about driving me home. It's comical when he makes this remark, but none of us who know him speak to him that way. That would be offensive and rude. But Jesus dared to call these Pharisees exactly what they were—blind men influencing the people in things they themselves refused to see and understand.

Nothing has really changed since the days of Christ. Blind men are still leading, and blind people are still following. Jesus' injunction to us is clear: "Follow me!" He says. "I am the light."

Who's guiding you?

Quarreling Along the Way

So much energy is wasted on petty issues. We get our nose out of joint about the silliest little things, and then we nurse that emotion for years. As time passes, the initial issue segways into other issues until we forget what the real matter was. We just stay mad and quarrel for the sake of the argument or the felt hurt.

The predicted famine came, and because of Joseph's wise leadership, only Egypt was prepared. The story is familiar about Joseph's brothers' journey to Egypt to buy provisions, of his sly way of returning their money, and of their fear of retribution from this powerful man of Egypt. Through skillful questioning, Joseph ascertained the knowledge he craved—his dad (Jacob) and his kid brother were alive and well. A beautiful reunion between Joseph and his ten older brothers ensued. Joseph then sent his brothers home to get Dad and Benjamin and instructed them to bring their entire families back to Egypt for the duration of the famine. What had begun many years earlier as an ugly backlash of jealousy now had the potential of a beautiful ending.

Joseph knew human nature and he knew his brothers: *As they were leaving, he said to them "Don't quarrel on the way!"* (Gen. 45:24b) What was Joseph really saying? "Don't mess this up now, boys! This is beautiful. What's in the past is over. Stifle the "if only" discussions. God was in this whole episode, and God desires that this reunion be a thing of beauty to everyone who witnesses it."

Thanks, Joseph. We needed that. Leave your grudges and hurts in the past. Don't sweat the small stuff. There are bigger fish to fry, and unity is more important than our petty opinions and differences. It's a mind set—and a "heart set."

Leave the past in the past; move on down the road.

JANUARY
24

Want to Live Long? Then...

We called her Mammy Bonney. She was to me what southerners call a "shirt tale relative." Mammy Bonney was my grandmother's brother's wife's mother. That made her no blood relation to me whatsoever, but she was a part of my childhood nevertheless. Whenever we traveled to Oklahoma to visit Uncle John and Aunt Cora, we saw Mammy. She lived with Uncle John and Aunt Cora, and she endured to the ripe old age of 103. To her last day, she was alert and beautiful. Her sky blue eyes had faded with the years, and her hearing failed, but her mind stayed alert to the end. Once, she was even featured on "This Is Your Life."

One day when I was thirteen and Mammy Bonney was 99, while we were playing dominoes, I asked her this question: "Mammy, how is it that you have lived so long?" "Oh," she responded with no hesitation, "I learned young to respect and obey my parents. That's what the Bible teaches, you know." What an impression that made on me—so much so that I can still visualize Aunt Cora's house and the exact spot where Mammy and I were playing our game. It's a memory that remains with me and returns for an occasional visit.

Proverbs 3 teaches us several of God's basic principles: There is wisdom in obedience to parents; there is wisdom in faithfulness to the Word; there is wisdom in trust in the Lord, there is wisdom in a "healthy" fear of the Lord; there is wisdom in giving God his tithes and offerings. And one of the results of this wisdom is long life. Of course, we have no guarantees, but we do have His word. Proverbs 3 is a set of beautiful promises. Some day each of us will be featured on "This is Your Life," and there will be an accounting made of all the acts of our lives.

This is your life: Live it well.

God's Good Intentions

In Van Dyke's classic, *The Other Wise Man*, Artaban expresses the feelings of most of us: "The ways of God are stranger than the thoughts of man." We can never get inside the mind and heart of God and decipher what in the wide world He is doing. And yet, He knows—all the time. He's got this whole big deal under control—including your life and mine. We just don't see all that He sees.

After Jacob died in Egypt, and his sons returned his embalmed body to the family crypt in the cave near Mamre, Joseph's brothers were overcome by fear and trepidation. Now that the old man was dead, Joseph's ten older brothers were scared to death. Joseph deserved revenge and retribution for all they had put him through when he was sold into slavery. What would he do to them now? They were well-aware that Joseph had the power and authority and means to unleash on them and their families enormous pain and disgrace and humiliation.

For once, Joseph's brothers did the sensible and prudent thing. They fell on the mercy of the court. In truth, mercy was all they had going for them. They thought that Joseph might kill them, so they offered to be his slaves. After all, they reckoned, servitude was better than death. Long ago, though, Joseph had buried the hatchet. Of course, he had suffered. He suffered a lot! But, God was faithful, and Joseph's life became its own reward. Joseph was mature enough to put the past in the past. His beautiful words ring down through history: *You intended to harm me, but God intended it for good to accomplish what is now being done.* (Gen. 50:19-20). Whatever is in your past, you *can* "get over it," and set God free to accomplish good in your lives and the lives of the others around you.

Bury the Hatchet! Get Over it!

Roaming Around with Angels

Why do some people seem to get all the breaks? Looks, money, health, good families. Interesting that you should ask. Others wiser than you have asked the same question. One day a group of angels came to God, and Satan snuck along with them. "Where did you come from?" asked God. Satan's answer is alarming to the contemplating heart: "From roaming through the earth and going back and forth in it." Did you ever wonder if Satan is busy? His answer should set your questions to rest. He's busy! And up to NO good.

Job was one of the "beautiful people," and Satan challenged God for him. "You've put a hedge around him. Let me at him, and I'll show the world once and for all, that *any* man will curse God if things get bad enough." God agreed that Satan could "mess with Job." He couldn't touch Job—just his possessions. In short order, Job suffered four major losses. When it appeared that Job could handle no more, his circumstances got worse—much worse. He suffered dreadful boils, his wife turned against him, and he lost all his kids. The good man suffered almost beyond human endurance. But his perseverance and devotion in the face of tragedy continue to be an example today.

I have a friend who for over 45 years has suffered like Job. She and her first husband adopted his brother's two children when he and his wife were killed. Her three husbands have all died difficult deaths. She lost her younger brother in a car accident. Her parents died when she needed them most. Her oldest son died of cancer. She herself suffered cancer as well. Recently, I visited my friend. She had a smile on her face and a lilt of laughter in her voice, and she brought cheer to my day. My friend's life has proved God: *She still maintains her integrity, though you incited me against her to ruin her without reason* (Job 2:3b).

Your suffering may be a test. Will you pass?

Heaven in a Child

The Pharisees simply would not leave Jesus alone. Many people followed Him because they were amazed by His teaching and miracles. It's safe to assume that the Pharisees followed Jesus as well because they always seemed to be in the crowd. Their intentions were to make Him look stupid or to ambush Him with a contradiction of scripture. Jesus was sharp and Jesus was wise. They just couldn't catch Him. He either taught in parables or answered their questions *with* scripture. A pretty good example for us today, don't you think?

On one particular day, the Pharisees just about wore Jesus out asking about divorce and marriage. At last He escaped from them and attempted to spend some time with the children. I'm sure Jesus thought that a little time spent with kids would be rejuvenating and mind-settling after all the posturing of the Pharisees. Most likely the disciples were trying to protect Jesus, but they didn't understand. Of all people, you would think the disciples would have been glad to see Jesus sit down and play with the kids. But, they tried to turn the parents with kids away. Their intentions were good, but their comprehension of the kingdom of God was shallow.

That day by the shore of Galilee Jesus taught us all an important lesson. Heaven is in a child. We see heaven in the sparkle of their eyes as they experience the wonders of nature. We experience heaven in the sincerity and naiveté of their questions and the open honesty of their belief system. We see heaven in the purity of their lives and the unmarred potential for good. Are you bogged down with the Pharisees in your life? Spend a little time with a child.

God reveals Himself through a child—it's a promise.

Rewards of the "Ministry"

Anyone can become cynical about his or her chosen profession. Youth is idealistic, and people commence careers—even the ministry—with high hopes of making an impact. We sincerely believe that we won't become bitter and disillusioned as so many seem to be. But it happens. Circumstances interrupt and people disappoint us. Before we know it, we are "bashing" our chosen profession and pointing out its flaws. I've seen in again and again.

It's always sad to see a crestfallen senior adult, but it's even sadder to see disillusionment in the ministry. The rich young ruler said he wanted to follow Jesus, but he wasn't willing to pay Jesus' asking price: "give all you have and follow me." What about those who do forsake family and future and financial gain to give their entire life in full-time Christian work? Ministry is predominantly people work, and people can be hurtful, revengeful, disappointing, and discouraging. It's pretty easy to grow weary in well-doing.

Recently, a pastor's wife shared with me honestly: "I didn't even want to go to church this morning. These people don't understand or appreciate what my husband has given up to be their pastor. I just don't want to face these people today. They are too fickle." Honest words. I'm glad she felt comfortable and safe saying them to me, but Jesus reminds us that there *are* rewards in "ministry:"

Everyone who has left… for my sake will receive a hundred times as much and will inherit eternal life. Perk up, Christian worker; life is short, and the rewards for your service are long. Only heaven will reveal the full results of your labors. You will have all eternity to share the fruits of your faithful life. God promises you a "hundred times over" reward, and that reward is people.

Cheer up weary pastor. God's in your life.

Go Ahead: Kill Me!

Poor Job. It wasn't enough that God allowed Satan at him; his friends took after him as well. You know the feeling. When circumstances are the worst, some of your friends drop by to tell you what "they would have done," or what you did wrong to bring this on yourself. There's a name for these people: They're called "Job's comforters." In truth, they're no comfort at all. They are a drag and a pull downward in our depression. We dread to see them coming.

During Job's time of oppression and depression, he was visited by a parade of self-righteous people who had his predicament all figured out. If he would just listen to their advice and counsel, this horrible ordeal would be over in short order. He could get back to his life of ease, prosperity, and health. It wasn't that simple. God permitted Job to be persecuted as a testimony of faith. He didn't do anything wrong; he hadn't sinned. Job's neighbors couldn't understand this.

And Job didn't understand it either. But God knew what He was doing when He opened Job's life to Satan. He knew this man Job, and He knew he was made of the right stuff. Job remained loyal to God even as his condition worsened. Perhaps Job figured, "I'm in this so deep now, nothing or no one BUT God can rescue me."

Suffering Job has given us some great quotables. Job's neighbor, Zophar, logically explained how he could get back into God's good graces. At last Job had enough; *Though he slay me, yet will I hope in him...* (Job 12:15). Job understood God when he didn't understand his own circumstances. "Whatever occurs," he was really saying, "God is always there. And if He wants to take me, I'll just be with Him a little sooner than I had expected. So, Zophar, take your advice elsewhere because I'm not quitting now. I'm sticking with God."

Stick with God. He truly never fails.

Shattered Plans

*Heartaches, broken pieces, ruined lives are why you died on Calvary.
Your touch is what I longed for; you have given life to me.*

At the *Lafayette Hotel* in Long Beach, California in the early 70s, our banquet speaker taught us this new tune. It was brand new then, but since that night, I've sung it a hundred or more different places with thousands of others. We've lifted our voices and our hands heavenward, and tears have slipped down our cheeks as we've sung this sweet little tune with its beautiful words. We really believe it—until the heartaches and broken pieces invade our lives.

"Lord, I was singing about the lost, wasn't I?" Yes, but not always. Like Job, heartaches and disappointments and "tests of faith" call on all believers. Sooner or later, our words are reminiscent of Job, *My plans are shattered, and so are the desires of my heart* (Job 17:11). Cheer up! The final days of Job were better that his first.

Perhaps you're hurting so deeply you think there will never be a tomorrow. For reasons totally out of your control, it appears that your life is ruined and in broken pieces. You paid your tithes every week, but because of a dishonest business partner, you've had to declare bankruptcy. You took your children to church and taught them the ways of God, and now they have turned their backs on him and struck out with their backs to you and God as well.

All of us yearn for God's touch on our lives. Heartaches and broken pieces aren't reserved for sinners, and God's touch isn't exclusively for them either. He wants to touch you wherever you are; He wants to give you back a new life—perhaps a different one than you had planned—but nevertheless one in which He is in total control.

Allow Him to touch you today. He can do it!

It's About Time...

As tour leader to Israel, my husband and I have shared the joy of "walking where Jesus walked" with scores of people. One of the biggest thrills of each trip is the *Palm Sunday Walk.* We park the bus on the Mount of Olives, walk down a steep road, pass a Jewish cemetery, and stop at Gethsemane. It's not possible to take the entire walk because of a major highway that intersects the Kidron Valley. Our walk is enough, though, for modern pilgrims to comprehend what happened at the triumphal entry of Christ.

From Jerusalem, the Mount of Olives is directly across the Kidron Valley. Jesus was clearly visible to anyone looking that day. Crowds began to swarm out of Jerusalem to link up with His entourage as they approached the city. Mob mentality prevailed. We've all seen it. It can be frightening, and those who become a part of a mob can't believe what they did or why they ever acted so impulsively.

People got caught up in the drama that day. Here came the healer, the preacher, the prophet. Maybe, just maybe, He really *was* the Messiah. And so they joined the parade. They chanted *"Blessed is He who comes in the name of the Lord, Hosanna in the highest* (Matt. 21:9). This parade atmosphere was short-lived, though, when Jesus stormed the temple overturning the money tables of the religious profiteers. The leaders were shook up—indignant the Bible says. This can't be happening in our little world—this religious kingdom we've so neatly arranged to serve our selfish desires and ambitions.

When Jesus arrives, He upsets the norm. It's the same today. People are revealed for what they really are. People and relationships are healed, and things are different. Many "religious people" are fearful that Jesus might come into their church and lives and upset things.

Let Him come; it's about time.

Reflections on the Word...

February

Job 19-42, Exodus 1-40, and Leviticus 1-5
Matthew 22-28 and Mark 1-9
Psalms 18-27 and Proverbs 3-6

My Prayer Time for February...

Thanksgiving _____

_____

_____

_____

_____

Intercession _____

_____

_____

_____

Ministry _____

_____

_____

_____

Encouragement _____

_____

_____

_____

_____

He Knows Me

It's an unspeakable comfort when someone vouches for your character. When we were kids, we often would tell our friends, "I'll tell my mom; she knows I wouldn't do such and such!" Our childish words expressed our belief that Mom would always protect us.

Job's smug accusers continued to descend on him in a perpetual flood. "Mr. Job, you must have done something wrong. If you'll just confess…" "No, I didn't," protested Job. Job's friends persisted: "This much bad doesn't come into the life of a pure person, Job. Come on. 'Fess up. What did you do that has brought all this deep despair and helpless agony on you and your family?"

It's refreshing and rare when a person stands up and defends what's right. After all, why would we want to stick our necks out by getting involved in someone else's misery? It's not always easy and it's not always popular, but we are liberated by a friend's defending words, "I know that person and he or she would never do what they are accused of doing."

Job knew himself and he believed that God knew him as well. Job's only defense was his life and his belief system: *But he knows the way that I take; when he has tested me, I will come forth as gold* (Job. 23:10) Job responded to his "comforters." They could sue him; they could accuse him; they could ignore him; they could be condescending to him, but Job knew in his heart that he had done nothing wrong. What he didn't know was "Why?" And yet Job believed that ultimately God would avenge him. And God did.

What a comfort to us when we can say, "God knows me; He knows my heart; and He will prevail in my life."

You, too, can "come forth as gold."

The Capstone

I'm not a student of archeology, but I've been privileged to travel and experience some amazing ancient ruins. In Israel, Egypt, Rome, Athens, and Ephesus, I've walked through reconstructed streets of ancient cities and seen the remains of theaters, forums, and agoras. The guides are impressive in their knowledge, and the little I know, I've learned from them. They just seem to know everything.

The buildings and temples were supported by gorgeous marble columns, and the streets and marketplaces were lined with them. As a guide describes the significance of a specific site, he or she draws attention to the columns, pointing out the capstone—the ornate carved piece that crowns it. The capstone identifies the type of column—Ionic, Roman, or Doric. There is no real noticeable difference among the columns except for the capstone.

Jesus was the master of word pictures. During His day, Israel had a huge Roman presence, and that presence was reflected in their architecture. Jesus used the crowd's architectural familiarity to explain His parable of the tenants. In this hypothetical story the ungrateful renters killed their servants and finally killed the son of the landowner as well. What was Jesus teaching?

Jesus' deity and supremacy are not nullified because the world disregards or disrespects Him. *The stone the builders rejected has become the capstone* (Matt. 21:42b). We may disregard or disrespect Him, but He will ultimately be above and over all. God Himself yearns to lift His son above the whole world and crown our lives with Him. Make Jesus your capstone today, and permit Him to identify you. He will crown your ordinary, day-to-day life with the beauty of His glory and love and compassion.

Let Him crown your life.

When Life's not Fair, God Is!

Life is NOT fair; that's an undeniable fact. We learn this very young when we feel that a sibling got favored above us. We learn it from Day One of school, when another kid gets the seat we want. We learn it in middle school when our best friend gets the part in the school play that we are certain we deserve. We learn it in high school when another kid gets to play more in the big game than we do. We learn this when we plan for college, and we are aced out of that major scholarship that we know we deserve.

And then real life begins. Sometimes our dreams are shattered by events that are completely out of our control. At other times the poor decisions we make along the way haunt us with crushed relationships, career disappointments, financial losses, and more. Perhaps a loved one is struck down by a catastrophic disease or a senseless tragedy. Life just isn't fair! And on and on the story of life goes.

When we dwell and obsess on life's unfair circumstances, we quickly begin a spiral downward into an endless cycle of despair, depression, and loneliness. David understood these feelings. Life wasn't always fair for him either. Some situations were out of his control; at other times, David just flat out messed up. He was human, and his words are refreshing: *He rescued me from my powerful enemy, from my foes, who were too strong for me... the Lord was my support* (Psalm 18:18-19). He is the one we can absolutely count on who will absolutely never forsake us.

David continues: *The Lord has dealt with me according to my righteousness, according to the cleanness of my hands he has rewarded me* (Psalm 18:20). God knows! He is always fair; He is going to have the last word, and He will justify your life fairly. You bet! Life's *not* fair, but God *is*! We can rest in His ultimate fairness.

God never plays favorites.

Practice What You Preach

Jesus was haunted and hunted incessantly by the reprehensible Pharisees. He called them hypocrites. They wouldn't leave Him or the people alone. Jesus said it first: "Practice what you preach!" The Pharisees knew the law in side and out, and they preached it vociferously day in and day out. Apparently, this law they preached wasn't for them—they acted as though they were above the law.

Jesus knew the law well. The Pharisees weren't counting on that. They were accustomed to dealing with people through intimidation, but Jesus refused to be intimidated by these arrogant, supercilious men. They simply did not frighten Him, but He sure scared the daylights out of them. Continually, He laid their lives down along side the law they preached, and they continually failed to measure up.

Jesus put them on notice: "You put heavy loads on the people, but you never carry your own weight. All you do is for men to see; if it can't be seen, you don't do it. You pay your tithes, but you are totally devoid of virtue, justice, mercy, and faithfulness. Everything on the outside is "According to Hoyle," but your insides are a great big mess full of greedy self-indulgence. You are blind guides! You don't practice what you preach." Ooh! The Pharisees hated that!

We're impressed when an "important person" gets his or her hands dirty along with us ordinary folks. This speaks volumes, for we are all just ordinary men and women. Jesus nailed it: *The greatest among you will be your servant. For whoever exalts himself will be humbled, and whoever humbles himself will be exalted* (Matt. 23:11-12). Wash out your cup; allow the mercy and love and faithfulness of God to flow through your life. That's the true and only way to be a witness in a hurting and dying world.

Get your hands dirty in His work.

Cold Love

Cold love is a complete and total contradiction of terms. Love is warm and love is cozy and love is sentimental and love is sweet and love is honest and pure. Cold love? What is that?

I was raised in Alaska in the '50s, and my comprehension of war is keener than some of my contemporaries. I've experienced blackouts, air raid drills, and city wide evacuations. On that remote far-flung piece of real estate, we had a healthy, built-in fear of Russians—our enemy. The Russians were coming, we were told, and Alaska was the front line. My parents were pragmatic and mature about all this. When we were home, we weren't afraid. Blackouts became quality family time as we pulled down black shades, cooked with *Sterno*, and ate by candlelight. What did we have to fear? We were safe in our father's house.

Jesus realized that ultimately the world is ending—an end destined to be cataclysmic. He reported what we witness daily: nation against nation; global famines and disasters. Christians will be persecuted; people will turn against one another. In short, the end times won't be pretty. Pretty ugly, maybe. Jesus smacks us broadside: *Because… of wickedness, the love of most will grow cold* (Matt. 24:12).

In the last days many people who call Him Savior will succumb to fear. Their love and testimony will grow cold. So, what's cold love? It's total absence of trust accompanied by overwhelming fear. Why and what do we fear? If we are in Him, we are safe in our Father's house. The end days can be quality time with the Father just like our times in Alaska years ago. I want to be equipped for today. *God, please enable my love to stay warm and loving and relevant despite world conditions around me. Amen.*

Keep your testimony alive and warm.

Be at the Gate on Time!

A number of years ago we vacationed in Hawaii with some friends. What a terrific time the four of us had together. It was beautiful and relaxing; too quickly the day came for us to fly home. We arrived at the airport early, checked our luggage, and then began to roam around the airport waiting for the departure announcement. What fun we were having—buying that last souvenir, eating fresh papaya, laughing and enjoying one another's company.

At last, we strolled to the departure gate. Were we ever surprised? Our huge plane was backing away. This wasn't possible. We had tickets, AND we were at the gate on time. Four adults went into high gear quicker than you can imagine. Jennie and I jumped up on a ledge facing the pilot as he pulled away from the jet way. We made every hand gesture thinkable to attract his attention and let him know that passengers were left behind. Gary and my husband literally ran to find an agent to halt the plane and allow us to board. And they did! Because the plane had pulled away early, they were compelled to pull back to the jet way, open the door, and let us on. We were paying passengers, and our tickets were in order.

What a relief, but what a feeling! I'll always remember looking into the face of the pilot and realizing that we were actually being left behind. If you have to miss a plane, I guess Honolulu is a pretty good place for that to happen, but the deserted feelings I had that day were real. In our case, the pilot and gate agent made an error, but there is going to be a day, when we had better be prepared. One fine day, He's returning, and the marriage and the celebration will be simultaneous with that return. If we aren't prepared when He comes, there will be no time to run for the ticket agent. It's over. What a sinking feeling that will be! I want to be ready.

Got my ticket; my luggage is checked; I'm at the gate!

The "I Am" of the Storm

Storms happen. They're devastating, hazardous, and destructive, but worthwhile things come from storms. Storms are nature's ways of clearing forests, aerating the ocean, or simply washing the land. God is the creator of storms, and He has a reason for all His creation. When we are in a storm, we aren't thinking about its potential benefits. We're thinking about survival!

I saw a sign that read "Cheer Up. Things Could Get Worse." I did, and *they* did! That's the way it was with old Job in his catastrophic storm. As soon as one wave of disaster cleared the deck of his life, he was hit from another direction by a more deadly wave. His life seemed doomed, going from bad to worse. After Job's neighbors visited and revisited him, each rendering his calculated and sanctimonious spin on Job's state, God came. Job deserved an explanation about the dreadful events that were happening to him. There's an eye to many storms, and it's a calm place. In the eye of his storm, Job asked God that basic human questions, "Why? Why, me?"

God's answer wasn't what Job expected: *Brace yourself like a man; I will question you, and you shall answer me* (Job 40:6). Where did that come from? But God said it. God wants to be certain that He has chosen the right candidate for His tests. It would be a pity to fail when the world is watching; the stakes are too high. His questions in our storms lend us occasion for self-review and afford us an opportunity to prove God. He's not just in good things, but He's in *all* things! We flail out at Him: "Where are you, God?" When we listen with our heart, we hear His calm reply: "I'm in the storm, and this is for your good and my glory." God was in Job's storm, and He's in yours. You may not even want to think about His questions, much less answer them. But, you, too, can pass your stormy test?

The great "I Am" is available for your storm.

FEBRUARY
8

Tea for Two

Ever go to a pity party? Not many come—just one—you. Poor pitiful Pearl! It's more fun with just one. The party lasts longer. No one feels responsible to cheer you up or make you smile. One is good. You can wallow in the "nobody cares about me" syndrome best when you're alone. "After all," you think, "I'm rarely seen; no one appreciates all I do; my successes are devalued; I'm worth little." We know the drill, and we've all attended these parties.

When we stay depressed, people who love and care about us become concerned. Self-pity isn't healthy anyway you cut it. The Israelites were suffering in Egypt. Things began great, but after Joseph and his Pharaoh died, generations passed, and now the current regime was oppressive. God loved Israel and cared about their predicament.

I've seen parents get interested in strange things. People who never cared about sports become fans when their child is involved. They attend games they don't understand and stand and scream when their kid's team scores. Why? Someone they love is involved, and now they care. On the other end of that continuum, I've seen parents get involved in abuse support groups to help their teenager who succumbed to a destructive habit. Why? They care about their kids.

God cares about every detail that affects you. Believe it! He said it to the Israelites in their persecution, and He's saying it to us now: *I have indeed seen the misery of my people in Egypt...and I am concerned about their suffering* (Exodus 3:7). What's concerning you? It doesn't matter—big or small—it concerns God because it concerns you. Take it to Him. Awareness that God is concerned is liberating when we allow Him to share and define suffering. He wants to make your party a celebration of His grace and mercy.

Put Him at the top of your party list.

The Word in Real Time

Who's the Boss?

We chuckle when we hear the schoolyard chant, "You're not the boss of me." The truth is, however, that each of us is accountable to someone or something. There's an invisible chain of command, and it's incumbent on us to know it well. We cringe and grit our teeth when we hear the little word *submit*. There's an innate quality in all of us that loves to be in charge. We don't want anyone or anything telling us what to do. Life never goes too well, though, until we recognize that accountability is a major part of maturity.

The Israelites in Egypt *knew* they weren't in control. That was evident. The Egyptians feared the Israelites because there were so many of them; so they made them servants and slave laborers. The Israelites knew they were God's people, and yet they were confused about *who* was in control. The Israelites thought the Egyptians were in charge. Wrong! They saw themselves as slaves because they had forgotten "whose" they were. They were God's chosen people. What? "You've got to be kidding," they said to Moses. "We aren't chosen; we're slaves." They just simply didn't get it. Poor, Moses. He had to deal with these pitiful, whining, fickle people.

God spoke to the people through Moses: *I am the Lord...and I have remembered my covenant* (Exodus 6:2 & 5). The Israelites *thought* the Egyptians were their Lord because long ago they had ceased believing that they were God's chosen people. The evidence of God wasn't there. But God was there! They just didn't recognize Him.

Who's the Lord of your life? Is it a person or a situation or a habit that seems to control your every move and thought and action? God reminds us today just like He did through Moses years ago, "My promise is sure; I will not forget you. I am the Lord."

Be honest: Who's your boss?

The Silent Jesus

Intermittently, things begin to unravel in our lives and spin out of control. This happened to Jesus in His final days before the crucifixion. To the "sane" observer of this episode in Jesus' life and ministry, nothing was going right. Everything was wrong.

For openers, one of Jesus' best friends turned Him in. That had to cut to the core. In a surge of misguided loyalty, Peter struck out at the soldiers. In the humiliating betrayal, Jesus was forced to do damage control because of an overzealous follower. Next, they drug Jesus into church court (the Sanhedrin) as though He had been hiding. This power play wasn't necessary; He'd been in church regularly. He wasn't hiding. The chief priests were desperate for *anything* they could fabricate to shut Him up once and for all.

At last, two people timidly came toward the authorities and accused Jesus of saying that He would "destroy" the temple. That was good. Now they had definitive evidence to hold and try Him. Great! When the high priest queried Jesus as to whether He said this or not, Jesus remained silent. There's a time to speak in self-defense, and there's a time for silence. The timer was set; the game had begun; the players were in place; the inevitable would happen. They might as well get on with it. Later, Jesus spoke, and when He did, they called Him a blasphemer. Jesus knew that nothing He could say would satisfy them. They were thirsty for blood; they wouldn't be quieted.

It's the most difficult thing in the world to remain silent when we are falsely accused. Since Jesus is our greatest example, we can learn a lesson here. Sometimes, very little we can say or do will make any difference. It's best to cut our losses, deal with the inevitable, and leave the retribution to God. He can handle it.

Discretion is still the greater part of valor.

11

Here Comes Trouble

For one brief moment, you almost feel sorry for the Egyptians. Reminiscent of modern dictators, all Egypt suffered because of an arrogant, egotistical leader. Israel's 430 year visit to Egypt was finished. Pharaoh refused to acknowledge the obvious fact that they were going home. When God is moving, nothing will stop Him— not temperaments or authorities or bodies of water or weather. Absolutely nothing can thwart the movement of God.

For a while it appeared like Pharaoh was in charge. His sorcerers replicated the first plagues. See there, Moses, you're God's not so powerful. Wrong! When Pharaoh's men couldn't duplicate the swarms of gnats, they admitted they were over their heads: *This is the finger of God.* (Exo, 8:19) These men were frightened by God's little finger. Still, Pharaoh remained resolute in his belligerence.

The plagues rolled on one after the other like a ruthless Sherman tank: blood, frogs, lice, flies, anthrax… Pay attention, Pharaoh. You're running out of options. Swallow your pride; get a grip; not much is left short of total disaster. Pride and power are heady things, and once experienced, they are difficult to relinquish. Pharaoh was not about to give up without a fight. These indentured servants were necessary to keep the GNP and the economy on an even keel.

God is still trying to get man's attention. Intermittently, events turn our hearts and minds to Him. For a fleeting moment we're humbled by unmanageable circumstances. But life moves on, and soon we forget. If Pharaoh had only known what was next, he might have acted differently. Pharaoh didn't know the future, and neither do we. God holds the future, and He's still in charge. Take a lesson from Pharaoh before it's too late, and turn to God while there's still time.

Trouble's coming. You can bank on it.

Messing with People's Kids

Somewhere our there in the great unknown there is an unwritten rule book. *The book* contains the "dos and don'ts" for families, churches, any group. It's prudent to adhere to *the book*. There's hell to pay when we don't. *The book* lists the people we talk politics with and those we don't. It even tells us with whom we never again mention the Christmas of '88 if we know what's good for us. One of the real biggies in *the book* is, "Never Mess with Other People's Kids." Don't even go there. That always gets people's attention.

God is aware of *the book*, and He knows how precious our children are. Nine times He struggled for Pharaoh's attention. Nine times should have done it, but it didn't. Pharaoh continued his unbending adamancy that the Israelites would *never* leave Egypt. Their departure wasn't negotiable. There's a basic truism: When God has had enough, that's it! When God's efforts to get Pharaoh's attention failed repeatedly, He orchestrated a night that divided history.

The Israelites didn't know what God was doing, and the Egyptians assuredly didn't know. But God knew what He was doing. When He told the people to sacrifice an animal and paint some blood over their doorpost, He was liberating the Israelites once and for all. The next morning dawned—a day to remember: A day of sadness and mourning for the Egyptians, but a day of celebration for the Jews.

Whether we choose to recognize it or not, there is going to be a day of judgment for us all. He yearns to "pass over" our door and spare us His judgment. He gives us opportunity after endless opportunity to put our house in order. What a high price the Egyptians paid and what an amazing lesson for today's far-sighted Christian. When the final Passover comes, will the blood be over your door?

What's over your door?

God in "Real Time"

A popular term today is *real time*. I like it. In essence, it's saying that life is unfolding before us as we live it. God has always worked in *real time*. It's easy to dismiss a section of scripture as just a "Bible story." Don't fool yourself. The men and women of the Old Testament weren't super people any more than we are. They didn't know from day to day what was coming down the pike; neither do we. When we get a handle on the concept that the Bible happened in *real time*, it comes alive in a brand new fashion.

The Israelites were so fickle. God delivered them from Egypt. He gave them daily rations on their road home. They should have been secure in the knowledge of His loving care. As they marched toward the Red Sea, the people sang and rejoiced. Until they saw Pharaoh coming, that is. What an opportunity to live in *real time*. I wish they had. Woops! Foiled again. They turned on Moses and blamed him for their predicament. They even claimed they liked Egypt and never wanted to leave. Fickle, fickle people.

Moses was weary, yet he understood the concept of *real time*. He had not a clue how they could evade Pharaoh, but he believed that if God could do what He had already done, there must be something terrific ahead. If I had been Moses, I would have resigned—or at least scolded the people. Moses trembled as he stood before the people and spoke: *Do not be afraid. Stand firm and you will see the deliverance the Lord will bring you today.* (Exo. 14:13).

Whatever you're facing, God is there. This is *real time*. The God who delivered you from a debilitating habit; the God who healed your marriage; the God who solved your financial dilemma; the God who restored your church, is real today. Fear not! He can do it again.

He wants to do it again, and He will.

14

The Transcender of Stones

Israeli tour guides share a local legend about creation: "When God created the world, He had five bags of rocks. Four He scattered around the Earth and the last He dumped in Israel." It's obvious. Israel has more than its share of rocks. It makes sense that something as familiar as rocks would be common to the Israelites.

Moses struck the rock and out came water. After they crossed the Jordan River, God told the Israelites to build an altar of rocks to commemorate the victory. Again and again, throughout the Old Testament, the Children of Israel built a stone altar. Everyone loves to hear about little David killing the giant with one stone. We thrill to the story of Daniel in the lion's den. Even though the den was sealed with a stone, Daniel's God spared Him.

Jesus talked about stones. He ordered the people to roll the stone away from Lazarus' tomb, and then He raised a dead man. When they taunted the adulterous woman, He said that the one without sin should "cast the first stone." And they all walked sheepishly away. Bible stones are symbolic representations of something impenetrable. Rivers don't part—especially at flood stage. Giants aren't felled by a little stone. Sealing a lion's den or a grave with a giant stone should have been enough to kill Daniel or keep Lazarus dead.

The Romans were resolute. There would be no "monkey business" with Jesus'remains, and they sealed His tomb with a stone. A giant stone and guards couldn't stop Him. A stone didn't keep the angels away from Daniel; it didn't stop Jesus from raising Lazarus, and it certainly didn't keep Christ in the tomb. Is anything too hard for Him? Not really. If He can roll the stone back from Daniel and Lazarus and Jesus, He can move any obstacle in your life. Let it be.

He's Still the Transcender of Stones.

when started reading 07

This Is a Holdup

Early TV westerns molded our lives. It was common to hear a kid holler "Hold 'em up" at his pals while he pointed an imaginary weapon. Everyone understands the universal sign of surrender. Enemies who don't know a single word of the other's language know to "hold 'em up" when a weapon is pointed in their face.

A battle waged between the Anmalekites and Joshua. Accompanied by Aaron and Hur, Moses retreated to a hill to watch the battle. When Moses lifted his hands heavenward, Joshua was winning, but when Moses grew tired and lowered his hands, the battle would swing in the enemy's favor. Aaron and Hur saw this and together began to hold up Moses' hands. God prevailed and the Amalekites were "blotted out of memory from under heaven."

"Pastor" Moses was the spiritual leader of Israel. With leadership comes many burdens, for true leadership is a heavy responsibility. When Moses initially held up his hands, he was pointing to heaven, indicating that the battle was God's. When Joshua's warriors looked to the hill and saw Moses' lifted hands, it gave them courage. But, when Moses wearied, they wearied. It's true that followers look to their leaders, but it's equally true that our leaders grow weary. Aaron and Hur set a beautiful example when they lifted Moses' hands.

Our leaders need us as much as we need them; we must lift them up. The battle is not just that of the leader. The battle is the Lord's. When the leader gives us a "heavenward signal," it gives us courage to carry on. What's our part? To lift them up; to be supportive of leadership; to be encouraging; and to be understanding. *Moses built an altar and called it "The Lord is my Banner, for hands were lifted up to the throne of the Lord. "* (Exo. 17:15-16).

Hold 'em up for your pastor.

16

Dark Clouds and God

Each Monday noon in Kansas, we hear the wail of tornado sirens. Practicing for disaster is a necessity in "tornado alley." Tornados are less deadly now—not because tornados are less violent, but because warning measures are better than years ago. The prudent Kansas resident knows when to take cover. Dark, ominous clouds and strong winds are major indicators of stormy weather. In the spring, they come out of nowhere, and they capture our attention.

Time and again dark, foreboding clouds rumble across the skies of our lives until all semblance of normalcy is obliterated by inky blackness. This darkness seems to come from nowhere, but God is there. The Lord said it to Moses, and He says it to us: *I am going to come to you in a dense cloud, so that the people… will put their trust in you"* (Exo. 19:9). And then God began to speak with Moses, giving him guidelines that we still follow—the Ten Commandments.

If God visited Moses in a cloud, can He not visit you in your cloud? Life is often dark and foreboding. In our clouds, we have the opportunity to absolutely depend on the one who will absolutely not forsake us. Clouds are unwelcome, potentially destructive, and lonely. God speaks to us in clouds in ways we would never hear otherwise. When He speaks with us, our world hears—not an audible voice, but they hear the responses of our lives in our dark times.

No one welcomes or invites clouds any more than people in Kansas invite a tornado. When dark clouds rumble across your life, you can rest in the awareness of His protection. Your defense mechanisms will be stronger with each new storm. No one chooses to return to one of life's storms, but we can look back and realize that His sweet presence was with us in a measure that was beyond our ability.

God's in your personal dark cloud.

On Patching Old Clothes

Patching and alterations are budget stretchers. When Johnny rips a hole in his jeans, a patch over that hole works as well as a new pair of jeans. When a man wears out the elbow of his favorite sweater, a leather patch on that elbow extends the life of the sweater and even gives it a little pizzazz. When we gain or lose weight, it's a judgment call about which clothes to take to the alterations lady. If a garment is newer or more prized, it's worth the money, but if it's an old piece, it's not really worth our time or money to have it altered.

John's disciples were fasting, and that's a good thing—both spiritually and physically. Jesus' disciples, though, were not fasting. Rather, they were following Him, absorbing His amazing stories and teachings. Enter the self-righteous, pompous church leaders: "Jesus, why aren't your people fasting? If you are such a great teacher, shouldn't your disciples be as sanctimonious as our disciples?" Jesus knew His days were numbered, and He knew that soon the prophecies of His death would be fulfilled. So, He began talking to his accusers about weddings and wineskins and old clothes. "Stay on the subject, Jesus! We want to know why you aren't fasting like us. Don't try to tap dance around our questions; we want an answer!"

Jesus wasn't tap dancing. He was teaching a key spiritual truth. "I'm here!" Jesus was saying. "Why weep at a wedding? Why add the new to the old?" Jesus didn't come to "patch up" the old. No. He came to make everything new. We struggle to hide a sin by covering it over with something "new." That never works. Jesus understood it then, and He's teaching us now. Whatever you are trying to alter or change in your life, give it to Him, and allow Him to do anything that is necessary. Perhaps He will patch it up, or maybe—just maybe—He will toss it out and begin a brand new work in you.

What are you taking to the alterations lady?

Clouds, Fire, and Glory

In the dark, difficult seasons of life, we can feel totally alone. People are close, but we feel lost in a cloud of despair. Like storm clouds on the horizon, life begins to rumble with ominous warnings of doom. Like thunder on a sunny day, disaster may strike out of nowhere; a dark cloud begins to swallow us in crushing loneliness.

Days were enjoyable for the Israelites on their journey toward the Red Sea. The angel of God was with them as they traversed the desert—guiding, protecting, and providing for them. Their angelic escort would follow them all the way, but for six days a cloud "out of nowhere" swirled around Mt. Sinai. Later, the people recognized this cloud as God's glory, but at the outset, they only saw the storm.

Storms are terrifyingly unpredictable. God's voice called Moses *into* the storm. He was obedient and vanished *into* the cloud. The people remained behind, confused and questioning why God would take Moses when they needed a leader. Matters only got worse. Mt. Sinai erupted volcanically and fire "consumed it." Standing below, the people felt doomed and abandoned. It was over. They were stranded in the desert, alone and minus God's spokesman.

Has a fire or a storm capriciously exploded in your life? Sure it has. Whether *in* the cloud or down below looking up *at* the cloud, we feel confused and lonely. When we remain true, in due course we discover that we are never alone—that God is *in* the cloud with us. One day, we'll walk back down the mountain—battered and scarred —but with a glow that only comes from surviving a storm. That day we will own the knowledge of God's glory in a new and beautiful fashion. The price of experiencing His glory is always high, but He knows what is best, and He's in control of the storm.

There's glory in your dark cloud.

Open Grazing and a '46 Hudson

I was only four, but I remember it vividly. It was October 1947, and our family was wending our way from San Antonio to Seattle where we would board a plane for Fairbanks, Alaska. My father was a new missionary to this far flung part of the world, and we were on the move. Everything was new to me. In truth, life was never the same for any of us after that October. We were trading our *warm* life in the Rio Grande Valley for the *frigid* unknown North.

In the open spaces of Wyoming where you can drive mile after mile without any sign of life, I was asleep. Through my haziness, I heard Mother's voice: "Wake up, Kathy, you must see this." When I sat up, I was mesmerized. Our '46 Hudson was awash in a sea of bleating sheep. In all directions, all I could see and hear were sheep. In the West before the Interstate system, open grazing was prevalent. Shepherds led their flocks from pasture to meadow any way they chose. Our car was inching through a flock of sheep at five mph.

Psalm 23 presents a striking metaphor: He is *still* the shepherd, and He leads us where He will. Sometimes He leads through stunning scenery and we "ooh and aah" at His wonders. Other times He leads through the valley. We are fearful that we will even survive—much less sing again. When danger comes along, He protects; when we are hurt, He soothes. He promises that goodness and mercy will follow us, and that we will ultimately be with Him forever.

Spiritually speaking, "open grazing" is prevalent. Life takes us where it will. As long as there is "open grazing," we may find ourselves in potential danger, but the good shepherd is with us, regardless. Are you wandering spiritually across a Wyoming highway where a careless driver could do you in? Fear not!

The shepherd is always watching His sheep.

Exodus 27-28
Mark 5:21-6:6a
Psalm 24

On Touching Jesus

Shackled by a heavy burden, He touched me. In the 1970s this was one of the biggest "religious hits," and we all loved to sing it. There is something soothing about the touch, and Jesus' touch far surpasses even the kindest human touch. There was a sick woman in Christ's time, though, that taught us all a lesson about touch.

Jesus was in a great crowd. A synagogue leader named Jairus pushed his way through to Jesus and begged Him to come and touch His dying little girl. Jesus was busy! Hundreds of people were around Him. Besides that, Jesus was in the company of an important man. A suffering unnamed woman was also in the crowd. There was no way she could push or elbow her way through His disciples and the important people to get the Master's attention. She was desperate for a touch. And desperate situations necessitate desperate actions.

"If I can't get Jesus to notice me," she reasoned, "maybe I could just touch Him. Surely, His healing power is mighty enough that it will flow from Him into anyone who touches Him." She reasoned well, for Jesus felt her faith drain a measure of healing power from Him. "Who touched me?" Christ queried. When Jesus scanned the crowd to see who had touched Him, His disciples derided Him. "Really, Jesus, you must be especially tired today. Can't you see there are hundreds here? Who knows who touched you?" But Jesus knew, and this nameless woman fell fearfully at His feet, confessing her faith.

Talk about a confession of faith. An unnamed woman gave the world a snapshot of blind faith. While we are waiting for Jesus to touch us, we may pass up our golden opportunity of faith to touch *Him*. Reach out and touch Him. He loves you; He cares about you; and your faith will make you whole.

Reach out and touch Him today.

Priests, Disciples, and Dusty Feet

Exodus 29 offers a laundry list of consecration rules. Moses presents exhaustive rules and regulations regarding sacrifices, purification, and fasting days. When all terms are met, and all due respect is properly given, then: *They will know that I am the Lord their god...* (Exo. 29:46a). These are God's instructions regarding the sacred and holy. If the world is to see God, these rules must be respected.

Years later, Jesus launched His ministry by sending the disciples out two by two. Like God consecrated and dedicated the holy through Moses, Jesus commissioned His disciples to testify about Him. His instructions were implicit: *Take nothing for the journey except a staff...* (Mark 6:8a). Holiness and simplicity are twin characteristics that should filter through Christian ministry. As His disciples, we don't really need much, but we surely need Him.

Even when we respect the holy and do everything "according to Hoyle," Jesus warns that people will still reject us. It's inevitable. Rejection is a downer. It's difficult to handle, and it can discourage even the most faithful follower. The fact remains. Some people just "flat out" won't like us. There is persecution in the Christian ministry—both in the world *and* in the church.

Jesus' words are liberating: "When you've given it your best shot and people continue to disrespect you and the message, move on!" This is not a holy injunction to be a quitter; rather, it is Jesus' pronouncement that our departure can be a testimony. What is He saying? "Don't waste your time or Mine. Time is short. When they've heard and reject, go on to someone else. When you leave, be symbolic. Shake the dust off as a testimony against their disbelief and/or abuse."

Clean your shoes and move on down the road

22

Jesus and George Washington

On a bluff by the Potomac River near Arlington, Virginia sets Washington's plantation home, Mt. Vernon. This majestic mansion and its spacious grounds were George's favorite spot. It was to this place that he retreated; here he gardened; here he wrote his memoirs; and here he died. Yearly, thousands of visitors enjoy the beauty and dignity of George's mansion on the Potomac.

George's life wasn't always the life of a country gentleman. During the Revolutionary War, he was the man of the hour—the one the patriots looked to for leadership. In the Constitutional Congress he kept factional passions at bay while a workable document for a new nation was contrived. In his presidency he tended to the people of a new land with the powers of our newly established government.

Jesus' ministry was taxing and demanding. He was also the man of the hour; people looked to Him for guidance and healing. Celebrity is never without its challenges. One day, weary of the crowds, Jesus withdrew with His disciples to a solitary place. 5,000 fans and their families followed Him. The disciples were distraught: "What can we do? It's late. These people have no food. If we aren't careful, there will be a riot. Jesus, we must do something—now."

Jesus was nonplussed by their protestations. These were His people; He was responsible *for* them and *to* them. They would be fed. Jesus knew what the disciples couldn't comprehend: One day He would rest eternally in His beautiful heavenly home by the River of Life. Today, He had work to do. He fed the people physical food, while inviting them to live with Him *forever* through the gift of eternal life. George's mansion is beautiful and worth visiting, but He has a mansion prepared for you that is beyond human imagination.

You, too, have a retirement home on a river.

A Promise and a Glow

When we see the glow that accompanies good news, we recognize it. Newlyweds have that certain glow; a new mother has a special look. When someone has good news, we see it even before they tell us. The countenance reveals the contents of a man's soul. If conditions are dire, it shows. If news is good, that shows as well.

Moses reluctantly accepted leadership. Sensitive and aware of his inadequacies, he was the perfect leader for Israel. Moses pled with God: *if you are pleased with me, teach me your ways so I may know you....* (Exo.37:13). Bless his old melancholy heart. He speaks again: "If you don't go with me; don't send me." Thanks, Moses for that timely reminder. Life is too tentative and the road too dangerous to go it alone. "I must have the Savior with me for I dare not go alone."

For forty days, Moses was buried in a cloud away from his life. Moses was *with* God, but he was hidden in the "cleft of the rock" because the glory of God was more than he could tolerate. When his fasting and dialogue with God were completed, he journeyed down the mountain into the "real world" of responsibility. Moses didn't recognize it, but the people did. He had "the glow."

As he emerged from the cloud, his face glowed with God's glory. It was a difficult forty days, but Moses passed God's test, and God made mighty promises to Moses. When we least expect it, God may lead us up a mountain alone, and soon we disappear *with Him* into a dark cloud. In the shadow of the rock, we are nearer to Him than we ever would be in our day-to-day worlds. Are you hidden in a cloud today? He's there. This may be your big break. Listen to Him. His promises are sure, and when this test is past, you will shine again with a glory that comes only through adversity.

Have people seen "the glow" on your face?

Exodus 35-36
Mark 7:31-8:13
Psalm 25:16-22

Willing Givers

It's true, "God loves a cheerful giver," but He has received many offerings from grouches. God's financial plan is the fairest ever conceived. Everyone is equal—rich and poor, young and old, influential and unnoticed. Why, then, do so many Christians struggle over tithes and offerings? The answer is simple and yet profound. Giving is an issue of the heart. Some give readily out of love and devotion, while others give out of obligation or fear of reprisal.

Moses dealt with the issue of giving long before Jesus. It was time to build a tabernacle—their new sanctuary. That wasn't going to drop down from the sky; the funds must come from the people. The people's hearts were enthusiastically behind this ancient building program. Moses: '*This is what the Lord has commanded... Everyone who is willing is to bring to the Lord an offering* (Exo. 35:4-5).

The overwhelming response is a paradigm for today. Through the next several verses marches an historic parade of willing hearts:
> Vs. 21: Everyone who *was willing*...brought an offering.
> Vs. 22: All who *were willing*—men and women alike—came and brought...
> Vs. 26: All the women who *were willing* and had the skill...
> Vs. 29: All the men and women who *were willing* brought to the Lord freewill offerings for all the work of the Lord...

The scripture's wording infers that some *weren't willing* to participate. Too bad. They're the losers. God's work continues whether we're involved or not. We're never really involved until our heart is willing, and what a blessing we miss when our heart is not willing. Enthusiasm is contagious; people love to be involved; it's great to see God's work progress. Lord, prepare in me a willing heart.

Be a willing giver!

Denial? You've Got to Be Kidding!

This is not the age of denial. I'm not sure many people even understand the word unless it is used in court to "deny the charges." This is a day of instant self-gratification, the day of "buy now; pay later." Some are trapped in a hopeless financial quagmire because of this prevailing tone. They cannot live without a Tahiti honeymoon, a new car, a thousand inch plasma TV, a new house, and on and on. The human appetite is enormous, and one wish granted only leads the lustful eye on to the next treasure to capture.

"Things" are not life's beginning and ending. As we mature, we learn. The good learner quickly realizes that much of the stuff *of* life isn't necessary *for* life. Jesus understood the root of man's passion for more and the almost paranoid fear of denying any wish of the heart. But His perception of the human heart went far deeper than stuff. Humanly, we can ultimately conclude that all stuff is valueless. Jesus taught that the ultimate struggle of man is not denying stuff, but rather it is the citadel of self: *If anyone would come after me, he must deny himself and take up his cross and follow me… What can a man give in exchange for his soul?* (Mark 8:34-35) Wait a minute, Jesus! I'll give up my stuff, but are you really asking me to give up my self? That's a huge price, and I'm not sure I can afford it.

Jesus remained adamant. Do you want communion with Him? Communion will never be achieved through the good deeds we do, or by the occasional token gift in the offering plate. That's too easy, and too "this worldish." Jesus is crystal clear. To share glory with Him and His father, we must deny ourselves and follow Him—wherever He leads and whatever it takes. Not an easy task. But the rewards are priceless—and eternal.

Jesus isn't kidding: Deny yourself.

The Holy Sound and Light Show

A spectacular show dazzles children and adults alike. Many times I've stayed late in *The Magic Kingdom* just to experience the electric light parade. On July 4th, grown men become boys as they play with fireworks. As if the pyramids of Gisa themselves weren't enough to stretch the minds of man, *they* have a sound and light show. God visits us sporadically in lightening or in the Aurora Borealis with displays that can't be duplicated by pyrotechnicians.

Jesus took Peter, James, and John to a mountaintop one day, and God visited them. Thousands didn't rush to see it in a theme park, but the three of them would never forget this dazzling display of His greatness. In front of them Jesus was transfigured into the splendor of His divine glory; He literally radiated God's glory. As the three stood speechless, shielding their eyes against the brightness, a voice spoke from the cloud: *"This is my Son I love. Listen to Him!"*

"Terrific!" Peter responded, "This is too good to be true. Here we are—just the four of us—and now this fantastic, other world-like sound and light show. Let's stay right here and build a few monuments; we don't need to return. It's entertaining here, and it's comfortable." Jesus knew, however, that His day of suffering was near. God was revealing to them a glimpse of the Kingdom of God.

Now and again, we witness a "holy sound and light show." Most likely it isn't what the disciples shared, but similar. We're overwhelmed by His beauty and His awesome power. We want to stay and bask in this light and the sound of His voice, but we can't stay on the mountain. There's work to be done. Visitations of His presence are reminders that when we pass through life's valleys, He is there. They provide comfort for life and continuance of the journey.

Relish His presence.

I Smell Something Good

The words, "I smell something good cooking," conjure up a host of positive memories for most of us. We recall coming home from school and being welcomed by the smell of freshly baked cookies. Perhaps we recollect the savory smell of Mother's Sunday dinner roast as we come into the house from church. Cooks love it when someone stops dead in his or her tracks, and says "What's that smell? It smells delicious."

God enumerated an elaborate series of offerings that the people were to bring to the temple. There was a burnt offering, a grain offering, a fellowship offering, the sin offering, and a guilt offering. Each offering had definite directives regarding its presentation, and although the directives varied, each involved fire; we would say "cooking."

Tithes are our responsibility, but an offering is a gift. God's word is clear that each man or woman should bring one-tenth of his income into the storehouse—no questions. But offerings are different. Offerings are the physical evidence of the overflow of a heart of love. Offerings are gifts that come from our hearts. We've all been left speechless by a gift presented to us with tiny little hands that lovingly crafted something that we don't even recognize. But, we love it, because it came from a child's selfless, loving heart.

Numerous times in scripture, God calls offerings a "pleasing aroma." What does that mean? I think it means what it says. God sensed—He smelled, if you well—the intent of the giver's heart, and He accepted the gifts of love and sacrifice when He recognized that they came from a pure heart. People recognize sincerity, and they can also sense a perfunctory, duty-bound act. We simply can't hide our heart—either from God or man.

What aroma is your life emitting?

That Look of Love

If you've had a warm, tender loving look sent your way by someone, you know it. You never ever get over the comforting feeling that love emotes. True love is rare, and when someone reaches into the deepest part of your being, making a connection, you feel it. It goes so deep that there is a near physical pain.

In Capernaum, a wealthy young man questioned Jesus, *"Good teacher,"* he asked, *"What must I do to inherit eternal life?"* It was evident; this young man wanted to be a part of Jesus' message. He simply didn't know how. A noteworthy dialogue ensured. Back and forth they went with Jesus qualifying the man's statements, and the young man grappling to get a handle on Jesus' meaning. Suddenly, a light went on: "You mean, Jesus, that following the commandments will guarantee eternal life? Goody. Goody. I'm in. I've done it all."

The young man didn't get it. Jesus gave the young man "the look." It wasn't the look we might expect—that look of exasperation we give when we explain something clearly and our listener doesn't grasp it. It wasn't the look of disgust we give when someone displeases us. Not at all. Jesus saw straight through to the young man's confused heart, and He loved him. That look must have burned in the young man's heart for years to come. He was face to face with the Son of God, discussing matters of eternal proportion, and he still didn't get it. Jesus could have rebuked him, but He loved him instead.

Humanly, we grow impatient or even annoyed with people who don't grasp Jesus' message. Impatience, exasperation, or annoyance simply don't cut through confusion; love does. Our eyes reveal our hearts, and that is what the world is searching. When your heart is filled with love, your look will show it.

What does your look reveal?

Reflections on the Word...

Reflections on the Word...

March

Leviticus 5-26 and Numbers 1-31
Mark 10-16 and Luke 1-8
Psalms 28-39 and Proverbs 6-8

My Prayer Time for March...

Thanksgiving_____

_____

_____

_____

Intercession_____

_____

_____

_____

Ministry_____

_____

_____

_____

Encouragement_____

_____

_____

_____

_____

Leviticus 5:14-7:10
Mark 10:32-52
Proverbs 6:12-19

20/20 Blindness

J ames and John had visions of grandeur; all Jesus' healings gave them a rush. But they still didn't understand *who* He was. Jesus was going to Jerusalem to be sanctified; their request was completely disjointed from His purpose: *Let one of us sit at your right and the other at your left in glory* (Mark 10:37), they requested. After all they had shared with Him, James and John didn't have a clue. If they had understood, they would have thought twice before making this self-serving request. Jesus replied: *You don't know what you are asking,* (Mark 10:38) Then, He chastised them: *Whoever wants to become great among you must be your servant.* (Mark 10:43b).

After this exchange between man and the divine, they were accosted by a blind beggar. Bartimaeus stood by the Jericho highway doing all he knew to do—begging. When he heard a sudden commotion, Bartimaeus spoke, "What's all the noise? What am I missing?" When he was told that this was the healer from Nazareth and His entourage, he spoke up: *Jesus, Son of David, have mercy on me* (Mark 10:47) he pled. That's all he had to do. He wasn't asking for position or glory; he needed healing, and this was his golden opportunity.

Even though the crowd rebuked the blind man, Jesus heard him and healed him. Just like that. No fanfare; no begging for position; just an honest plea of faith. And faith made him whole. What a contrast between the sighted who spent weeks with Jesus and never *saw* His mission and a blind man who *saw* with eyes of faith.

Seeking glory and position and recognition render us blind to His mission. Visions of grandeur leave us as spiritually blind as James and John appear to be. Jesus implores us to believe without seeing, and in so doing, we shall see.

How's your eyesight?

On Moving Mountains

For seven years we lived in the shadow of *Mt. St. Helens*. Daily, we watched it from our backyard as it intermittently spewed smoke and ash into our beautiful Washington environment. Then, on May 18, 1980, *Mt. St. Helens* blasted its way into world news and history when it erupted and blew its top. Those memories are vivid whether we saw it up close or in some distant place via TV.

A massive black plume of ash swept across the skies, darkening communities many miles away. As ash began to settle, it rapidly choked the Tuttle River, and only a change in the wind saved the twin cities of Longview and Kelso from certain flood and destruction. Ultimately, all the ash in the Tuttle River was dredged or diverted to the Pacific Ocean. Literally, the mountain was moved to sea.

When I was a girl and my father drove past the beautifully cone-shaped Mt. St. Helens with its nearly perfect mirror reflection in Spirit Lake, I would not have believed the aftermath of May 18, 1980. No one who visits the site of that eruption or flies over it can dispute that a gigantic portion of that beautiful mountain is gone forever—lost in the depths of the sea or piled in a burm along I-5.

It's difficult to comprehend the impossible. By its very nature, impossibility can't be done. Jesus taught repeatedly that with Him *anything* is possible. *I tell you the truth, if anyone says to this mountain, 'Go throw yourself into the sea,' and does not doubt in his heart but believes that what he says will happen, it will be done for him* (Mark 11:23). This verse becomes easier to understand in light of Mt. St. Helens' eruption. You name it: What's the biggest obstacle in your life—that immovable person or situation that's beyond your human capability? Nothing is too big for Him. Ask. Believe.

What's your mountain?

Stand at Attention!

We have lived in two cities each with a huge military contingency—San Diego, CA and El Paso, TX—one Navy city and one Army town. In El Paso, I taught school on the post, and I couldn't even pass the *Ft. Bliss* post gate without the appropriate sticker on my car. When the MPs saw it, they saluted, and I drove on through. In the military there are procedures to follow and rank to be respected. That's the military way, and every buck private learns in short order that the military way is to be strictly followed.

We cherish an image of our loving heavenly father. It's warm and it's good and it's comforting. He is indeed all those things and more. God does, though, have standards and protocols that we're expected to respect. Nadab and Abihu, Aaron's sons, neglected to obey God's dictated plan of sacrifices, and they paid with their lives for their disregard of the holy. God admonished Aaron and his other sons with words we could heed today, *you must distinguish between the holy and the common* (Lev. 10:10).

God's house; holy communion; marriage; store house tithing; corporate worship—on and on the list continues—are all things God expects us to respect. This is a day of the casual, and that's not all bad. We can become too casual, though, with the things of God and treat them with mundane and run-of-the-mill superficiality.

Psalms 29 is a great contrast to Nadab and Abihu and perhaps the 21st century worshipper. *Ascribe to the Lord the glory due his name; worship the Lord in the splendor of his holiness* (Psalm 29:2). The *Message* translation shouts: *Stand at Attention!* That says it all. Pay attention to God's customs and commandments. It's not our duty; it's our responsibility.

Who's your commander?

The Tax Man Cometh

Dreading taxes is an American "right of passage." The listed cost is never the total—tax is added. The varied taxes give us pause for a long sigh: sales, value added, income, social security, property, excise, road tolls—the list is hopelessly endless. Regardless of their burden, taxes benefit us: a terrific road system, quality education, medical facilities, welfare, social security, and more. We are so accustomed to these entitlements that it would be nearly impossible to live without them. And yet, taxes aren't American or new.

After Jesus' triumphal entry and cleansing of the temple, the Pharisees and Herodians resolved to get rid of Him. With fawned sincerity and deceitful agendas, they went after Jesus: *Teacher, we know you are a man of integrity, not swayed by men. Is it right to pay taxes to Caesar or not? Should we pay or shouldn't we?* (Mark 12:14) Jesus wasn't swayed; He perceived their conniving, sinful hearts.

Jesus knew they were endeavoring to trap Him; He told them so. Their sneaky trap became His object lesson. Taking a coin, Jesus held it up: *whose portrait and whose inscription is this?* (Mark 12:15b) Jesus knew what their answer had to be. They were trying to ambush Him, but the Pharisees and their cronies were trapped in front of their constituents. *He* was always turning *their* words around. How embarrassing for these "religious" men.

I can visualize Jesus flipping the denarius back and forth between finger and thumb as His look pierced their everlastingly evil hearts: *Give to Caesar what is Caesar's and to God what is God's.* (Mark 12:17). Gottcha! Jesus knew their wicked hearts and the selfish motives of their questions. His answer is as pertinent today as it was then. We are responsible both to God and to our government as well.

Pay your taxes; give your tithes—it's not an either/or!

Tiptoe through the Tithers

When our grandson was born, the gifts my son and his wife received were almost embarrassing. Jokingly, my son and daughter-in-law told us, "The baby has more clothes than both of us combined." There was one specific gift, though, that touched them deeply. Our son's grandmother—a humble widow on a fixed income —gave them a gift certificate for $25.00, a small gift compared to many they received. Why was it so significant? Her gift was sacrificial and from a heart of love. She would have it no other way.

Jesus knew that giving would always be a problem in the church. One day He stood by the offering plate and observed. A parade of haughty rich people in fine clothes marched with fanfare to the plate and placed their large gifts so that everyone looking could see them give. Somewhere in the middle of this procession, a poor widow slipped in line. The rich people weren't sure how she got there, and her presence sort of made them look bad, but what could they do but tolerate her? She was virtually unnoticed that day. Unnoticed, that is, by everyone but Christ. When she timidly placed her fractional gift in the plate, He noticed!

There's an attitude in the church that sickens God: When one gives a large gift they then have a superior status or an entitlement to direct those funds where they choose. If we are not cautious, we begin to tiptoe around the big givers, kowtow to them, and tolerate their whims. How wrong we are. Jesus doesn't "give a hoot" about the size of your gift, the flare with which you give it, or what you wear the day you present it. Jesus cares about your heart. He really doesn't want our gifts; He wants us. When He has us completely, He has our means. Yes, "a little child shall lead them," but we can learn from this humble widow as well.

Want a blessing? Give from your heart.

Stop Watching the Clock

I once had a summer job in a California insurance company as their permanent "girl Friday." I moved from department to department filling in for vacationers. Many days I worked eight hours in the typing pool on an IBM Selectric typewriter. Employees prepared documents or dictated letters; we typed them. Not the most challenging job, but honest summer work for a college student.

It was easy to distinguish between who just had a job and who was seeking advancement. As the day wore on, the typing pool girls perked up. It was an amazing evolution. Around 4:00 PM, the clock magnetically attracted them with concerned diligence. 5:00 PM was quitting time. When I say quitting time, that's what I mean. In utter astonishment I watched girls lift their hands from the typewriter at 4:55, leave a letter in the carriage, turn off the machine, put on the cover, and walk out the door. Amazing!

Jesus understood this thing of "clock watching." We are curious. We want to know when, who, how, and why. Jesus taught that matters of the last days are His department and under His control. No one knows the day or time of His return. We are to concentrate on our purpose and leave His purpose to Him. And what's our purpose? He said it: "Be on your guard!"

Jesus reminds us that there is enough to do just to keep on our toes and be on guard. The exact day and hour of His return are irrelevant. There will be persecution and distress and famine and peril. We must be ready. He's saying to us what a supervisor might have said to my friends in the typing pool: "You want a promotion? Do your job and do it well? Keep your eyes on your work and off the clock. I'm watching and there are rewards to those who faithfully serve."

What's your business? Mind it.

The Scapegoat

In William Golding's thought-provoking novel, *Lord of the Flies*, we are stunned by the horrific exploits of a band of children who crashed on an island and make a striking transition from civilized to barbaric. Golding illustrates with Piggy, the scapegoat. Without society's constraints, man is inherently savage. It gives us some sort of savage comfort to find someone other than ourselves to blame, ridicule, or scorn.

Leviticus is a tedious book of laws, cleansing rituals, and endless regulations. We wonder; can we learn from it? Suddenly, when we've about given up, a gem of truth leaps out. Reconciliation of God and man through Christ's death is first symbolized in Leviticus when the priest's sins are confessed over a live goat. The innocent goat is dispatched into the desert to die—a graphic and prophetic picture of Christ's death, resurrection, and atonement.

Golding's characters are an allegory of Satan's struggle for man's soul. From the get-go, Jack is savagely angry with no concern for order. Simon sustains his positive outlook through goodness, insisting that they will be rescued. Ralph, Jack's antagonist, doubts that possibility. Simon helps out when it is needed, but usually stays to himself rather than get involved in the conflict. In his attempt to maintain order, Ralph struggles with Jack continually. Roger has no mercy and intentionally kills Piggy, their scapegoat.

Every facet of human nature is captured in these characters. When Piggy died; in actuality, each one was guilty. The "atonement goat" or the scapegoat presents a prophetic snapshot of Christ's sacrifice made for all. He was blameless—just like Piggy, but He died. And in His death and resurrection, He is the atoning sacrifice for all our sins. There is no more basic or humbling biblical truth.

Who are you? Jack, Simon, Ralph, or Roger?

Leviticus 17-18
Mark 14:17-42
Psalm 31:9-18

I'm too Sleepy!

Remember how you resisted when your parents woke you early to help them with a chore? You were obviously younger than they and had a ton more of energy, but somehow you just couldn't "rise to the occasion." It was okay to get up early on Christmas morning; it was okay to leave at the crack of dawn for a school trip or a family vacation. Those times were fun and they were about you.

When your parent asked for a little time, a spirit of resentment boiled over. This person who gave you life and would sacrifice anything for you should be respected, and yet you thought: "Why are they invading *my* space and asking for *my* time?" Sometimes you even said it. These thoughts and comments reflect immaturity and lack of judgment that should be discarded somewhere in that magical never-never land between adolescence and adulthood.

It was Jesus' last night before His arrest. The Last Supper was over; the betrayal was perpetrated, and Jesus was praying—talking to His Father. One last time Jesus begged that the "cup be taken from Him *if* it was the Father's will." He didn't ask much of the disciples; in fact, He didn't even ask them to pray with Him. He simply asked them to watch. Not a hard thing to do—just keep your eyes pealed for trouble—that's all. But they weren't up to the occasion. They failed the Master. When He needed their support most, they simply weren't there. They were there in body, but not in spirit.

Many followers today are like the disciples in the garden. We're present in body but not in spirit. Jesus has sacrificed His life so that we might live. Truthfully, we want to be diligent and watchful, but life interrupts, and we grow weary and tired. We should be willing to do anything for anyone, anytime.

Sleep later. Be alert today.

I Didn't Do It!

My mother reminded me often, "A guilty conscience needs no accuser." Defending ourselves is as much a reflex as pulling a hand back from a hot stove. No one appreciates being blamed for something he or she didn't do, yet we aren't all innocent all the time. When we're guilty, it shows, but we hate to admit it. It goes cross-grain with pride. Many could double as "D Queen of D' Nile."

It was Jesus' last night; His disciples didn't know it, but Jesus knew. After He shared communion with them and after Judas darted away to commit his dastardly deed, Jesus retired to the Mount of Olives with the eleven. He was tired, and He knew the inevitable was just around the corner. He needed some rest. Peter was stunned when Jesus turned to him and said: *you will fall away...*

"No, Lord. Not me! I'm your most faithful follower. I'm true blue. You can count on me. Whatever the others do won't affect me. I'll be here to the end." Peter was adamant. How could the Lord say such a thing? It was unthinkable. Jesus persisted, *I tell you the truth, tonight before the rooster crows twice, you will disown me three times* (Mark 14:30). Peter was hurt. "I'll die with you if needs be."

That dreadful night progressed. Jesus was arrested and taken before the Sanhedrin, leaving His confused disciples in the courtyard. Peter did it: he denied Christ three times. Then he heard the morning quiet broken by a rooster's undeniable "Cock-a-doodle-doo." Poor Peter! His own humanity hit him between the eyes. He'd done exactly what he said he would never do. He was guilty of a betrayal that could never be refuted. And so are we. Daily, we deny Him in many ways. This account isn't an indictment of Peter, but a reminder to us all of how prone we are to denying Him. Stay true. Whatever.

If you did it: admit it; fix it; and move on.

Don't Cut Off the Buttons!

My father was a missionary to Alaska in the 40s and 50s when Alaska was far from a shopping epicenter. The term *shopping mall* had not yet been invented. We had "a" grocery store, a hardware/department store where we couldn't afford to shop, a smattering of drug stores, and a plethora of bars. It was a rough northern outpost. Because of these geographic and shopping restrictions, churches on the "outside" often sent us missionary boxes.

These boxes were anticipated for two reasons: (1) The homemade quilts people sent us were useful and appreciated connections from home. (2) These packages were a source of entertainment. People sent us the strangest things: Once an entire box of 1920s women's bathing suits; another time, fifty sock puppets; even a box of empty coffee cans. But the clincher was a rather sloppily organized box of old clothes. The thing that singled this box out as different was that someone had grabbed each garment and cut off the buttons. The cutting was so haphazard that a hunk of fabric went with each kidnapped button. Useless to us. A waste to the sender.

God has a whole lot to say about the condition of our sacrifices. He even says that some of our sacrifices are "unacceptable." *Do not bring anything with a defect, because it will not be accepted on your behalf* (Lev. 22:20)! God wants our best. He is interested in nothing less—the best of our time, talents, resources, and our hearts. He's a jealous God, and He will not compromise His standards in any area. My mother frequently said, "If you can't do it well; don't do it at all!" That's God's message regarding gifts. Bring your gifts with a happy, generous heart—not for a tax donation receipt. God sees our motives and He insists on gifts of the truest, purest, and highest nature. Nothing less is acceptable.

Leave the buttons on your giveaways.

Leviticus 23-24
Mark 15:1-32
Psalm 31:19-24

You've Got the Wrong Number

It's annoying and it happens daily. In the middle of a project or reading a book or watching TV, you're interrupted by the phone. If your "caller ID" doesn't identify the call, you feel compelled to answer; after all, it might be important. You hear an unfamiliar voice, "I'm sorry, I have the wrong number." Your concentration was interrupted by someone else who made a mistake. It's just as frustrating to the one on the other end of the line as it is to you.

Think about it: Whoever made the call had something important to say to someone. By a simple human error, the caller got connected to the wrong party—a minor annoyance if you're calling to chat or ask a simple question. What if, though, the misdialed call was a matter of life and death? In an emergency, it's vital to have the right number and the right connection.

As Jesus hung on the cross, balancing between God and man, He cried out, *My God my God, why have you forsaken me?* (Mark 15:34b) The worst human agony that we endure will never compare to His torment and humiliation. Jesus knew His earthly mission—but this? It was too much. We can resonate with that. "God, where are you?" we call out in our own anguish. Jesus questioned and so can we.

The soldiers near the cross thought Jesus was calling Elijah, the prophet who was transposed directly to heaven. It wasn't Elijah's number Jesus was calling—He was calling His Father. Jesus dialed the right number when He needed it most. There are situations in life when we simply cannot afford to make a mistake. We need the Father, and we need Him now—not a prophet, not an evangelist, not a singer—the Father! When tragedy strikes or when disappointment comes or when pain overwhelms, we can't afford to misdial.

Put His number on your speed dial.

Promise – Promises

A man's word was once his oath, his solemn pledge. To a large extent, those days are long gone. For some, a promise is as good as the current weather conditions. If things go well, the promise is kept, but if there is a change in the wind and it is more expedient to go another direction, then the promise is tossed out like yesterday's trash. At a young age, we learn which people we can trust and which ones to consider their word with a "grain of salt."

God is good to His word. You can bank on Him. If He promises it, He'll come through in a remarkable way. In the Old Testament, God's covenant—His pledge or His promise—appears like one continuous thread. We see this covenant with Abraham, Isaac, Moses, Joshua and more. God's promised reward is for us as well as the patriarchs: *…I will keep my covenant with you* (Lev. 26:9).

Christ's disciples personally heard all His predictions about His own passion, death, and resurrection. Yet, they still didn't fully grasp the magnitude or the surety of these promises. When Jesus' mother and Mary Magdalene went to the tomb, they were astonished to find it empty: *Don't be alarmed, the angel said…He is risen! He is going ahead of you into Galilee. There you will see him, just as he told you* (Mark 16:6-7). Christ promised it and it was so.

Following His resurrection, Jesus hung around Galilee a few more days before He rose into heaven as prophesied. During that brief period between the cross and the ascension, Jesus made some BIG promises to the world. He promised to be with us to the "ends of the earth." He said that "whoever believes will be saved." He promised that in His name we would be able to drive out demons and heal the sick. You can count on it: His promise is true; He won't forget you.

You can take His promises to the bank.

Speechless in Jerusalem

Surprise, surprise! Occasionally a woman past forty-five hears the words, "You're not sick; you're pregnant." Oops! We wanted a child when we were young, but now? This can't be. Such thoughts must have occurred to the priest Zechariah when he heard the doctor's report. He and Elizabeth had been married for years, but no kids. They had adapted to their childless home and uncluttered lives. A baby? Why now? God had a plan, and He had a promise for Zechariah and Elizabeth: *He will be a joy and a delight to you… He will be filled with the Holy Spirit even from birth* (Luke 1:14-15). What parent wouldn't be overjoyed to hear those words?

Kids come to us without promises, guarantees, or warranties. We're led by a little wild person through terrible twos, horrendous teens, and the struggling young adult phases. Elizabeth's special baby, though, wouldn't pass through any of the normal stages of maturation. He would be unique. Zechariah simply refused to believe their baby news and demanded a sign: *How can I be sure of this? I am an old man and my wife is well along in years* (Luke 1:18). Big mistake. Gabriel rebuked his disbelief and tied his tongue until after the baby's birth. "Zechariah, you wanted a sign? You got one."

It may not be a late-in-life baby, but God still works miracles. His word is packed with promises of His presence, His blessings, and His protection. What more can we ask? Yet, we're prone to reflect Zechariah's attitude. "Come on God, this thing you're proposing isn't possible now—or ever. Please don't tease me. I've grown accustomed to living without. I know it can't happen, so please, let's leave well enough alone." At the birth of John, God loosened Zechariah's tongue, and he spoke. When miracles happen in our lives, we will want to talk about it and tell everyone we meet.

Brag about your new baby.

Ordinary People

If you've passed your fourth birthday, you've had a rude awakening: you are painfully ordinary. We have so many commonalities that we notice them even at an early age. Consciously or subconsciously, we strike out early to make a mark and be different from the pack in some small way. Despite our ordinariness, God gifts each one of us uniquely, and He has a mission for each of our lives.

Mary was an ordinary teenager from an obscure village. Her childhood wasn't noted by anyone other than her adoring family. She was just a humble girl, but God saw something special in her and sent an angel: *You who are highly favored.* (Luke 1:28). Mary was highly troubled by the message and by the messenger: "I'm just a young teenager—a girl—from a small village," Mary thought. Despite her protestations, the angel continued: *Do not be afraid, you have found favor with God* (Luke 1:30b).

Favor with God. What beautiful words. Those words sound terrific, and yet how can we—so ordinary and so strikingly human—ever attain God's favor? When Mary questioned the angel, the answer was intense: *The Holy Spirit will come upon you, and...will overshadow you* (Luke 1:35). That's it. His Holy Spirit takes the ordinary you and the ordinary me and overshadows us. What a metaphor. Now, *He* is seen; not us. That's heady and that's powerful.

Are you ordinary? Yes! Does He want to favor? You bet! Does He long to overshadow your personality and do something spectacular *through* your ordinary life? Another resounding, "You bet!" God has no one but ordinary people like Mary and you and me. Refuse to be restricted and earthbound by your ordinariness. Allow His favor to shine on you. The world will be amazed; God will be glorified.

He casts a long shadow.

Humility & Youth

A young Quaker preacher ascended the stairs of the high pulpit with his Bible under his arm to deliver his first message. His head was held high; he *knew* that his message would "Wow" the congregation. Looking down into the faces of his friends and neighbors, his arrogance faded, and his delivery bombed. Humbly, he came to a stumbling conclusion, ducked his head, and descended the stairs. One of the elders approached the young preacher: "If thee would have gonest up as thee camest down, thee would have comest down as thee wentest up." There's a lot of truth in those words.

Mary was greatly humbled by the knowledge that she would bear the Son of God: *My spirit rejoices in God my Savior, for he has been mindful of the humble state of his servant* (Luke 1:47). Mary was young, but she knew who she was—a poor, humble peasant girl. "Why me?" She must have pondered. But God had a plan, and Mary accepted her place in that plan.

How different are Mary's reactions to God's blessing and assignments than some of our reactions. We come to expect blessings from God. "It makes sense," we think, "that He would choose us to do a great or significant task in His kingdom." Dangerous territory. When we entertain such thoughts, just like our young preacher friend, we are setting ourselves up for a mighty fall and dreadful disappointment. Mary says it better than we: *He has brought down rulers from their thrones but has lifted up the humble* (Luke 1:52).

Do you want to be used of God in His kingdom? Have a humble spirit about *anything* (big or little, great or small, seen or unseen) that He asks you to do. With this spirit, God will use you.

God delights in the humble.

His Name is Jack

When my mother was young, my widowed grandmother married a widower, and together they had a son. When her old country doctor asked Gramma the baby's name, she replied, "His name is Jack Vaughn." The doctor pitched a fit. "Jack Vaughn? No way. A boy should be named for his father." Not even Gramma knew her husband's real name; he simply was called, "CC." After CC died, Gramma and Jack moved from Oklahoma and began a new life in Oregon. When Jack registered for the draft, there was confusion; no record of his birth could be found. At last, it was discovered that a baby named "Charlie Clyde" had been born on Jack's birthday—to my grandmother! The old doctor had registered a bogus name. The *faux pas* was corrected, and my uncle continued to be Jack.

Zechariah was incredulous when an angel announced that he and Elizabeth would have a son. Unbelievable. They were old and had been childless all their married life. Zechariah questioned the angel, and God struck him dumb. Not before, however, He revealed the baby's name—John. During Elizabeth's pregnancy Zechariah was speechless until the infant's circumcision. The neighbors were positive he would be named Zechariah, Jr. After all, the first boy is always named for his father. Zechariah stunned the crowd. He took a tablet and determinedly wrote, "His name is John!" With that one obedient step, Zechariah's speech returned.

God often instructs us to do things that surpass experience, understanding, or common sense. He expects complete and blind obedience. Zechariah didn't understand what God was doing, but God got his attention when he struck Zechariah temporarily speechless. Your world, too, will be speechless when they hear about God's miracles in your life and see the evidence of His working.

Blind obedience leads to miracles.

The Lord's Blessing Be Upon Ye...

The United States has a large Irish presence. They were one of our biggest immigrant groups and were also despised and looked down on in New York City and other areas. The fact that they were loathed only caused the Irish to band together more. Today, their mistreatment is pretty well lost in history's annuls. We do remember, however, that each March 17 we must wear green. The Irish, though, have contributed more than the color green to our national complexion. Despite their hardships, the Irish have a reputation for being "lucky." Thus, the expression: "The luck of the Irish be with ye".

A true believer is constantly conscious that life in Christ is not one of *luck*, but rather one of daily and countless blessings. The world is looking for the lucky break, the winning ticket, the mother lode strike, the quick fix, the junk bonds, or the slot machine that returns a fortune for a dollar's investment. True accomplishments come the old fashioned way—through work. As we live in Christ and are obedient to His word, blessings follow just as achievements come from our physical and mental endeavors.

Moses gives a beautiful poem in his priestly blessing: (Num. 6:24-26).

The Lord bless you and keep you;
The Lord make his face to shine upon you and be gracious to you.
The Lord turn his face toward you and give you peace.

Headaches and burdens often follow "luck." The big win increases our taxes; a bigger house doubles our maintenance time and money, and the junk bonds can jeopardize our reputation. Luck can't give us God's gracious and compassionate protection; it can't make His face turn toward us or give us peace. Today is St. Patrick's Day. It isn't luck that the world needs; it's His blessing.

Bless someone today.

An Old Man and a Baby

When my father was 81, my brother's wife had a baby—a girl. At age 81 my father had five grown grandchildren and a great grandchild; "grandfatherhood" was old hat, but there's something special about progeny—especially at such an advanced age. My parents have a bond with this child that they haven't had with any of their other grandchildren. She's given them a new lease on life—a senior serendipity that keeps them young and focused on the future.

Simeon was old when Joseph and Mary brought baby Jesus to the temple for His consecration to the Lord. Today we call this baby dedication or baptism. It's a sacred time in which serious parents recognize dependency on God and ask His guidance in raising their little gift. Hearts melt as babies are presented for dedication. Old men and women remember their days with little ones, realizing the challenges and pitfalls that await these eager young parents.

As Simeon clumsily took baby Jesus in his arms, the spirit of God came on him, and he praised the Lord. Instinctively, Simeon recognized who he was holding—the son of God. This little baby was the living evidence of prophecy. His prayer was touching: *My eyes have seen your salvation…, a light for revelation to the Gentiles and for glory to your people Israel* (Luke 2:29b-32). Everyone—including Joseph and Mary—marveled at Simeon that day. How did he know who Jesus was? All his life, Simeon had studied the scriptures; when Jesus was placed in his arms, a divine transaction occurred. This helpless little baby was the promised Messiah. He just knew it.

What has God put in your life? Do you know the scriptures well enough to recognize Him when He is literally placed in your hands? It happened to Simeon, and it can happen to you as well.

Jesus is in your hands today.

Losing the Divine

On a family vacation one year, we lost our son. My parents took him in their car, and we kept our daughter with us, but our two cars got separated on the plains of Wyoming. It took the better part of a day before we finally connected. In retrospect this is humorous, but when it happened, we were anxious. "Where's our child? I thought he was right here with me, and now he's nowhere to be found." What an empty, helpless feeling! The day we lost our son, he wasn't upset. All day long he was with his grandparents, safely enjoying the privilege of being an "only child" for a brief period. He didn't understand what the big deal was. After all, he was safe.

Joseph and Mary attended the Passover in Jerusalem every year. When Jesus was *bar mitzvah* age, they took Him along. This was a big deal for Jesus *and* his parents. They probably prepped Jesus like we do today: "Remember, son, this is a significant occasion. Don't do anything to embarrass yourself or your family. There will be a big crowd, so stay close. We don't want to lose you."

Jesus' parents trusted him with the other boys and went their way, meeting friends, socializing, and enjoying the feast. When the Nazareth delegation set out for home, the atmosphere was charged with memories that would last all year. A few miles down the road, Mary and Joseph noticed that Jesus was absent. No Jesus. They were perturbed and fearful. Where could the boy be? Jesus knew where he was. He was tending His Father's business; it was that simple.

What a lesson for us today! We begin our journey with Jesus among us. If we fail to keep Him close, He slips away and into His Father's business. Joseph and Mary *thought* Jesus was with them, but in the busyness of their lives, they lost Him.

Don't let life rob you of His company.

Grounded by Clouds

I t's fun to travel when everything runs smoothly. For many reasons, though, countless delays are par for the course: road construction, low fuel, restroom breaks, or car troubles. And that's only the beginning. For those of us who fly a lot, there are airport delays, security checks, and the every present dilemma of weather. There can be a perfectly fitted airplane on the tarmac with a complete crew and a manifest of passengers ready to board when we hear: "Grounded because of weather." Another delay. We grumble even when we know it's for our safety, but dark clouds can't be trusted. No one really knows their contents; visibility is limited, and wind sheers are possible. We want to arrive at our destination; the delay is justified. We want to get there—not crash somewhere along the way because of haste or rashness.

God provided Israel a cloud as their wilderness guide. After resting on the mountain and then on Moses, the cloud finally hovered over the Tent of Testimony. This cloud is your guide, God clearly said: *whenever the cloud lifted, the Israelites set out; whenever the cloud settled, the Israelites encamped.* (Num. 9:17). Time was irrelevant when it came to the cloud. Through it, God was guiding them.

Clouds darken our lives like God's cloud darkened the Tent. Sure, clouds are annoying and interrupt our plans, but God's plan is bigger than ours, and it involves clouds. In clouds God is saying, "Stop!" You don't know what dangers are in dark clouds. Sometimes a disaster or disappointment stops us in our tracks for days, months, or even years. We can't move. We feel as though our lives are on an indeterminable holding pattern. And then one blessed day, a strong wind comes from no where, and the cloud begins to lift. We see the sun, and He says, "Now's your time; you can move on."

When your cloud lifts; move on!

Lunch with a Lesson

Whining is wearisome, childish, and self-centered. When a child doesn't get what he wants when he wants it, he whines. Whining wears adults down until they ultimately capitulate. A wise parent sometimes gives into a whining child to teach him a lesson. "Okay, you want a pet, you're getting a puppy, but it's yours to care for." Uh oh! That's not what the kid wanted. Not responsibility? He just wanted a puppy—all fun with no investment of time or money.

God provided plenty for the Israelites when they left Egypt. No one was hungry or thirsty, even though the fare was boring. Manna, day after endless day. Sort of like eating mashed potatoes for a month. How dull. Whining is non-productive at any age, but a particular bad fit on an adult. The "Children" of Israel whined, *If only we had meat to eat! We remember Egypt… now we have lost our appetite; we never see anything but this manna!* (Num. 11:4b-6).

Exasperated, God conceded. It was lunch with a lesson. "You want meat; you've got it. When this is over; you won't ask again. You're whining attitude disgusts Me; in time, you will rue this day." They got meat—and not just a little either. By nightfall the whiners were standing in quail three feet deep. Yuck! God wasn't finished. This wasn't just one meal; they had quail for an entire month. Like a parent knows what's best, God knew what was best for the Children of Israel. He answered them with an unforgettable object lesson.

Have you ever whined? Be honest. Most of us have; we can remember the lessons God taught us when we asked for more than we needed or for something that wasn't good for us. As we mature into fully devoted followers, we begin to comprehend the fact that He has our lives in control, and He always knows what's best.

Be careful what you whine for; you might get it.

The Minority Report

Negativity is deadly and contagious. Impossibility thinkers are a drag, and their negative "can't do" attitude permeates every fiber of a group. I was once the secretary for a progressive organization. This group was amazing. We accomplished events for teenagers that were unparalleled at the time. Despite all this success, one committee member saw only pitfalls and challenges. Our president was a man of humor. Often, he addressed our negative member: "Well," he would say, "What's the negative report?"

The mission of the twelve spies was perfunctory; their task was to bring back a condition report. Moses' committee misunderstood their mission. The land was already theirs. They reported on the abundance of the land; they even returned with grapes so large they had to be carried on a pole between two men. Those are whomping grapes! The spies stopped reporting and commenced commenting: "The people are HUGE, and we are as insignificant as grasshoppers compared to them." With these comments, they spread a bad report.

Caleb was unrelenting. Come on boys, *we should go up and take possession of the land, for we can certainly do it* (Num. 13:30). Yet, the impossibility thinkers prevailed; God now became a major player in this historic drama. Moses pled with God to be lenient with these small-minded people. Finally, God agreed—but with conditions. Only Joshua and Caleb would enter the Promised Land. The naysayers and their descendants were doomed to die in the desert. It's unwise to comment on God's ways. When He gives us something, it's ours. If they are giants, it's just His way of showing the world what He's ultimately capable of conquering. Don't do anything to compromise the personal promise land God has for you.

With God, you're no grasshopper.

You've Gone too Far!

We're stunned to hear about yet another church split. How could this be? These events aren't new; they were present during Moses' time. Levi's son, Korah and his cohorts were insolent, and they formed a gang of 250 against Moses. There is pseudo-safety in numbers, and if 250 people think the leadership is bad, it must be so. This motley crew spoke to Moses, *You've gone too far. Why did you set yourselves above the Lord's assembly?* (Num. 16:3b).

Moses was distraught. He hadn't asked to lead, but God appointed him; until God said differently, *he* was the leader. God proposed a test for Korah and his buddies; each man was to present his burning censor to the Lord, and God would choose the holy one. God's choice would indicate who their true leader was. Moses spoke to Korah: *You Levites have gone too far*. Korah was undeterred and remained defiant: "Bring it on. I'm as good as you and Aaron."

God told Moses to separate himself from Korah's evil men so that they could be destroyed. Moses spoke: "If these people die a natural death, I am wrong. But, if they're swallowed by an earthquake, that will be God's sign that He is with Aaron and not these evil men." As quickly as the words left Moses' lips, an earthquake struck, and the only ones destroyed were Korah and his band of dissidents.

God chooses leadership for the church. It's all too common for someone to rise up with the attitude and bearing of Korah: "I could run this thing better than the pastor. Follow me." Unless there are moral or illegal issues, our place is to follow God's chosen leader— not some upstart without training or understanding of the situation. In God's time, He will change leadership if necessary; in the meantime, we owe our pastor our prayers, our support, and our love.

Don't go too far: Love your pastor.

Tax Collectors, Doctors, and Sick Folks

The hyper-religious Pharisees and defenders of the law dogged Jesus incessantly. It was the day the paralytic's friends lowered him through the roof, and they had been watching all day to catch Him. Jesus healed the man *and* forgave his sins. Uh oh, Jesus, you shouldn't have done that. You've made the "powers that be" mad.

The Pharisees were speechless, the crowd was awed, and Jesus was weary; yet, this remarkable day wasn't over. As Jesus and His disciples left the paralytic, they saw Levi, the tax collector. He was a man avoided like a leper. Jesus approached Levi. In His unorthodox style and with simple words, He pierced to the core of this abhorred man, *'Follow me,' and Levi got up, left everything and followed him.*

There was a divine transaction between Jesus and Levi that day. Levi was never the same again. To thank Jesus, Levi threw a party. Who did he invite? His friends! Another opportunity for the Pharisees to hound Jesus: *Why do you eat and drink with tax collectors and sinners?* Duh! What a stupid comment. Levi's friends were sinners; he didn't know any "church people" to invite to his party; he invited his friends. By now, Jesus had had enough of the Pharisees. Why didn't they just go home and give it a rest? *It is not the healthy who need a doctor, but the sick,* Jesus responded.

We Christians need tax collector friends in addition to our "church" friends. Whenever I'm home, I eat breakfast at a little diner. It's overpriced and not one bit fancy. People smoke there. Few Christians come there, and yet everyone there is my friend. What's the message? If we really want to make an impact in the world, we must get away from our insulated, safe "church world" and out among tax collectors and sinners.

You may meet a tax collector at the diner.

Wisdom or Precious Gems

A few years ago, my parents were convinced that the most lasting future investment was the purchase of precious gems. So they paid a high price for a diamond, an emerald, a ruby, and a garnet. Each of these gems was flawless and large for its genre. After they purchased them, my parents stored the gems in a bank safety deposit box. They were supposed to hold their value regardless of the stock market. But it didn't flesh out quite like that.

For several years, these gems sat in a dark bank vault. Occasionally, I overheard an animated discussion about their future value. At last my parents agreed to enjoy them. They made a ruby ring for my mother and an emerald ring for me. The diamond and garnet were sold—for less than their initial price. What had been intended as future investment became a financial exercise in futility.

Solomon understood this concept: *Choose my instruction instead of silver, knowledge rather than gold, for wisdom is more precious than rubies, and nothing you desire can compare with her* (Pro. 8:10-11). A lot of life is spent in pursuit of things that ultimately matter little. We store up for ourselves treasures on earth, but the best choice is not things—it's Him and the wisdom He gives.

My pastor father had little as I grew up. Yet, my parents worked diligently to instill in us values and appreciation not only for the Bible but for literature, music, culture, and travel. We had music lessons and attended concerts when we couldn't afford them. We visited national parks and enjoyed family picnics beside arctic streams. My dad read to us from great works of literature, and daily we read the Bible together. These things can never be taken away; they are priceless and nothing can compare with them.

What legacy are you leaving your family?

Enduring Promises

The poet, Robert Service, said it in *The Cremation of Sam McGee:* "...a promise made, is a debt unpaid..." I love that line. It says it all; you're duty bound to keep your word. Hardly a 21st Century mantra. Today's promises are so conditional. We're hard put to find an individual or group who keeps a promise when it is no longer expedient. Because of this prevailing atmosphere, it's difficult to trust—and that includes trusting God and His Word.

Psalm 37 is a hallmark section of scripture that we return to often for comfort, reassurance, and support. David begins with what Dr. Earl Lee, my college pastor, called the *Cycle of Victorious Living*: "Fret not; trust in the Lord; delight in Him; commit to Him; wait on Him; fret not." This continuous cycle is a lifelong buttress for each of us with the ins and outs and ups and downs of daily living.

Psalm 37 continues, *I was young and now I am old, yet I have never seen the righteous forsaken or their children begging bread...the Lord will not forsake his faithful ones* (Psalm 37:25 & 28). David began serving God as a teen, and he was as human as any one of us. He had countless victories, but he also had some debilitating, humiliating human disasters. In his old age, David could look back and see that God's promises were secure, regardless of his own wavering temperament. If God said it; God meant it. God remained constant.

Where are you today? Are you young? Take the word of a man of old who experienced all the variances of life: His promises are indeed a "debt unpaid." Whatever He has promised, He will do. Are you facing your last years in a life of loneliness and quietude? Look back. He's been with you all the time, and He will remain with you to the end. He just won't go away.

God is a man of enduring promises.

Talking to Asses

It's a sign of aging to talk to oneself. Some of us are lonely, and some of us just like the sound of our own voice. We bestow human attributes on our pets also when we talk to them, acting as though they not only understand us, but expecting an answer. No one really expects their pet to answer with words. We know they can't talk, but there's a crazy sort of therapy in talking to pets. We would be shocked beyond belief if a pet actually answered us. It's out of the question. But God uses incidents that are totally out of the question to stop us dead in our tracks and get our undivided attention.

God was angry with Balaam for visiting the princes of Moab. So, He sent an angel to block his path. Balaam didn't see the angel, but his donkey did. First she pressed against one side to avoid the angel, crushing Balaam's leg. When that didn't work, she laid down in the road and refused to budge. Whatever the donkey did, the angel remained invisible to Balaam. The idiocy of his donkey's actions angered Balaam so much that he beat the animal. After all, that's how a rider gets his mount to move; it's a time proven practice.

Exasperated, the donkey spoke to Balaam. Donkeys don't speak; everyone knows that. But this one spoke, and a full-blown conversation ensued between Balaam and his mount. At last, God opened his eyes, and Balaam saw the angel that was blocking their way. How like God. He will use anything or anyone at any time or anywhere—as ludicrous at it might seem—to get our attention.

The next time you're stopped dead in your tracks by an unseen obstruction and are frustrated by yet another blind delay, stop. God may have placed something or someone in your pathway to humble you and open your eyes to what's ahead.

God may use the ridiculous to get our attention.

Airport Placards

Often I'm met at an airport by a stranger—my "new best friend." Until the minute we meet, we're unknown to each other. How helpful it is when my host or hostess has the forethought to print my name on a placard and hold it up for me to see. When I see my name, I know this is my host, and he or she is relieved to know that they have successfully identified their guest.

The Jewish people had been waiting years for the Messiah. When would His plane arrive? What would He be like? How would they identify Him? John the Baptist was in the same predicament as the public. He didn't know who the Messiah was or when He would arrive. When reports of Jesus' healings and teachings filtered back to him, John wanted to be positive that Jesus was the Messiah. He sent his disciples to Jesus with this message: *Are you the one who was to come, or should we expect someone else?* (Luke 7:18).

Jesus reply was typical: "Tell what you have seen and heard." In a word, Jesus was saying, "My deeds are my introductory placard. They have my name on them." He acknowledged John's inquiry while highlighting His mission: *...there is no one greater than John; yet the one who is least in the kingdom of God is greater than he* (Luke 7:28). Jesus knew who He was; He knew His mission as well.

The world is standing at the jet way asking, "Are you the one?" They're hoping someone will recognize them and introduce them to their host. They want comfort and rest after their long, weary journeys. We know Him, this "host of the world." What an honor to stand at the jet way of people's torn lives with placards held high. These placards aren't about us; they bear His name. We have an awesome privilege to properly introduce Him to our worlds.

Whose name is on your airport placard?

MARCH

29

BIG Forgiveness!

In our "buy now, pay later" society, it's easy to get caught in the debt trap. No one sets out intentionally to owe thousands. Through life's surprises, mismanagement, or the mistakes of others, it's easy to become awash in an ocean of debt—no land in sight. What a boon if "out of nowhere" a rescue ship cruised by and snatched us from our sea of debt. That's a fantasy world for sure.

Simon, the Pharisee, invited Jesus to dinner, and Jesus accepted the invitation despite Simon's doubts. As His host, Simon should have had a servant wash Jesus' feet. But no such gentilities were offered. Word of Jesus' presence spread and a sinful woman heard where He was eating. Uninvited, she burst through the door and anointed His feet. She was so humbled by His greatness that the magnitude of her sinful life overcame her. She wept and washed His feet with her tears, drying them with her hair. Whoa! "What in the world are you doing in my house? Who invited *you?*" Simon questioned.

Jesus' emotions were drawn in magnetically charged counter poles. On one extreme, the woman's honest humility moved Him. On the other hand, Simon's arrogance and lack of hospitality angered Him. So, He told a parable: "If two men owed money—one several thousand dollars, the other just a few dollars, and the lender forgave them both, who is forgiven most?" Foiled by divine reason. *I suppose the one who owed the most,* Simon was forced to reply.

The last thing Simon wanted to do was admit that Jesus was right. But He was. And He's right today. Regardless of your sin, forgiveness is available. When we humbly realize the magnitude of our sins and accept His forgiveness, it is BIG for every single one of us. It's almost too much to comprehend that He should forgive us.

Christ's forgiveness is HUGE!

Numbers 27:12-29:11
Luke 8:1-18
Psalm 38:13-22

Mary, Joanna, and Susanna

My entire life has been lived in the "parsonage." that magical never-never-land created just for pastors' families. What an amazing array of individuals I've had the privilege (or curse) of meeting. Everywhere I've lived—either as pastor's daughter or pastor's wife—I've come to realize that some of the most forgiven and humble people are some of the biggest supporters of the church and its pastor. Curiously, many of these people are women.

After Jesus' ministry reached full stride, He had no time to pursue a trade in order to support the ministry. Jesus knew the urgency and time limitations of His mission, so He trusted God to provide. Enter Mary Magdalene, Joanna, and Susanna. As Jesus preached and taught in village after village, several people supported Him. Three are mentioned specifically: Mary Magdalene, a woman cured of evil spirits; Joanna, the wife of King Herod's household manager, and another named Susanna. The Bible gives us no details about Susanna, but enough is told about Mary and Joanna to know that each of them had a story, and each of them had a changed life that compelled them to be dedicated to the loving support of Jesus.

Pastors are gifts, and their lives are packed with situations that most people never even consider—much less encounter. Financial encumbrances and emotional isolation only inhibit a pastor's ministry and divide his time. Money is a necessity, but there is even more that our pastors deserve and need. These women supported Jesus out of their "own means." They got it. What they could give was little, but they willingly gave. We can safely assume that some of their giving was monetary, but encouraging, believing, and emotional support accompanied their finances. Love and support your pastor; it will set him free to be all that God intended him to be.

You can be a Mary, a Joanna, or a Susanna.

MARCH

31

Numbers 29:12-31:24
Luke 8:19-39
Psalm 39

The Test of Fire

I was raised in Alaska; we had no gold, but I still learned a lot about that precious mineral that has driven man to the ends of the globe with a lustful fever. Gold is difficult to mine, and once mined, it must be refined and purified. As I grew, I learned that all ores are similar to gold in their need for refinement. Digging a precious ore from the earth is only the beginning of the process of refinement.

The Old Testament is replete with lengthy explanations of wars, ceremonial cleansings, and religious observances which seem irrelevant in our world. Suddenly, out of no where, a remote lesson leaps out at us. It's relevant—like reading today's newspaper. Moses avenged the Midianites, killing every man, but the people brought back spoils and plunder, including women and children. Moses was angry. The Midianite women were the problem; they had followed Balaam's advice, turning them against Israel in the first place.

Many times we don't finish a battle, short-circuiting victory. God was clear: This battle would be finished only when all the Midianite boys and women were killed. With the aid of Eleazar, the priest, Moses detailed the purification process. The Israelites' spoils and plunder were hammered from precious minerals, but the shapes tooled by the Midianites were evil. They must be purified: *Gold, silver, bronze, iron, tin, lead... anything else that can withstand fire must be put through the fire, and then it will be clean* (Num. 31:22).

Once our battles are won, we must submit to a spiritual purification and cleansing by fire. Purification isn't easy and it hurts. Yet, from the fires of our own private battles we can emerge a newly fashioned image of God—made from the same stuff—but retooled through fire into His likeness and suited for His purposes.

God wants to purify and reshape us all.

Reflections on the Word...

The Word in Real Time

April

Numbers 31-36, Deuteronomy 1-34, and Joshua 1-18
Luke 8-24 and John 1-2
Psalms 40-53 and Proverbs 8-10

My Prayer Time for April...

Thanksgiving _____
_____
_____
_____

Intercession _____
_____
_____
_____

Ministry _____
_____
_____
_____

Encouragement _____
_____
_____
_____
_____

The Word in Real Time

Expecting Jesus

An expectant crowd is exhilarating. I've stood along parade routes awaiting my son's marching band—just to see him strut his stuff. I've waited at an airport, excited to get my first glimpse of a friend after a long separation. My children loved to have guests. After we cleaned the house, cooked the meal, and set the table, we waited and *expected* the invited guests. I still can hear one of the kids shout from an upstairs bedroom window, "They're here!"

The word was out about Jesus; He was front page news. There was hardly a place where He could get rest, for everyone was looking for Him: *When Jesus returned, a crowd welcomed him, for they were all expecting him* (Luke 8:40). This "everyone" included not only the people desiring healing, but the seditious Pharisees. It seemed that everyone had a vested interest in what Jesus either could do *for* them or what they could do *to* or *against* Him.

Jarius was in the crowd *expecting* Jesus to heal his dying daughter. A woman with a hemorrhage of twelve years was also *expecting* His touch. The second appeared to stymie the first and keep Jesus from visiting Jarius' home. These two strangers are forever intertwined; their personal *expectations* intersected at Jesus' feet. The woman's interruption wasn't a problem for Jesus. He understood both Jarius and the woman—their hearts *and* their expectations.

What are your expectations of Him? Do you even have any? Has life beat you down so that you plod from day to tedious day, never expecting, never receiving. To paraphrase, "You have not because you *expect* not." *Expect* His blessings; *expect* His healing; *expect* salvation for your family; *expect* freedom from addictions. Nothing can stand between the truly *expectant* heart and the healing Jesus!

Come thou long expected Jesus.

APRIL

2

APRIL
2

Numbers 33:1-34
Luke 9:10-27
Proverbs 8:22-31

Divine Mathematics 101

Math. The very word strikes terror to some. They're afraid of math; the mere thought of it conjures memories of homework and blackboards and tests and endless struggles. Mathematics, on the other hand, makes perfect sense for others who literally thrive on it. Whether we have pleasant memories of math or whether we don't, mathematics is an integral part of daily life. We need it for just about everything, everyday. It's a permanent component of our lives.

Jesus' disciples had issues with math. Thousands followed them to Bethsaida; Jesus couldn't escape. As they rested on the hill, Jesus delivered The Sermon on the Mount. They were captivated as Jesus taught about the Kingdom of Heaven. A corporate consciousness permeated the crowd; this was greatness! As the sun set, the worried disciples spoke: *Send the crowd away so they can... find food and lodging, because we are in a remote place here.* (Luke 9:12). There weren't enough fast food joints in all Galilee to feed them, and there certainly weren't enough motels. If they didn't feed them soon, a riot would ensue. Jesus' response was frustrating to these practical men, "Give them something to eat." Really? Where do we get food? Jesus, you're not in the *real world*. We have a situation here!

Jesus knew what was available, and He knew who He was. They still didn't get it. He instructed the disciples to divide the group, and then He multiplied what they had—five loaves and two fish. The very first "fast food" experience. This orderly division of the crowd and the divine multiplication of the bread and fish produced more than enough sustenance for them all. Amazing? Not really, when you fully understand Jesus. Are you coming up short today? What's available in your situation? It may not seem like enough to you, but with God *anything* is enough.

Little is much when God is in it.

104   The Word in Real Time

Numbers 35 -36
Luke 9:28-56
Psalm 40:9-17

A "Safe Place"

The yellow "Safe Place" sign is a symbol of encircled arms. This symbol is printed on cards and distributed to students with "Safe Place" addresses like the corner 7-11 or K-Mart. The concept is simple, yet profound. Students are instructed that if they are ever in danger—real or imagined—they can turn to the "Safe Place" for immediate protection. These signs symbolize hope for kids who don't know where to turn when they need help.

Six of the Levite's 48 cities were consecrated "cities of refuge." God established detailed laws regarding hostilities of any kind. If a person was guilty, he was sentenced to immediate death. If, though, a person was provoked in an altercation, he had the option to seek shelter in a city of refuge. As long as the high priest lived, and as long as the provoked person stayed within the city limits, he was safe. If he left its walls of safety, however, he was on his own.

Our homes must be safe places. As I travel and speak, I receive prayer requests everywhere. Repeatedly, I am overwhelmed and angered by the secret sins committed regularly behind the doors of Christian homes. This duplistic behavior must stop. It sends the absolute wrong message to everyone in our lives. When a home is not a "safe place," children are literally taught to live a lie, and that will ultimately disillusion and destroy them.

We have an obligation to create contemporary "Cities of Refuge." The local church is such a place. We must guard it with everything we have in order that it remains a "safe place" in our world. Some churches have allowed animosity and bitterness to pervade them so much that the "safe place" has become a place of harm. We must guard against this with every fiber of our being.

Is your home and church a "safe place?

What's the Cost?

My Augusta, Georgia host worked for "the club" at the U. S. Masters Tournament. *If* you're invited to join and *if* you make the mistake of asking the fee, you are disqualified. Cost is not discussed; it's just paid. I've always had to live on a budget; I can't imagine what it feels like to buy anything or do anything regardless of cost. Most of us count the cost, save for the big trip or new car, or sacrifice for music lessons or braces. When confronted with a financial decision, our reflex response is the same: "What's the cost?"

It costs to be a fully devoted follower. Jesus was confronted by the question of cost centuries ago, and people are still asking the same questions and making the same propositions to Him: "I'll go with you anywhere." Jesus response was to the point, *Follow me.* And that is His message to today. "Now, Lord? I intend to follow you *anywhere* ultimately, but first I want to finish *my* plans." We don't articulate those specific words, but actions really do speak louder than words. Luke recorded some of their flimsy excuses: "I've got to take care of my dead father; I must say goodbye to my family." Jesus was disgusted and angered by their lack of commitment. *No one who puts his hand to the plow and looks back is fit for service in the kingdom of God* (Luke 9:62).

What was He saying to them and to us? There's a cost to being a fully devoted follower. If you begin this walk with hesitations and constantly look back at your old life, you're not "fit" for His Kingdom. Powerful words with a powerful impact on our lives. To each follower, the cost is something different, but there is a cost. Jesus said it, "We must deny ourselves daily..." There are rewards for those who "lay up treasures in heaven." Our treasures are people and no cost can be levied on a life that is forever changed.

It will be worth it all when we see Jesus.

Divine Mathematics 102

We're prone to adjust and alter situations and circumstances to comply with our own agenda or priorities. Psychologists call this *rationalization;* theologians call it *situation ethics.* God is as crystal clear about adjustments and variations to His law as Uncle Sam is about our adjustments to the Income Tax Code. We may not like it; it may not suit us; but it's the law, and as citizens we're compelled to obey.

Near the end of the Israelite's wandering as they were preparing to cross the Jordan River, Moses reviewed God's laws. He reminded them of God's words: *Do not add to what I command you and do not subtract from it* (Deut. 4:2). To quote Dr. Seuss, "I meant what I said, and I said what I meant... an elephant's an elephant, 100%." God reminds us that His word is final and it is total. We can't change an elephant, and we have no authority to change His word. We're not given the privilege to pick and choose what we want to obey and/or what we would rather ignore. Moses continued with God's reminders: *I have taught you decrees and laws... so that you may follow them... Observe them carefully, for this will show your wisdom and understanding to the nations* (Deut. 4:5-6). Do you pray to be a witness? Then read, study, and adhere to His word. It's the law.

Moses' words are as relevant today as this morning's newspaper. More than ever before, it is spiritually imperative to be scripturally sound. Everywhere we turn, someone is propounding his or her interpretation of the Word. If we're unfamiliar with the Word or don't consistently read and study it, we can be swayed by false doctrines, contemporary trends, and situational rationalizations of His omniscient word. This is spiritual quicksand. It will not hold us up when we need it the most.

His formula is accurate: Don't add; don't subtract.

Complicated Simplicity

Children are refreshingly black and white. Their unsophisticated, unpolluted minds believe what they're told. Adults often find this humorous; yet secretly we wish to turn back our own clocks to a less cluttered, less educated, less cynical time. Adults make things more complicated than necessary. It becomes increasingly difficult to take things at face value and accept them as they are stated, and that includes God's Word. Enter Jesus and His complicated simplicity: *Ask: it will be given to you; seek: you will find; knock: the door will be opened. Everyone who asks receives; he who seeks finds; and to him who knocks, the door will be opened* (Luke 11:9-10). Hum? I wonder what Jesus really means? Really? It's black and white.

If you sincerely want something from Him, ask. If you are earnestly seeking an answer, you will find it. If you knock on Christ's door and beg His forgiveness, He will open the door for you. In case they still didn't get it, Jesus taught them a parable that resonates with our modern lives. Jesus: "Do you love your kids?" His followers: "Of course, Lord!" Jesus: "If they ask for pizza, would you give them caster oil? If they asked to be on the ball team, would you refuse?" His followers: "Of course not, Lord. If it's in our ability to give, and if it will benefit the kids, we'll do anything, go anywhere, or make any sacrifice on their behalf."

Hello! Jesus isn't any more difficult than that to understand. We love our kids, and our heavenly Father loves His kids. Do you want God to bless you? Ask Him. He wants to bless you, but He needs to know that you *really* want Him. As you seek and knock, He's right there ready to open the door and help you find whatever it is that you are searching. He loves you and wants the very best for you.

He's at your door.

Talk about Awesome!

We say it everyday: "That's awesome!" The word *awesome* is one of those "fad words" that gets overworked until we lose the impact of its real meaning. In case you are among the millions who have forgotten its meaning, here it is: *Awesome: profound and reverent respect for the supernatural and respectful fear inspired by authority.* Rich Mullins penned these words and music, "Our God is an awesome God!" Whoa! When we insert the dictionary definition into the words of the song, we stand amazed. God is truly awesome!

God instructed us in many areas. *Love the Lord your God with all your heart, with all your soul, and with all your strength. Talk about Him when you sit at home and when you walk along the road, when you lie down and when you get up* (Deut. 6:5-7). Good parents recognize their responsibility to their children. We shelter them, protect, nurture, educate, and guide them. Moses is recapping an important piece that we dare not omit. Teach them that God is awesome.

What becomes important to kids is what is important to parents. Early they learn to value what we value. We are their first and most influential teachers. Our lives, conversations, mores, and values shape their young lives. It's effortless for us to talk about our jobs, our finances, family issues, or the kids' schooling. There's something bigger and more important that our kids must learn from us: Our God is an awesome God.

Pray "believing prayers" with your kids and grand kids; focus on God's answers when they come. Enjoy God's creation with them; talk about the beauty of nature and all that He has created just for them and you to enjoy and experience. "Our God is an awesome God" is more than a mere line in a song. Let the world know.

Our God is indeed an awesome God!

April Splendor

It's spring—that magical time of the year when the earth awakens from its winter rest. One day as I was driving to breakfast, I became immersed in God's spring canvas of yellow and white and pink and green. The sky was blue; the birds were singing; all was right in God's world. As I drove along with a song in my heart, I was so captivated by the beauty of it all, that I lost connection with my purpose. Suddenly, I was several blocks beyond my destination, lost in God's magnificent springtime.

The trees and bushes and flowers that fascinated me did nothing whatsoever within their own power to attain their beauty. It's spring, and in the spring trees and bushes naturally are beautiful. During the long, cold winter months, I've never heard a tree fret about its Easter outfit. It just happens. How unlike nature we are, and how much we can learn from it. He's the creator of everything. Here we are, the most sophisticated and intelligent of the lot, and yet we are the ones who worry and fret the most about whether and when He is going to take care of our needs.

Jesus understood this: *Consider how the lilies grow. They do not labor or spin. Yet I tell you, not even Solomon in all his splendor was dressed like one of these. If that is how God clothes the grass of the field… how much more will he clothe you? Do not set your heart on what you will eat or drink; do not worry about it. …Your Father knows that you need them* (Luke 12:27-31). We labor and we spin and we fret and we worry. His injunction continues, *Seek his kingdom, and these things will be given to you* (Luke 12:32). As winter dissolves into spring, I need this reminder. We are concerned about things that should concern Him. He's in charge of the entire cosmic universe—including you and your situation. Aren't you glad?

Don't Worry; Be Happy!

The "Remember When" Game

During the Korean War in Alaska, I experienced air raids; I recall the Russian's threats of front line attacks. I came of age during the 60s with its civil unrest. I remember Kennedy's death; I remember Watts: I remember the day Martin Luther King was shot: I remember when Bobby fell in Los Angeles. We relate experientially: what we experience is relevant to us and what we don't experience seems disconnected and somehow irrelevant.

After years of teaching, I know this to be true. My last fifteen years were in inner cities where I taught racially diverse and ethnically divided clientele. It was a challenge to relate to today's kids the events the 40s, 50s, and 60s that so radically altered all our lives. As an educator, that is my profound responsibility. If today's kids don't understand their parents' sacrifices, then all their efforts are in vain.

Before Moses died he reminded the Israelites who they were and where they had come from. While they wandered in the wilderness, two new generations were born. These generations had no personal memory of persecution in Egypt, and they didn't understand God's provision for them. Moses felt a divine compulsion to remind the Israelites: *Remember that your children were not the ones who saw and experienced the discipline of the Lord: his majesty, his mighty hand, his outstretched arm, the signs he performed... (Deut. 11:2).*

We heard about the Depression nearly every day of our lives; my parents wanted us to know what had impacted our lives. "Remember when" is a fun game. Play a spiritual "remember when" game with your kids and grand kids. Remind them how God has worked in your life. Tell them about His majesty and His outstretched arm. Pass it on. Don't let the story die with your generation.

Share what you've seen and heard.

The "Aha!" Experience

Aha experiences are rewarding to teachers. Time wasn't wasted; the kids got it after all. I've explained a subject perfectly, only to see blank faces. They didn't get it. My explanation was flawless, but still they stare. When least expected I've heard: "*Now* I get it! If nine times six is fifty-four; then six times nine has to be fifty-four." Duh! I've taught that all semester. Thank goodness for "Aha!" experiences. Without them, teachers would throw in the towel.

There is something God-driven in Christians—an urgent desire to do something *great* for God. If only we had the ministry of Dr. "So and So;" or if we could sing like a gospel "star." If only we had the finances to build a church; if we had the courage to witness to our neighbor. Intrinsically, these desires are identical. We want to make a difference and do something BIG for God, but we're intimidated by our own limitations and by our lack of understanding of faith.

I can see Jesus scratching his head and rummaging through their experiences to conjure up one more simile. Aha! This will work: *What is the kingdom of God like? What shall I compare it to? It's like a mustard seed, which a man planted in his garden, and it grew and became a tree... It's like yeast that a woman mixed into a large amount of flour until it worked all through the dough* (Luke 13:18-20). Jesus must have thought: "I've explained the Kingdom of God a dozen ways. This is as down-to-earth it gets. They'll get it now."

If the tiniest seed can produce a large tree, and if a dab of yeast can cause an entire lump of dough to rise, then a little faith is all you need to get started. We're stopped short of great things for God because we're searching for BIG faith. Start with small steps and see the great things God can and will accomplish through your faith.

Just a little faith—that's all.

The Word in Real Time

You're being Watched

A deserter was brought to Alexander the Great. As the young man stood trembling in Alexander's presence, he addressed him, "Soldier, What is your name?" Cowed and frightened, the deserter stared silently at the floor. Again, the great leader addressed him and received the same silent response. The third time, Alexander demanded, "Soldier, state your name or off with your head!" The hesitant response came in an uneven whisper, "My name, sir, is Alexander." The legend continues: Alexander the Great rose to his full height and shook a trembling finger at the deserter: "Soldier, change your behavior, or change your name!"

The Pharisees were always watching Jesus. They stayed nearby in order to catch Him in an inconsistency either in His own life or in interpreting scriptures. On one particular Sabbath, Jesus ate in the home of a prominent Pharisee. This wasn't any ordinary church member—he was a member of the official board. As always, the sick found Him: this time it was a man with dropsy. "Okay, Jesus, what are you going to do with this? You say you know the Bible; we certainly know it. The scriptures say you can't work on Sunday. Healing is work. So, what are you going to do now? You're trapped."

Jesus responded to their hearts even though they never verbalized their objections: *If one of you has a son or an ox that falls into a well on the Sabbath day, will you not immediately pull him out? And they had nothing to say* (Luke 14:5-6). Jesus was always being "carefully watched," and so are we. The world desires to know one of two things: Is our God real, or are we a fake? When you name Jesus as your Savior, people begin to watch. Jesus knew they were watching, and He knew that this was not a "win-win" situation. He did what was right in the eyes of God, and that was the most important thing.

Does your behavior suit your name?

God's "un" Favorite Things

Rain drops on roses and whiskers on kittens. These are a few of our favorite things. Some things, though, make us sick to our stomachs. It's hard to love a child molester or a philanderer or a murderer. We find them vile, unfathomable, and detestable. How could anyone stoop so low? What causes such deplorable behaviors?

Some things, though, we ignore: the newspaper horoscope, "900" fortune teller lines, Quiji boards. What could these hurt? They're harmless entertainments; no one truly believes in them. Therein lies the problem. A little boy fell out of bed every night. Nightly, his mother was awakened by his cries, consoled him, and tucked him back in for the night. Exasperated with this pattern, the harried mother asked the boy why he kept falling out of bed. "Oh," he replied, "I guess I'm just staying too close to the 'gettin in' place."

God warns about staying too close to the edge: *Let no one be found among you... who practices divination or sorcery, interprets omens, engages in witchcraft, or casts spells, or who consults the dead. Anyone who does these things is detestable to the Lord.* (Deut. 18:8-12). Dabbling in the occult, witchcraft, or fortune telling is on the edge. Sooner or later, you will fall out of fellowship—a fall more catastrophic than that of a child falling out of bed.

We must know what we believe and why we believe it. Winking at Satan's allures will eventually pull us downward into a pit of despair and captivation. God's word is clear. This passage doesn't require a theologian to explain it. Simply put: Stay away! "How can I do that," you ask? Dig into His word; put your total trust in Him. There's enough guidance in the Word of God to handle any situation of life. Don't make Him have to repeat Himself:

Stay away from the 'gettin in' place.

Come to the Party

San Diego was a designated Vietnam POW reentry point, and by the mid '70s, POWs became to arrive at Miramar Naval Air Station regularly. With tears of joy, I sat in my home and watched the C-141s touch down on US soil, delivering their precious cargo. What a mixture of emotions. Men were reunited with family and country that they hadn't seen in years, and they had missed so much. Personal views of the war were temporarily shelved in lieu of the euphoria of these "Rip Van Winklesque" homecomings. No one was critical or refused to come to the party.

Jesus told about a similar reunion. Two brothers were separated by their own choices: The younger brother traveled far away and lived a wild life, depleting all his funds. The older brother stayed home and worked with Dad. But they *both* received their inheritance. Out of the blue one day, the kid returned, and Dad threw him a party. Rejoice! The runaway was home again. Everyone celebrated—minus one. The older brother was mad and refused to attend the party. How could Dad give this wasteful scoundrel a party? After all, *he* was the one who stayed home and tended to the family. His dutiful life had become a burden; his joy was gone. No one ever gave him a party. Long ago, he too had left Dad—in his heart. Envy festered as he fantasized about the sinful life his little brother had chosen. His attitude: *So, this is what I get for being loyal?*

The church is jammed packed with people who are doing all the right things for all the wrong reasons, and they refuse to attend the party. When a sinner comes to Christ, or when someone "succeeds" in the kingdom, it makes them mad rather than gladdens their spirit. Without fully knowing what's happening, you can become like the older brother—a resentful saint.

Rejoice! There's a party going on.

Finders Keepers – Losers Weepers

inders keepers; losers weepers. American kids learn this phrase early. We chanted it and teased one another when we found something that wasn't ours. We held the object high and goaded, "What's it worth to you?" That was harmless child's play, but "me first" attitudes slip into our adult years like grease off a skillet.

From Day One, man has been asking, "Who is my brother?" Moses dealt with this: *If you see your brother's ox or sheep straying, do not ignore it …Take it home with you and keep it until he comes looking for it. Then give it back to him.* Just finding something doesn't automatically make it ours; there is an obligation to find its owner. More importantly, when you discover that someone is missing something intangible, are you willing to give of yourself to help them find it?

I once led a group of women on a mission trip where we worked at a halfway house for crack moms and their babies. We were stunned by what we found. To a person, we were abashed at the overwhelming amount of "stuff" these women had been given. There were dozens of boxes of infant shoes, and more clothes for each child than ten babies could wear. There were new strollers, high chairs, and state-of-the-art toys. What an eye-opener for women who thought that dollars and a bit of elbow grease was needed most.

We soon realized that these women didn't need stuff—they needed us. Talk about being your brother's keeper. It's easy to throw money or theories at issues and people. These women didn't need money; they needed our company and acceptance. Before we left, we stood on the steps and took a group picture with the moms and babies. There wasn't a dry eye. We had given back to our brother what we found along the road of life, and God blessed those efforts.

Keepers, Weepers – Givers, Receivers

Father Abraham Had Many Sons

Once, a wealthy man moved back and forth in a chauffeur driven limousine. Each day he was delivered to the door of his high rise office. Since their fates rose or fell on his capricious moods, everyone catered to his whims. Each night his limousine returned him to his pent house. A maid had a lounging robe laid out and bath water run. A flawlessly presented and palatably delectable meal was ready. His stock portfolio was large and secure; he owned a condo in Maui; he had a corporate jet. Everything in his life was perfect.

Daily, the man passed a beggar pleading for a handout, but the arrogant man turned away as he stepped into his limousine, cell phone glued to his ear. He was a busy man with people to meet and places to go. One day the beggar was gone. *If* the rich man noticed, it was only that an irritant was absent from his watertight life; he had no time for "lowlifes." The beggar died unnoticed not only by the man but by hundreds of others. He wasn't just *any* beggar, though; he was a good man who had fallen on bad luck. At his death *the angels carried him to Abraham's side.* His agony was over. For eternity he dined sumptuously and slept happily in the "bosom of Abraham."

Later the rich man died also, but his fate was entirely different than that of the beggar. Suffering in hell, he recalled many things he had overlooked in his busy life. His tormented mind recalled the beggar, and he called out to the man he had ignored in life: *Father Abraham, have pity on me and send Lazarus… because I am in agony in this fire* (Luke 15:24). Help was not forthcoming. Father Abraham spoke: "In life you had everything; the beggar had nothing. Now he is contented and you are in hopeless agony. Conditions will remain this way forever; a wide gulf separates you. You could have bridged that chasm in life, but you chose not to. You sealed your own doom."

Are you a son of Father Abraham?

Deuteronomy 26-28:14
Luke 17:11-37
Psalm 46

Safe Sanctuary

The cries of Victor Hugo's grotesque hero, Quasimodo, as he escapes into the cathedral with Esmeralda, echo in our ears: "Sanctuary! Sanctuary!" God and the holy places were created as safe places for His people—places we can hide when we have no place to turn. We've all felt like Quasimodo: "Where can I go? Where can I turn? Everyone is pursuing me? Is there refuge and comfort for the hurting and weary?"

When we lived in Washington State, Mt. St. Helen's was virtually in our backyard; in Southern California, our home sat near the San Andreas Fault; in Alaska, we had threats of tsunamis resulting from earthquakes; presently, I live in tornado alley, Central Kansas. As fearful as nature can be, there are situations in life that tower over us, creating long foreboding shadows. Disease may destroy our body; kids may disappoint us and break our hearts; people in the church may disillusion us; business setbacks may ruin us financially.

King David, identified with our human feelings of fear; he nailed it: *God is our refuge and strength, an ever-present help in trouble. Therefore we will not fear, though the earth give way and the mountains fall into the heart of the sea, though its waters roar and foam and the mountains quake with their surging...* (Psalm 46:1-3). Do you feel like Quasimodo? Do you want a place to run? Run to God.

Suffering provides impetus for self-review and give us opportunity to totally depend on Him. Be content and focus on His plans rather than on your comfort. Suffering causes a true believer to look to God rather than to himself. There is no comfort compared to the comfort by which He comforts us, no freedom like the freedom to trust Him; and no confidence like the confidence to trust in Him.

He is your safe sanctuary.

The Equalizer

Supercilious hypocrites create an auspicious air with their self-righteous sacrificing. Backhanded statements about their generosity are a source of irritation. They demand that buildings or pews or various and sundry pieces of church furniture be named for them. They feel slighted when the pastor or community doesn't recognize their philanthropic efforts. They are confident of their own virtue and look down on everyone else. Jesus said all that; not me!

Two men prayed in the temple. The Pharisee prayed loudly so others could hear clearly; he thanked God that *he* wasn't a major sinner—a robber, an adulterer, or a tax collector. His reference to the tax collector was not randomly made. He was aware that nearby stood a detested tax collector, an abhorred individual who collaborated with their Roman occupiers. This man, too, was saying his prayers. The Pharisee was convinced that he was better than others as he prayed loudly: "I haven't committed any major sins—especially the turncoat activity of collecting taxes from my own people." The tax collector, though, knew that his life was deplorable both in the eyes of his neighbors and God, and he shamefully admitted his sin. So humbled was he as he prayed that the tax collector hung his head and beat his chest, *God, have mercy on me, a sinner* (Luke 18:13b).

God is the great equalizer; He knows our hearts. If you give to be recognized, He sees that. If you hope to get attention or maybe win in the next election, He sees that as well. The ground is level at the foot of the cross. There are no degrees of sin; there are no degrees of forgiveness. Use whatever term resonates with you, but the truth remains: He justifies, evens the score, and sets the record straight. When we pray our demeanor must reflect the tax collector—utter humility and thanksgiving that He would love a sinner such as I.

He's the judge, the justifier, and the equalizer.

A Wee Little Man

Zacchaeus was a wee little man... Those of us who went to Sunday school can pick up that little tune and finish the song. In the middle of ancient Jericho is the "Zacchaeus tree," a sycamore that has been there for over 2,000 years. Zacchaeus' story isn't a parable; it occurred in real time. This little man didn't intend to be canonized; his curiosity was peaked, and unknowingly he thrust himself into biblical history.

Who was this man; what was all the hullabaloo about? Zacchaeus' personality wouldn't allow him to rely on others' word; he had to discover Jesus personally. A less tenacious man would have dismissed the extra effort as wasted, but not Zacchaeus. He was small and couldn't see through, over, or around the masses, but he was resourceful. He found a tree and climbed it. Not even his physical limitations would stop Zacchaeus from at least seeing Jesus.

His intentions were to sit in a tree and draw his own conclusions; he wasn't prepared for what happened. From his tree perch, his eyes met Jesus' eyes. When any man truly looks into the eyes of Jesus, he will never be the same. Jesus called Zacchaeus by name and announced that He needed a place to spend the night. Stunned, Zacchaeus obeyed. Not only was Jesus his house guest, but He became a permanent resident of Zacchaeus' heart and life.

At what distance and to what extremes have you gone to see Jesus? What limitations or excuses are keeping you from seeing over or through or around the problems and situations of your life? There are no accidental encounters with Jesus. He yearns to come into your life, sit down and fellowship, and truly be your friend.

Plant a sycamore tree in your yard.

For Every Moses...

My father followed a pastor who had been in that church for twenty-seven years—a daunting task! Everyone in the community knew the retiree. He was loved and nearly granted sainthood. Interestingly, the transition was smooth, and it had little to do with my father. The pastor had groomed his people well. He pledged that his last Sunday would indeed be his last. He would conduct no more weddings or funerals. He was their friend, but unavailable to listen to complaints about the "new guy." He was unique. These transitions—whether church or business—are often pretty rough. It's human nature to hark back to the "good old days."

Born and raised in Egypt, Moses was God's chosen leader. Victoriously, he led Israel out of Egypt and through the Red Sea while Pharaoh pursued. Moses endured their wilderness grumblings and failures, and he faithfully delivered the Ten Commandments. He sent spies into Canaan and cleaned up the backlash of that mission. Poor, melancholy Moses. I wonder how often he wanted to resign, but he remained steadfast until his death. Even though the people grumbled against him, they were accustomed to his ways. What were they to do when Moses died?

God always has a plan. Moses called Joshua before the people: *Be strong and courageous, for you must go with this people into the land the Lord swore ...to give them... The Lord goes before you and will be with you; he will never leave you nor forsake you. Don't be afraid; don't be discouraged* (Deut. 31:7-8). These words were spoken to Joshua, but they were meant for everyone. Don't be afraid, Joshua is your new leader, and I am with him just as I've been with Moses. Are changes coming down the pike for your church, business, or family? God has a plan; He always does. For every Moses...

God always has a Joshua.

Superficial Diversions

Tax time. There are no two ways around it; we're responsible to pay; that's final. We understand the concept; it's the paying that's difficult. Taxes are an inevitable, perpetual nuisance, and commiserating about taxes is an American rite of passage. We wait until April 15 each year to mail our return. "After all," we reason, "our money might as well be in the bank as long as legally allowed."

Taxation is as old as the world. The Boston Tea Party and other acts of civil disobedience helped shape our country. In Jesus' day, tax collectors were everywhere. The Pharisees continually searched for a trick question to trap Jesus so that they could turn Him over to Pilate. Aha! Taxation is the ideal approach, the perfect trap. They stirred up the people with their phony concern and used innocent citizens to ask their crafty question: *Teacher, we know that you speak and teach what is right, and that you do not show partiality… Is it right for us to pay taxes to Caesar or not* (Luke 20:21-22)?

Jesus saw through their bogus concern. With a stroke of genius, He declared the separation of church and state, *Show me a coin. Whose portrait and inscription are on it?* Oops! The smug Pharisees were foiled again. They had trapped themselves. *Give to Caesar what is Caesar's, and to God what is God's* (Luke 20:24-25). Jesus' subtle message: The real issue here is your effort to trap the Son of God.

People are still looking for that silver bullet that will zap Christians speechless. Jesus longs to bestow His wisdom on us. We must be *into* the Word, though, to know the word. Don't allow someone's obtuse and mindless question about some remote scripture or controversial social issue to divert you from your true mission. Keep focused. Taxes and superficial diversions will always be with us.

Answer the unspoken question.

One Bride for Seven Brothers

Everyone grieves when a loved one dies. In a large part, things are never the same. We recall shared times and commemorate their lives with memorials. There's a hole in our heart and a vacancy in our lives. Grieving is a normal and necessary process, but somewhere along the line, the healthy griever realizes that "life goes on." Others need and deserve our love and attention. Eventually, a smile revisits our face, and we rediscover the silenced song of our hearts. We never forgot our lost loved one, but life is about living.

The Sadducees came to bat with a preposterous question. They laid out a virtually impossible scenario: If a man died, and each of his six brothers died, and if (according to law) each of them married the older brother's wife, whose wife would she be in heaven? Oh, brother! They had to cogitate a long time to conjure up that question. These incessant, absurd questions touched Jesus' last nerve. "Why don't you just give it a rest?" He must have thought. "There are countless issues of much greater significance."

This world is "earthly." But there is a radically different 'other world.' Heaven and earth can't be compared. The Sadducees' question was moot. In the other world, *they can no longer die; for they are like angels* (Luke 20:36). More than anyone, the Sadducees should have known that scripture. They pressed Jesus for His final answer: *He's not the God of the dead, but of the living...* (Luke 20:38). Once we are born physically, we live forever. Bodies die, but the spirit is eternal. The hypothetical woman couldn't be married to all seven brothers simultaneously. What a frightening proposition. Given the liberty of hindsight, I suspect the Sadducees were sorry that they ever asked such a ridiculous question.

He is the God of the living—eternally.

If You Don't Tell...

My older brother, one of his friends, and I searched through a burned print shop one day, salvaged some lead typeset and melted it into paperweights. What a disaster! Our concoction heated to its boiling point—620 degrees; and instantly, mother's kitchen erupted with lead. Molten lead was everywhere—the ceiling, stove, the counter top. We were in BIG trouble and scrambled to clean up the mess. We made a pact; "if you don't tell; I won't tell." All of us carried our secret into adulthood. It was simply not prudent to tell.

As the Israelites advanced toward Jericho, Joshua deployed spies to look over the city and land. Word of the Israelite's God preceded them, and the citizens of Jericho were filled with trepidation: *When we heard of it, everyone's courage failed ...for the Lord your God is above and on the earth below* (Josh. 2:11). Jericho's king then sent out a message to capture and kill these spies.

The spies visited the home of the prostitute, Rahab, and God spoke to her. When asked about the spies, she lied. "They were here, but they've gone; I have no idea which way they went. Hurry, maybe you'll catch them." Before Rahab aided the spies' escape from Jericho, she cut a deal with them: "I know the Lord has given this land to you, so if I keep your secret, please spare the lives of my family." It was agreed. *Our lives for your lives! If you don't tell... we will treat you kindly ...when the Lord gives us the land* (Josh. 2:14).

When you know something that's too good not to tell; wait before you speak. Your report may come back to haunt you. It's beneficial to your spiritual health to keep your word. It's not expedient to tell everything you know. If you promise secrecy; keep your word. It could save your life.

When you give your word, keep it.

Stuck in Winnemucca

Our wedding in a little Idaho college town was perfect, but disaster began immediately. It took four cars to get away from the church: one had four flats, one ran out of gas, and in the third we had a near tragic accident. At last, a friend took us to our car, and we spent the night in Idaho's only honeymoon suite where a frozen kitchen nixed our steak and eggs breakfast. To top it off, my mother called our first morning. Despite our bumpy start, we enjoyed our Sun Valley honeymoon and returned to our little rented cottage.

On Dec. 23, we left for California. Near Winnemucca, Nevada, our car broke down. A mechanic worked on it for 24 hours, but it broke again. My brother crossed Donner Pass in a storm to get us home. We finally arrived Dec. 26. On Dec. 30 we crossed the pass to Reno in yet another storm. After rescuing our car, we headed to Idaho, but the car broke again. On New Year's Eve we were stranded, and there was only one motel room available. Later, we coined a family phrase that has lasted: "I'm stuck in Winnemucca."

The Israelites could resonate with our experience. They were "Stuck in the Sinai" forty years, yet God had a plan. The Jordan was at flood stage; that didn't bother Him. It was time to move: *Consecrate yourselves; tomorrow the Lord will do amazing things among you* (Josh. 3:5). It happened. Their marathon trip lasted until an entire generation died. The Israelites followed the priests *through* the Jordan on dry land. There they built an altar to honor God's victory.

Have you been wandering in a desert for years? Does no resolution seem in sight? Don't give up. God has a plan for your life. There's no obstacle too big or too daunting for Him. When the time is right, nothing will deter God from working your long awaited miracle.

There's life beyond Winnemucca.

The Rebel Yell

In the Civil War, the blood-curdling Rebel Yell, punctuated with monkey screeches, was dreaded. With the yell, the rebels routed and intimidated an enemy twice their size. Passion for the cause buoyed the rebels to employ any tactic to crush the Union. Their yells were heard echoing through forests and valleys long before rebel troops were sighted. As the confederates advanced, their yells bolstered them with energy that surpassed size or military capacity.

Advancing into the Promised Land, Israel met many obstacles and one enemy after another. No city was as indomitable as Jericho, for "no one went in and no one came out." It was impenetrable and shut up tight. God's plan, however, was for Jericho to fall. It was a crazy sounding plan—nothing military about that; God must be confused.

The priests with their trumpets and the Ark marched around Jericho. Their instructions: "Keep quiet!" For seven days the people doubted: "What is this? This isn't strategy; it's stupidity." On the seventh day they marched around the city seven times, and then they shouted. *When the trumpets sounded, the people shouted. When they gave a loud short, the wall collapsed, and they took the city.* (Josh. 5:20). Talk about a Rebel Yell! God was with them all along.

Jericho's citizens had taunted and teased the Israelites. You can hear them, can't you? While they pelted the Israelites with rocks and debris, they shouted: "Hey boys, do you really think that marching around Jericho will make any difference? This is a secure city. You and your God look pretty dumb." Obeying God was humiliating, but they obeyed. He has victory for you and me as well. If you are faithful, one of these days, you will see it; the defenses of your adversary will crumble and fall. When they do, let out a Rebel Yell.

God is the ultimate "Rebel Yell."

25

My Enemy's Enemy is My Friend

It's a phenomenon of human nature that occurs with predictable consistency: When it's to a person's advantage, he or she will make friends with an arch enemy in order to annihilate a greater foe or achieve personal gain. We chuckle when we observe this in kids, but if we aren't completely grounded and know what we believe, it's easy to waver. This behavior is duplistic and destructive.

There was no love loss between Herod and Pilate. They'd rather not even see each other. The Jews questioned and pounded Jesus until they were blue in the face. At last, He answered affirmatively: "I am the Christ." Now they had reason to take Him to Pilate: "This man opposes Roman taxes, *and* He claims to be our King." Their efforts to appeal to Pilate's Roman loyalty only supported their selfish ends. They didn't care about His opinion about taxes. Their mantra: "Whatever is expedient." Pilate went straight to the core of the issue: *Are you the king of the Jews?* He didn't care about this Jewish king; Jesus was no real threat to Rome.

The Pharisees wanted blood. When Pilate discovered that Jesus was a Galilean, he used this loop hole to forward Him to Herod: "That's off my hands." He would nail this upstart "King." Arch enemies were now eternally "in bed together:" *That day Herod and Pilate became friends; before this they had been enemies* (Luke 22:12).

In this dog-eat-dog world it's imperative to be centered. In efforts to get our way, it's easy to compromise with forces of evil that we would never consider otherwise. It's possible, though, to stand with God, make tough decisions, and then rely on Him to work out the end result. Making friends with the enemy is an unnecessary selfish component in accomplishing your will rather than God's way.

Jesus, be the center of my life.

The Immobile Sun

When we are at the end of our human extremities, God can do the impossible. My family experienced this. After a routine operation, my mother suffered an embolism. When bone marrow shot through her brain, she was pronounced "brain dead." We were told to plan her funeral and wait, but God had other plans. Slowly, she began to revive. After six weeks of therapy, she is back to normal mentally, and nearly so physically. Unbelievable! She's the talk of her town; my mother is a walking, talking miracle.

Joshua was in a similar "impossible" situation. Adoni-Zedek, king of Jerusalem, knew Joshua had destroyed many foes. AZ formed a coalition with five Amorite kings, creating huge military might and out-numbering Joshua. That didn't factor with God. Joshua's army marched all night, taking their enemy by surprise. What a day! God sent hail that confused the battle. Toward evening, though, the job wasn't quite completed. Joshua knew he almost had his enemies defeated. He just needed a bit more time, but night was near.

Nightfall gave the enemy opportunity to regroup. But, Joshua knew that God could finish what He started—with just a little more daylight. So he asked God for the impossible: "Please make the sun stand still until this job is done?" An audacious request to say the least, but God did the impossible: *There has never been a day like it before or since, a day when the Lord listened to a man.* (Josh. 10:14).

Do you have an impossible situation? Are your energy and time spent just when victory is in sight? Not a problem for God. God has victory for any enemy you face. When you have exhausted your resources, ask Him for the impossible. Trust His character. If He can make the sun stand still and bring my mother back to life…

He still can work any miracle in any life.

27

The Et Ceterites

Remember this: "Whatever the task, it's worth completing, and it's worth doing right the first time. If not, don't start it at all." That was drilled into my brothers and me by our Midwestern, depression surviving parents. It's a solid philosophy that has held true in my life. They were right.

As the Israelites advanced into the Promised Land, they met one obstacle and one enemy on the heels of the last. Like a steam roller or a Sherman tank, obstacles came at them from all directions. Just as they defeated one enemy or overcame one difficulty, something else arose in their path. The Bible records a laundry list of thirty-one kings and kingdoms that they defeated—thirty-one! That's a bunch. And that's life. "When it rains, it pours." How true that is.

Just when we think all the problems, issues, concerns, and circumstances of our lives are all ironed out, here comes another one. Et cetera. Et cetera. It's unavoidable. The only thing that's really constant in life is change. From one day to the next, life can change drastically and permanently. God knows this and gives us examples through people like Joshua: *Joshua left nothing undone of all that the lord commanded...* (Josh. 11:15b).

How does God expect us to handle the unexpected—the *et ceteras*—of our lives? He wants us to face them squarely, deal with them, and move on. Too many of us are like the Children of Israel on Moses' side of the Jordan River—we whine. "Why this? Why now? This job is too big for me." Et cetera; et cetera. The God who defeated thirty-one kings for Joshua can help you to overcome any *et ceterite* in your life. He's the God of every situation and every crisis. You can lean on Him anytime, anywhere, for anything.

Got any rivers you think are un-crossable?

The Heavenly Ghost

I put my children to bed one night and then retired myself. Later, I awoke thinking I heard a noise. Fearlessly, I walked down the hall and adjusted the thermostat. As I stepped back into our bedroom, a man walked out of the closet. Screaming, I fell against the wall; I was surely a "goner." The noise I heard wasn't an intruder; it was my husband returning from a business trip. The man in the closet was him as well. What a laugh we had—at my expense.

Following the crucifixion, two men were walking toward Emmaus. Jesus appeared and walked with them, conversing as they walked. Not until they were eating and their eyes met, however, did they recognize Him. At once, they ran to Jerusalem to tell His disciples. As they burst through the door with the news, Jesus appeared—this time to the others. They were frightened; a ghost was among them. *Why do doubts rise in your minds? Look at my hands and my feet. It is I myself! Touch me and see; I am not a ghost* (Luke 24:38-39).

Nothing has changed. Christians today react the same way His disciples did: You mean you are *here*, Jesus? Here in the middle of *my* crisis? I thought I was seeing a ghost. I thought you were speaking metaphorically when you said you'd be with me to the end of the earth. I didn't think you meant it. Neat! Jesus with me; anytime, anywhere. When the disciples saw His scars, their confusion and fear changed to wonder. Definitely out of the ordinary, but surely it was not Jesus. Then He sat down and ate. That did it; they believed.

Jesus is in your present situation. He wants to eat with you and talk with you as well. If you need to see His scars, He will show you. He's not a ghost, and you need not be afraid. He's the living, breathing Son of God, and He's here to live and dwell among us.

Don't be afraid; Jesus is with you.

The Holy Harbinger

Extra! Extra! Read all about it! These words always peak our interest. Such headlines have attracted us all to the first flashes of the BIG news. They've announced the sinking of the Titanic, the Hindenburg, VE Day, Hiroshima, VJ Day, the Oklahoma City Bombing, 9-1-1, and much more. When we hear, "Extra! Extra!" we know that it means big news. Extra, Big News is enhanced by eye witnesses—people who were there and saw it happen.

For centuries God promised Israel a Messiah. They knew He was coming; they were expecting Him. So much time passed, though, that the Israelites were passé about this Messiah. Maybe someday, but not today. And then came John, the Messiah's holy harbinger: *He came as a witness…. He himself was not the light; he came only as a witness to the light.* (John 1:7). Extra! Extra! Read all about it!

What a harbinger. John wasn't cultured or even educated. By today's standards, he would be called *rabid*—a bit weird and off beam, if you will. Yet, God used John to announce Jesus' arrival. If John came today announcing the Messiah, we would most likely dismiss him as a kook or religious fanatic. God knew what He was doing. John was eccentric enough to draw a crowd and humble enough that he knew his place in the divine scheme of things.

John came and went. Jesus lived, died, rose, and now sits at the right hand of God. We know this; we know He's coming again. Does our world? We know there's a day of judgment. Does our world? In the divine scheme of things, John completed his task as messianic prophet. We also have a task in the same divine scheme. Perhaps you are a prophet, or maybe He simply calls you to live in a way that your life announces His imminent return. What are your headlines?

He's the really BIG news.

No U-Hauls in the Cemetery

I've been there more than once. That long silent procession to the cemetery behind a hearse. In West Texas, my husband conducted a funeral for a teenager, and he asked me to drive him behind the family car to the cemetery. As we pulled away from the church on the flat high plains, I caught a glimpse in my rear view mirror. It looked as though we were escorting the entire citizenry out of town.

There were no U-Haul trailers in that procession. Baggage isn't necessary for burial, only a body. When the spirit is gone; nothing of substance remains. But, oh the stuff we leave behind. As we pass through life, it's easy for even the most Spartan individual to amass quite an array of stuff. We acquire houses, lands, and large insurance policies. We buy stocks, bonds, and collectables. We take expensive vacations and drive fine automobiles. We're involved in high dollar entertainments and purchase pricey adult toys. But none of our stuff ever shows up in a cemetery. It's not needed there.

Wealth is worthless in the day of wrath, but righteousness delivers from death (Prov. 11:4). When all is said and done, stuff won't matter. There are things, though, that will matter—a lot! He will ask for an accounting of our time and our talents. He will hold us accountable for our actions—even our silent thoughts and attitudes. All that will matter on that day is our relationship with Him and others.

It's normal to compare ourselves with the world, but there's really no comparison. We have hope; the world has none. We have a heavenly home prepared with no more sorrow or pain or tears. The world has something else awaiting them. Most of all, we have eternity to share with Him. Solomon says it well: *When a wicked man dies, his hope perishes. The righteous man is rescued from trouble...* (Prov. 7-8a).

What are you leaving behind? It matters.

Reflections on the Word...

Reflections on the Word...

The Word in Real Time

May

Joshua 19-24, Judges 1-21, Ruth, I Samuel 1-31
John 2-20
Psalms 54-68 and Proverbs 11-13

My Prayer Time for May...

Thanksgiving _____
_____
_____
_____

Intercession _____
_____
_____
_____

Ministry _____
_____
_____
_____

Encouragement _____
_____
_____
_____
_____

Prove It!

The school yard chant is the same world wide. "My dad can beat up your dad." Prove it! "I'm stronger than you." Prove it! "My mother is prettier than your mom." No, she's not. Prove it! *Proving it* is a childish way of "one-upping" another. Successfully *proving it* gives us a momentary sensation of superiority. A secure person is secure in and of themselves and has no real need to *prove it*.

Jesus' ministry began in a rather flamboyant episode. It wasn't His intent, but Mary had pondered her son's life mission in her heart from His conception. Like any mother, she wanted the best for Him, and she feared the worst. Mary had a feeling that the need for more wine was Jesus' place to shine. She expressed her ultimate confidence and motherly pride in Him when she said to the host, "Do whatever He tells you to do."

Jesus' public ministry was virtually launched by a few kegs of wine. Word was undeniably out. He was different, and people began to demand that He *prove it*. When Jesus saw the dreadful conditions in the temple courtyard, He lost it. Enough already. The church is a house of prayer—not a business! Still, the Jews demanded proof.

Conditions haven't changed since Jesus' first miracle. People still want to witness what He can do. That's good, and God uses His miracles to demonstrate His power. But, that coin has two sides. People are still abusing the church and manipulating others through it. In both cases, Jesus is teaching us that we can prove His power. We *prove it* through our lives, and we *prove it* by being true to the church's mission.

Is your life proof enough?

In Abstentia

When I graduated from high school and college, I marched in cap and gown across the platform and received my degree. I was there. Since then, I've had two other graduation days—days lacking regalia or parties. Neither time that I received an advanced degree, was I present to shake hands with the president and receive my hard-earned diploma. Nevertheless, I received the degree. I worked for it; I earned it; I deserved it.

Some of life's most significant lessons are learned through another's experiences. We are *in abstentia*, yet the lesson is just as valuable. Such was the lesson Jesus taught Nicodemus. Jesus' response to Nicodemus was intended for us all. Wise learner; take note. Don't make Jesus repeat Himself. Nicodemus, the seeking Pharisee, acknowledged Jesus' divinity: *We know you are a teacher who has come from God ...* (John 3:3). Characteristically, Jesus answered the unasked question: *No one can see the kingdom of God unless he is born again* (John 3:4b). Nicodemus: "How can this be—to be born again? That's impossible."

Jesus looked Nicodemus straight in the heart: "You are educated, can't you understand? I'm teaching you, but you don't get it. If I speak about earthly things and you fail to comprehend, how will you understand heavenly things? It's like this: The Son of Man must be lifted up so that all may have eternal life." Nicodemus' look provoked Jesus' tender words:

For God so love the world that he gave.... (John 3:16). God loved and gave the ultimate gift so that you and I may live. Did you get the lesson? There is a time that *in abstentia* won't be good enough.

Be present to receive your diploma.

It's Your Choice

It doesn't particularly matter which route you take to work as long as you get there. It isn't vital to your success in life which car you drive, where you buy groceries, or even the house you live in. Those things present an array of choices, none of which are life altering. They may make a short-term difference, but these decisions are not as important as who you marry, where you work, or the school you attend. Those things count big.

At Shechem, Joshua assembled the tribes and reminded the people of God's past presence. He reminded them that God had been with them all the way, despite all they endured. He rehearsed an exhaustive list of "et ceterites," their defeated enemies. At last in the Promised Land, it was high time for a victory celebration and covenant renewal.

It could have been easy to rest on their laurels and coast into temptation and spiritual mediocrity. Joshua yearned for the Israelites to reach for all God had for them, so he drew an eternal line in the sand: "Watch me. Regardless of what comes down the pike, I'm serving God. He's proven Himself in the past, and I fully expect that trend to continue. What about you? Are you going to vacillate between God and the heathens around you, or will you stand with me? As for me and my family, we're serving God."

It's vital that we review God's protections and provisions and renew our covenant with Him. It's equally important to take a stand as a public witness. The world is earnestly seeking fully devoted followers who step across that line in the sand whatever it may mean and follow God wherever He leads. Thanks, Joshua, we needed your example.

With some things, you really have no choice.

Spiritual Splinters

I was a tomboy; I loved to romp in Alaska's vast outdoors—shimmying across water pipes above roaring streams, hiking over glacial crevices, or speeding down hills with my feet on the bicycle handle bars. Hours in the outdoors guarantee a few injuries—the least of which may appear to be a splinter. A splinter, however, is major until it's removed. Removal may seem painful, but the almost certain prediction of infection if the splinter is not dealt with diminishes the thought of the momentary pain.

After Israel conquered the cities and tribes on the western side of the Jordan, they grew careless in following God's injunctions. His rules were explicit: When you conquer a city, completely drive out *all* the people, destroy their heathen altars, and inhabit the empty city. Surely, God wouldn't care if they conscripted the Canaanites into forced labor. They were merely maximizing their resources; God would understand.

God never understands disobedience. His words were a vivid wake-up call: *I will never break my covenant with you, and you shall not make a covenant... Yet you have disobeyed me.* (Judges 2: 1b-2). Oops! They disobeyed; there would most assuredly be consequences. "I won't fix this one for you. The aliens and their gods will be thorns in your sides." God said.

Perhaps an act of disobedience in your life has produced a splinter, and the pain and infection is incessant. God could remove it, but He chooses to leave it in your life as His daily reminder that He expects complete obedience. If that is your situation, you can face it and appropriate His lessons. What He says; He means.

Thank God for your splinters.

Wasted Demonstrations

As a teen, I was keenly aware of Martin Luther King, Jr., Ralph Abernathy, Rosa Parks, and Robert Kennedy. I was also aware of Angela Davis, Eldridge Cleaver, and Skokie Carmichael. They were daily news. Each had a cause for which they would go to any extreme; some even died or went to prison for their causes. Whatever we think of their politics, we can applaud their chutzpah and passion for the cause.

As a teacher I've witnessed a metamorphosis in youthful opinion. Teens today fail to connect with the '60s activists. There seems to be a lack of appreciation for others' hard fought causes. Freedoms fought for in the past are taken for granted today. What happened? Did America grow accustomed to her freedoms and fail to pass on the value of yesterday's struggles?. Jesus explained it well: *Others have done the hard work, and you have reaped the benefits of their labor* (John 4:37b).

Forgetting the recent past was evident in the lives of the Israelites. As time passed, they grew lazy and forgetful. *Another generation grew up, who knew neither the Lord nor what he had done for Israel...* (Judges 2:10). Whose fault was this? Who held the responsibility? The older generation—pure and simple.

We yearn for our children to be spiritually mature; and yet, we do them a disservice by neglecting to teach them the sacrifices of their elders. Don't allow the "spiritual marches" and battles of your youth to be for naught. Teach your children God's ways and encourage them to follow. They will surely benefit, and our world will benefit as well.

Don't be lazy; teach your kids God's causes.

The Waters Still Heal

Crossing the courtyard at St. Ann's Church, I lost my footing and took a fall beside the ancient Pool of Bethesda. Stunned and nearly out cold, I realized that although I was down, I wasn't badly hurt. In a twist of fate, I fell with my weight on the side where I carried a large water bottle. Miraculously, I bounced against the bottle, cushioning my fall.

My fall created quite a sensation, and a crowd formed quickly. How embarrassing to be lying flat with dozens of curiosity onlookers peering at me. My embarrassment only began there. A smart aleck friend chose to video my dilemma—with narration: "Ladies and gentlemen. You're witnessing it. She's down, but she's not out. The pool still heals." Ha. Ha.

It was believed that the Pool of Bethesda had mystic, therapeutic powers. When the desert winds blew across the waters, tradition held that the first into the water was healed. Daily, an invalid was left at the pool. Each day he watched some other lucky cripple grab the brass ring. With no help, he was trapped in his own despair—so close and yet so very far

Jesus was drawn to this man. "Do you want to be well?" He asked. Was Jesus blind? "Of course, that's why I'm here, but I'm a cripple." Jesus saw his self-pity not his lameness. "Stand up, fold up your mat, and get on with life." The waters didn't move, but his heart did. And he moved. With his tiny act of faith, the invalid was healed—physically and spiritually.

Jesus is still calling us out of our pity parties. "You're down, but you're not out," He seems to say. "Life may have dealt you an unfair blow, but faith can still make you whole, and the waters still heal."

Fold up your self-pity and get on with life.

Gideon from Missouri

When he was first tapped for leadership, Gideon protested: *...if the Lord is with us, why has all this happened to us?* (Judges 6:13)? He could have been from Missouri, the "Show Me State." Hesitantly, Gideon accepted God's call, tore down the altars of Baal, cut down the Asherah poles, and built an altar—an altar of peace.

Gideon's altar didn't promote peace; it only agitated the people. When the Israelites learned that Gideon was responsible for the fall of their god, they wanted to kill him and return to worshipping their heathen gods. Joash mocked the people: "If Baal is such a great god, he can take care of himself. Let's let Baal handle this; it will be a divine duel." Fortified by Joash's faith in him, Gideon spoke to God: "If you are really going to rescue Israel by my hand, please give me and this pitiful people a sign."

Gideon proposed the test of the fleece to God. "If tomorrow morning there is only dew on the fleece and none on the ground, I will know you are in this." And that's exactly what happened. Gideon's tentative nature needed more proof. Once again, he made a proposal to God. "Let's reverse the deal; if tomorrow morning, the dew is on the ground and not on the fleece, then I will know you are in this." Patiently, God went along with Gideon's Missourish "prove it to me" personality.

Many of us are like Gideon. When God taps us for a task, we don't feel up to it, and we challenge His authority and question our own abilities. God is patient and understands us. God promises that we can "prove Him." Spiritual fleeces are a wonderful tool for testing God's directives. Put Him to the test. He will show you unmistakably what His will is.

Lay out a fleece; allow God to "show you" His will.

Holy Commotion

God isn't the author of confusion. That's true, and yet the super-natural is confounding to man. The Midianites were down-right mean—that's a fact, and they were absolutely determined to defeat Israel. The Midianites outnumbered the Israelites and had more sophisticated weapons. It was just a matter of time until they would annihilate God's people.

God spoke to Gideon in a dream. "Yes, the Midianites are as thick as locust and have more camels than they can count. Not to worry. Spy out the land at night, and I will encourage you." With an army of only 300, Gideon had to know that God must truly have a plan because without Him this battle with the Midianites was a hopeless impossibility.

Clueless about God's plan; Gideon merely followed God's playbook as he addressed his little band: *Get up! The Lord has given the Midianite camp into our hands* (Judges 7:15b). When the Midianite army was fast asleep, Gideon struck. Talk about God in "real time." Gideon didn't comprehend God's ways; but he obeyed. Gideon shouted; broke his vase, and lifted high his torch. His little band followed suit. It didn't make sense, but God was in it. You know the rest: Confused and bewildered, 120,000 Midianites were overtaken by Gideon and 300 obedient men.

Are you battling an enemy stronger and better equipped than you? Are you pared down to nothing? Are your resources reduced and your will to fight gone? God's ways are stranger than the thoughts of men. Remember Gideon. When things are the most confusing, God has a way.

Make some noise; God's at work.

The Parable of the Trees

Abimelech tricked his mother's brothers into making him their leader. With his uncle's money, he hired a gang of reckless thugs as his cohorts in crime. These bad boys fell upon Abimelech's father's home, killing his seventy brothers except the youngest, Jotham. After his brothers' brutal deaths, Jotham spoke to the people of Shechem in a parable:

Once, the trees decided to choose a king, anointing the olive tree as "King of the Trees." The olive tree declined, "If I became the king, who would provide oil? Choose another." Refused by the olive tree, the trees chose the fir, who replied, "Should I withhold my sweet fruit from man just to be king? Find another." Then the trees invited the vine to be king. "You're kidding," said the vine. "If I were tree king, there would be no more wine." Rejected again, the trees approached the thorn and begged this detested bush to be king. The thorn pondered his unexpected honor: "If you want me to be your king, then sit beneath the shade of my prickly branches. If you choose not to sit there, then let fire fall from heaven and devour you." By default, the thorn bush became the leader of the trees.

Abominable Abimelech's gang continued to wreck havoc on everyone they met. Finally, he met his demise when a large rock fell on his head as he attempted to burn an entire city. And the moral? God ordains leaders. Taking matters into our own hands will always reap a whirlwind of devastation. When God anoints a leader, He will empower him or her. A leadership vacuum, produced by hesitancy, creates the perfect "break" for the renegade leader with a selfish agenda. Be prudent in allowing people to lead—examine their credentials, their hearts, and their motives.

Remember the lesson of the trees.

Out of God's Hands

Tough love is tough! Painfully, we force our children to face the music orchestrated by their own actions and deal with the consequences. I know a woman who was called heartless when she refused to help her son—a polio victim—get up from a fall. Despite her neighbors' objections, that boy grew up to walk normally. His mother knew what was best.

God invented the "D" word. From Day One, He used it in the garden, and He's been using it ever since. The disciplines God enacts on us are more painful than disciplines applied by parents to children. Fortunately, God and loving earthly parents usually give us an opportunity to try again. As parents, though, there comes a time when enough is enough. Your child is on your last nerve and nothing is working. It's in those times of desperation that you're forced to look straight at your child and say: "I love you more than you will ever know, but as of now you're on your own."

Words of abandonment are startling. The Israelites allowed one poor leader after another to lead them far away from God by worshipping Baal and other foreign gods. Finally, God had had enough and sold them to the Philistines and Ammonites. They were out of His hands, and God told them so: *You have forsaken me and served other gods, so I will no longer save you... Let them save you ...* (Judges 10:13). They had gone too far. Was there a back into His favor? Like a loving father, God pitied and reclaimed them. What a price they paid, though. How much better it would have been if they had trusted Him from the get-go.

His hands are the safest place ever.

God's Tongue Twister

Susie sells seashells by the seashore. Peter Piper picked a peck of pickled peppers. We all have childhood memories of struggling to say tongue twisters, determined that our next attempt would be the perfect delivery. The combination of similar vowel sounds and diphthongs twists our tongues; even in adulthood, we mess up attempting them.

God has employed every imaginable tactic to get people's attention. But a tongue twister? Surely not. But, yes. Jephthah was confronted by the wicked Ephramites: "Because you fought the Ammonites without asking our help, we're going to burn your house down." Jephthah had a comeback to all this huffing and puffing: "In the middle of the big fight, we called for your help, but you refused to come. I took the battle into my own hands, and the Lord gave us victory. So, what's this all about? Where were you guys when we needed you?"

A Hatfield/McCoy type feud between the Gileadites and the Ephramites erupted. Ephramite prisoners begged permission to cross the Jordan, yet they continually lied about their nationality. There was one tell-tale revealer of their true identity; they couldn't pronounce the Gileadite dialect properly. Jephthah ingeniously used their handicap and trapped them. His army asked the Ephramite prisoners to say 'Shibboleth,' but it never came out correctly. Their tongues twisted, and one by one, they said 'Sibboleth.' Busted! Mispronunciation was their death sentence.

Our words are self-condemning. It's probably not a tongue twister, but our true identity is exposed through what we say. People are listening, and your words just may be a major part of a major test.

Be careful what you say; it will save you.

Hidden Agendas

Intelligence is enhanced by education and life experience, but it isn't defined by them. Some of the wisest people have little to no formal education. On the other hand, some of the most educated people have little common sense. Some of the best advice I've received has come from an uneducated person, shared with poor grammar and lousy syntax.

In His society, Jesus was only a poor peasant from an obscure village. He spoke with a commonness understood by the masses, and yet His grasp of scripture confounded the Pharisees. They were incensed as He taught in the temple: *How can this man get such learning without having studied* (John 7:15b)? Their jealousy of Jesus' charisma spurred them to attack His credentials. By their standards, He had none.

The issue was not Jesus' knowledge of the scriptures, but rather their lack of understanding about who He was. They thought He was an unschooled upstart rearranging their neat little religious world. Wrong! He was the divine, the immortal, God made flesh. They knew the scriptures inside out, but in their blind jealousy, they lost sight of the divine.

All the Pharisees did and said was calculated and rehearsed with a personal agenda. Jesus wasn't self-seeking; they were. Now and again, we are humbled by an unassuming person who has little formal education, but owns a wealth of life experience. Who are you listening to? Do you feel superior to others? Jesus can appear in anyone at anytime. Don't miss seeing Him in a child or in a wise elderly "uneducated" individual.

What's your agenda?

Weakness from Strength

P*ride goeth before a fall.* These familiar words aren't learned in the telling; they're learned through the living. Such was the case with Samson. Menorah and his wife were so thrilled with their little serendipity, that they dedicated Samuel into the Nazarite order. Samson was dedicated to abstain from wine, not to eat anything from an unclean animal, and not to cut his hair or shave. These were the outward signs of the Nazarites.

God blessed Samuel with remarkable strength *and* His spirit. Samson, though, was a strong weak man. Regardless of God's spirit on his life, Samson ignored his Nazarite vow and rationalized his disobedient ways. His principal test came through Delilah, a seductive Philistine woman. The Philistine's plot to nullify Samson's strength was craftily orchestrated. Get the woman to weaken him, and he will talk.

Delilah used all her feminine wiles with Samson, and after four attempts, this weak strong man confessed the source of his strength. What could it matter if she knew the secret of his power? But it did matter. When he awoke, Samson expected things to be just the same, but something had changed: *He did not know that the Lord had left him* (Judges 16 20b).

We easily make one rationalization after another until, like Samson, we wander far from our initial vow to the Lord—our vow to be holy and separate and obedient. Samson needed God in a big way, but God had left him, and he didn't even know it. What an admonition for us today. We cannot afford to yield to temptation even once, because when we awaken from our careless sleep, we may discover that God's spirit has left us when we need Him the very most.

Will He be with you when you wake-up?

Will the Real Jesus Stand Up?

When TV was only black and white and had just three channels, there was a popular show called, "I've Got a Secret." In this pre-historic era, three people posed as the same person. Each participant made claims about his identity, profession, and family. The show's panel listened to each contestant's claims, considered them, and then voted for whomever they thought was real and legitimate. It was simple, but great entertainment.

Like people today challenge religions, the Pharisees challenged Jesus' validity: "You can't be who you say you are because you're your own witness—that's illegal." Jesus was confident in His response; *I stand with the Father... I know where I came from and where I am going.* (John 8:14). Their challenges and tricks fazed him not one iota; He knew who He was; He knew His job; and He knew the end of the story.

Again, the Pharisees challenged him: "Who are you?" Weary of their incessant, never-ending challenges, He never wavered. All the way to the cross He remained consistent: *When you have lifted up the Son of Man, then you will know that I am the one I claim to be...* (John 8:28). While Jesus was predicting His own death, He predicted that eventually all the scoffers will recognize that He is indeed the Christ, the Son of God.

People will challenge His validity and authority and supremacy right up to the Second Coming. He was the real deal then, and He's the real deal today. He has always been and will always be the real deal! People are looking, searching, and watching our lives to see if Jesus is real. Each day of your life, your Christian witness is on trial. It isn't a TV game; it's real.

Will the real follower of Christ stand up, please?

Watch my Lips!

The infant son of a friend of mine suffered from spinal meningitis. He survived, but with interesting side affects. His mother noticed that after his illness, her son reverted to infantile behaviors. One of these was baby talk. Determined that her son would speak correctly, she held his face in her hands and demanded that he watch her lips while she distinctly and deliberately pronounced and enunciated each word.

As their son grew, he often did not respond when spoken to—unless it was directly into his face. To their chagrin and to the doctor's utter disbelief, this little fellow had suffered more than suspected: He was nearly deaf, yet his speech was perfect. When he saw a person's lips, he completely understood their words. His deafness was undetectable. With flawless speech, he has grown into a productive and happy young man thanks to his mother's diligence.

The Pharisees suffered a major case of spiritual meningitis. When Jesus spoke, they simply didn't hear. They heard the words alright, but they refused to hear the intent. Repeatedly, He tested them, and the diagnosis was the same each time: spiritual deafness. Allegorically, Jesus took their face in His hands and spoke: *Why is my language not clear to you?* (John 8:43).

Jesus exposed their ailment. Their actions revealed their attitudes while Jesus' actions revealed who He was as well. We don't like to hear about the devil, but Jesus makes His point vividly clear: *The reason you do not hear is that you do not belong to God* (John 8:47). Churches are full of the spiritually deaf. It's possible, however, to have excellent spiritual hearing—by believing His words and acting on them appropriately.

Watch His lips; hear His heart.

Mother-in-law's Day

It's Mother's Day—that time of year when Madison Avenue bombards us with memories of mother, apple pie, and childhood. It's unforgivable for any red-blooded American to forget his Mom. This is one manipulative advertising campaign that we don't resist because 99 % of us love, respect, and even adore our mothers. I am doubly blessed because I have a wonderful mother and a precious mother-in-law as well.

Naomi and her husband fled to Moab from Judah during a famine. In Moab, their sons married Orpah and Ruth, both foreigners. Disaster dogged Naomi; soon her two sons and her husband all died. Alone in a foreign land, Naomi chose to return to her father's home. With a loving gesture, Naomi released both "the girls" from their obligations to her, and then she blessed them: *May the Lord show kindness to you, as you have shown… to me* (Ruth 1:8).

Tearfully, the three of them embraced at their parting. Oprah stayed in Moab, but not Ruth. Ruth had fallen in love with Naomi and her ways. Her words ring through history: *Where you go I will go, and where you stay I will stay. Your people will be my people and your God my God* (Ruth 1:16).

It is still possible to fall so in love with the Lord that nothing—categorically nothing—can separate us from Him and His ways. Our love can be so intense that we will follow Him to the ends of the earth, forsaking family and tradition and security. God had something beautiful and unimaginable prepared for Ruth in her foreign land. He still takes care of His own. Ruth's love for Naomi was selfless and unconditional. What an example!

Are you willing to follow unconditionally?

I Pledge My Sandal

A man's word is undoubtedly his most valued possession, defining both his character and his reputation. It means everything, and kingdoms have been exchanged because of a person's pledge. A pledge demands a symbol—a signature, a hand shake, an embrace, the piercing of an ear, a seal, and more. Judah had a unique pledge—they gave one of their sandals in pledge. Sounds strange, but I suppose it's as good as a notary public if both parties understand its meaning and implications.

When Ruth gleaned in Boaz' fields, she followed Naomi's advice and slept at his feet. Ultimately, Boaz noticed this foreign girl and spoke to her: "Who are you?" Ruth was a good student of Naomi's ways, and she understood that someone in her dead husband's family was obligated to "redeem" her. Ruth also knew that she was on shaky ground, and she responded appropriately: *I am your servant, Ruth… you are my kinsman-redeemer* (Ruth 3:9). Boaz was second in line to redeem her, and when the first kinsman-redeemer refused, Boaz gave him a sandal to seal the transaction. With the pledge, he became Ruth's bridegroom.

Christ is the bridegroom *and* our kinsman-redeemer. He will not barge His way into our lives until Satan releases us. That happens, when we demand that Satan let us go. Then Christ sets us free from the bondage of sin, its habits, and its ways. At that juncture we are embraced in a life of freedom and relief beyond belief or comprehension, for we have been redeemed by love divine. Let Him redeem you today.

Give Him your sandal.

Statue and Favor

Others tell us how quickly infants grow, but a reality sets in when we have our own little bundles of joy. Even when we lament that our "baby is growing up," we wouldn't want it any other way. Children are meant to grow and please their parents. Too quickly car seats, strollers, and cribs make way for tricycles, Barbie dolls, and birthday parties. Just as quickly, that stage gives way to skate boards, rock music, and dating. Soon our baby is driving off to college. If we've done our job well, our young adult wants to please us as much as we wanted to please him. That's a major component of the cycle of life and the metamorphosis of time and age.

Hannah was desperate for a child. God heard her prayers, and gave her Samuel. Hannah remembered her promise to God, and when Samuel was weaned, she bundled him up and took him to the temple to live under the tutelage of Eli, the priest. She reminded Eli of her prayer, the *Lord has granted me what I asked of Him. So now I give him to the Lord.* (I Sam. 1:27). Under Eli's care, Samuel matured and learned. The temple didn't seem strange to him; it was his home. He developed into a fine teenager—strong in body, respectful and contemplative in mind and spirit.

We come to Christ as babes. There's much we don't comprehend, so in a growing process we dig into His word, attend the means of grace, and fellowship with His people. As we do these things, the healthy Christian grows and matures in the Lord and finds favor with man as well. The church is full of baby Christians whose spiritual growth has been stunted by continual bottle feeding and pampering. Like Samuel, it's possible to grow up in the Lord so that we are productive and can count for Him.

How tall are you in the Lord?

Humpty Dumpty

Humpty Dumpty sat on a wall; Humpty Dumpty had a great fall. All the kings' horses, and all the kings' men, couldn't put Humpty together again. This verse has a political genesis. It's the story of an English cannon that fell from a wall at St. Mary's Church during a battle in 1648. The battle was lost because the king's men couldn't put the cannon back together.

Eli's sons were disrespectful toward the Lord's offerings, demanding the fat for their own eating and dining pleasure. They refused to listen to Eli's admonitions when he reprimanded them and continued spinning out of control. They were on a self destructive trip to ruin, but they weren't going alone. Ultimately, dear old dad went down with them.

The Philistines defeated the Israelites, captured the Ark, and killed Eli's sons—recalcitrant to their deaths. The heartbreaking news of his boys' deaths and the loss of the Ark was more than he could bear. Eli had his own "secret sin:" He, too, enjoyed eating fat. All that fat had done a number on him, and in his old age, he was fat and nearly blind. Aware that he couldn't put the situation back together, Eli lost his balance, fell backward, hit his head, and died. We could pity Eli if we didn't know that he was responsible because he allowed his boys to disobey the priestly laws.

Our children are our eternal responsibility. As parents and grandparents we have an injunction to live consistently before them. Compromise has dire consequences, and no one sees our true lives more or emulates them as much as our children. You can't control everything your kids do, but you can control what you do and what they see. Don't fall off the wall.

Leave the fat alone; young ones are watching.

The Ebenezer Stone

What a thrill! I saw the *Rosetta Stone* with my own eyes in the Egyptian Museum in Cairo. The discovery of this amazing slice of history in 1799 allowed archaeologists at last to decipher hieroglyphics. This rock became the "keystone" and fulcrum for hundreds of previously nebulous and undisclosed historic mysteries.

The Philistines defeated the Israelites, capturing the Ark—God's symbol of the holy. Circumstances did not go well for the Philistines while they held the Ark. They suffered plagues of tumors and rats, and three different communities were nearly annihilated. At last the Philistines decided that it was in their best national interest to return the Ark to the Israelites. What was holy to God's people was a bad luck charm for the Philistines.

"Arkless," the Israelites erected Asherah poles and idols to Baal. They begged Samuel to intercede for them: *Do not stop crying out to the Lord our God for us, that he may rescue us…* (I. Sam. 6:8). Samuel instructed them to destroy their pagan gods and serve God alone. God sent a thunderstorm that confused the Philistines, causing them to run. The Ark was recaptured and returned to its rightful place. Samuel inscribed the word "Ebenezer" on the stone and placed it between Mizpah and Shen. What does this mean? "Thus far the Lord has helped us."

Like the *Rosetta Stone*, the *Ebenezer Rock* was merely a rock until Samuel wrote on it. Samuel's words—like the writing on the *Rosetta Stone*—became abundantly significant. It is critical that we lean on the Lord and avoid pursuing foreign gods and idols. It is the *Lord* that has led us to the point we are today, and it is the *Lord* who will safely lead us home.

Do you have an Ebenezer Stone?

God's Candid Camera

We're all familiar with Alan Funt's ubiquitous "candid camera." His closing line has become a permanent part of our day to day vernacular: "Smile. Somewhere when you least expect it, you may be on candid camera."

Saul's father sent him to find some lost donkeys—a rather lackluster task to say the least. Saul was having no luck finding the lost animals and wanted to go back home so his dad wouldn't worry. God had other plans for the young man, Saul. Just the day before, God told Samuel that the next day he would meet an impressive young man from Benjamin. When he met this young man, God told Samuel, he would know him.

He was to anoint this young man King of Israel. When Samuel saw a young man who was taller than anyone else, He knew this young man was God's chosen king for Israel. He was God's man. So, Samuel anointed him king and prophesied: *The Spirit of the Lord will come upon you in power... and you will be changed into a different person* (I Sam. 10:6).

That's the way it is with us and God. Right in the middle of a routine, perfunctory task, God shows up. He often has other plans that send our life in a totally new and exciting direction. When we least expect it, He anoints us for an extraordinary task—one that we don't feel qualified to do, and yet with His anointing, He empowers us just like He empowered Saul to be king. When He comes to you along the way and offers to "change you into a different person," allow Him to work in your life.

Smile; you may be on God's Candid Camera.

Buy One; Get One Free

M ost people simply can't resist a sale. Even when we haven't carefully done the math to see if it is really a sale or just an advertising gimmick, there's something magnetic and enticing about getting something "for free." I've known people who bought something they didn't even want just to get another one like it for free. Crazy, but that's human nature.

Jesus spent an inordinate amount time and effort attempting to explain the trinity to His followers and protagonists. If they could only grasp this principle, He reasoned; then they would get it. They either really didn't understand the trinity, or perhaps some were afraid to admit they understood for fear of retribution from the Pharisees.

Jesus must have been in total exasperation with the people when He cried out: *When a man believes in me, he does not believe in me only, but in the one who sent me. When he looks at me, he sees the one who sent me* (John 12:44-45). They knew who God was; they knew the scriptures inside and out. Maybe this word picture would help. They had questioned everything: His miracles, His message; His identity. Jesus knew that they believed in God; that should do it. But it didn't.

Do you want to see God? Look to Jesus. Do you believe in Jesus? Then, you can believe in God as well. Jesus and God look alike because their Father and Son. There's a strong resemblance. It's the best deal ever offered to man—this concept of the trinity. Do you want your neighbor to see God? Then let Jesus be seen in your life.

He's a deal you cannot refuse.

It's a Panic Attack!

Panic is paralyzing, and we all experience it at one time or another. In extreme cases, though, a life experience can traumatize us to such a degree that the very thought of it throws us into confusion. Taken to its limit, these situations are clinically called panic attacks. Anyone who has suffered from a panic attack knows that they are real and can be debilitating without professional intervention.

Jonathan and his armor bearer snuck away from Saul's army and decided that the two of them would surprise the Philistines. They would creep down the middle of the ravine where the Philistines were camped on the opposing cliffs and surprise them. Jonathan's reasoning: *Nothing can hinder the Lord from saving, whether by many or by few* (I Sam. 14:6b).

When Jonathan and his armor bearer appeared in the ravine, it startled the Philistines and sent them into a state of panic. Surely, they reasoned, if two men were emerging out of the desert holes, then the entire army of Israel must be right behind them. The Philistines were in such panic and confusion that they began killing one another. When Saul witnessed this confusion in his enemy's camp, he moved.

Corporately, we often hunker down, intimidated by an enemy that seems stronger and more equipped than we are. There we sit until some trusting soul acts on God's word. When the church sees one or two stepping out against unbeatable odds, trusting only in God's word, it encourages everyone. Perhaps you are a Jonathan. Then move. If you are one of the silent crowd, and you see a believing soul moving, then follow. God can work through the enemy's confusion as much today as He did years ago.

It's His battle: follow those with courage.

You've Got Dad's Hands

My husband's birth father abandoned him and his mother when he was born. Until the day he died, David's father never contacted him or sent support as though he and his mother never existed. In the past ten years, my husband has met a sister who was raised by his father and knew him intimately. We have become fast friends with her and her husband.

Noteworthy and uncanny things have come from this new kinship. There is an unspeakable bond between David and this new found sister; but they have little in common. He was raised the oldest of five siblings; she was raised an only child. He was raised by a Christian mother; she was raised by non-church attendees. He's a Protestant minister; she's a practicing Catholic. They have little in common, and yet they relish being with each other. They don't have any shared history, but they share the same blood, and that blood ties them irrevocably together.

When we are together, David's sister often begins to weep tears of joy. "You don't understand," she says. "Seeing you is like seeing Dad all over again. You walk and talk like him; you have his sense of humor. You've got his hands. You're exactly alike."

Jesus taught that when we know the Father, we will know the Son. It's that simply—and that complex. The Christian walk isn't about what people see; it's about what they feel from our spirit. We go through life wondering if we make a difference. When Christ is in you and if His blood flows through you, you can't help but make a difference. When people say they see something special in you, they aren't talking about you. They're talking about the Father reflected through your life—the hope of glory.

You, too, resemble the Father.

Nature and Nurture

Spring is a refreshing time. Regardless of whether we are an avid gardener or whether we just piddle around a bit in our yards, there is something stimulating about spring and new life. We never grow weary of the metamorphosis of spring as we see the dead come to life one more year. It's as predictable as tomorrow's sunrise.

Jesus understood man's intrigue with nature and the outdoors, and He knew his audience as well. Many of the people He spoke to were master gardeners and vineyard owners. They knew about old growth and grafting and the necessity of being connected to the vine. In John chapter 17, Jesus paints a magnificent word picture of the garden. He is the vine—the part of the plant that is securely connected to the growth source, the soil. We are just the branches. Everyone knows that freshly cut branches and flowers are pretty for a brief time, but they don't last. They're dead.

Nature must have connection—nurture—to survive. And so it is with our Christian walk. The disconnected from the vine look pretty good for a brief time, and then they inevitably wither and die. That's nature. Cut flowers are for a season. But the vine is for a life time. God doesn't want us to be a flash in the pan. He wants us to grow through His nature as we permit Him to nurture us through His word and His body. It is then, and only then, that we will bear fruit. Do you feel as though no one is ever affected by your life? Are you weak and withering and dying on the vine? Let the nurture of His nature permeate and course through you so that the world will see the beauty of this thing He calls the "Body of Christ."

Connected to the vine, you will produce fruit.

Not afraid; Prepared

Jesse sent his young son, "Cheese and Crackers David," to carry lunch to his big brothers who were fighting with Saul's army. God had visited David more than once with divine power, and he had been anointed with oil by Samuel. Still a shepherd boy, David trusted God and believed in Him. What he saw when he came to the battlefield shocked and alarmed him. The entire army of Israel was being intimidated by a braggart.

David was appalled at the weakness displayed by Saul's army "What's going on here?" he asked. "Surely, our God who delivered me from the lion and the bear can deliver this uncircumcised Philistine into my hands." His brothers mocked him, but Saul was intrigued by David's chutzpah. Saul summoned him to the throne room and put his entire armor on the boy. Poor David; he couldn't fight in Saul's armor any more than you can effectively work outside the arena of your own gifts and personality.

David appealed to Saul: "Mr. King, if you will just let me be myself, God will deliver us from this giant today." Cautiously, Saul agreed. David took his crude weapon—the slingshot—and chose five smooth stones. Skillfully, he loaded the first stone, took careful aim, and felled the giant. "Why," might you ask, "did David need five stones if he was so sure of God?" Good question. I'm glad you asked! Goliath had four brothers. David wasn't a coward; he was prepared.

God invites us to go up against all kinds of giants; with Him we can be successful giant slayers. What about the next giant coming through the valley of your life? God wants us to be continually prepared for anything that comes along, anytime. Pick up several stones and face the world.

Keep some stones in reserve.

MAY

27

Faithful or Fickle

People who seem to know such things report that if in a lifetime you have three true friends, you are indeed blessed. We understand "fair-weather friends;" many of us have known such people. When things were going well, and when being our friends didn't cost them anything, or when we had something they wanted, then we were friends. But, let the wind shift just a little; let circumstances change, and our "friend" was gone.

This was not the case with David and Jonathan. Something beautiful transpired in their relationship, and nothing—not even Jonathan's jealous father—could sever that friendship. After David killed Goliath, he became a national hero. Their mantra: "Saul has killed his thousands, but David has killed his ten-thousands." Saul resented the attention David was receiving, but Jonathan celebrated David and cherished their friendship.

David was forced into hiding. Despite his father's empty promises and threats, Jonathan remained truthful and faithful to this special brotherhood. Nothing could break the bond between these two. It cost Jonathan a lot to be David's friend. His father cursed him and banished him from his rightful line of succession. Yet, Jonathan remained undaunted by his Dad's paranoid outbursts.

What kind of friend are you? Are you "there" when circumstances are good or convenient for you? Or, are you "there" regardless? God's love sticks with a friend whether they are right or wrong. What about your church? Bars and coffee bars are full because people are accepted just like they are. Are total strangers doing a better job at friendship than your church? We can learn from Jonathan.

You can be a faithful friend.

Eating Humble Pie

We like to be in control of our lives. No one chooses to look stupid, say something embarrassing, or act inappropriately. But, we do. And when we do, we have to swallow our pride, admit our mistake, and then move on with life. What if, though, God impresses us to do something that looks crazy in the eyes of the world? Surely, He would never do that.

Actually, God did exactly that with King David. David had the creativity to act crazy and insane. Why in the world would God do that with someone like David? David retreated from Saul to the alien territory of Gath where the people were superstitious and heathen. At the time, David was already appointed king, and if these people would have recognized him, they most likely would have killed David. But, no one wanted to mess with the madman in their presence (I Sam. 21:14-15).

This whole episode was very humbling for King David, but he took soberly his anointing as king and was not willing to do anything to jeopardize God's entire plan for his life or the Kingdom. David's actions were God-inspired and undoubtedly saved his life.

Ours is not to question the "ridiculous" things God asks us to do. Heaven will be replete with revelations of how our lives—crazy though they may seem—have been used by Him. So, the next time God asks you to do something that might make you look a bit crazy or stupid in the eyes of the world, remember David. Perhaps He wants you to speak up at work, witness to a co-worker, or bite your tongue when you'd rather speak your mind. God has a plan in every detail of your life. Humble pie may not taste good, but it can be good for you.

What crazy thing is God asking you to do?

Tyrannized by the Urgent

So many things and people and situations tug and pull and jerk on our fragmented lives that quickly we find ourselves engulfed in an ocean of the urgent. A million things clamor for our attention and time; everyone and everything is the most important issue of the moment. Sorting through all these pressures without allowing someone else's crisis to control our own lives takes skill, concentration, and teeth-grinding determination.

Nabal's wife, Abigail, was an intelligent woman. She should have fully understood God's prescribed chain of command. Her husband, however obtuse he might be, was the recognized head of the household. When she realized that her foolish husband refused provisions for the refugee king, Abigail took matters into her own hands and offered David food. After all, the situation was urgent. Perhaps, Nabal might have continued to stupidly refuse food to David, but we will never know what might have happened if she had appealed to him.

Abigail forgot that God could handle any situation, even this urgent one. She surmised that there wasn't enough time to follow the law. Since this was urgent, God would surely understand. We get so impatient for God to work that one by one, we take matters out of His hands and attempt to manipulate and control them ourselves. There are consequences to this behavior: Abigail became David's third wife, and they had a forgotten son, Chileab. She never enjoyed the life of Queen Mother. So sad. What a lesson for each of us. The more urgent a situation, the more it needs God's complete attention and timing. Don't permit your sense of urgency to get in the way of God's time, His plan, and His perfect will.

Relax; God's in total control.

Anointed for Service

If God lays His hand on a person for full-time service, that person has no other choice. He or she will be miserable until they surrender to His call. An isolation and loneliness comes from being set apart, but the beauty of full-time service outweighs any difficulty. And difficulty there is.

The pastor, church leadership, and the families of same seem to be fair game to many churchgoers. Second guessing the pastor and the leadership is sport. Roast pastor for Sunday dinner is normal fare for far too many. Criticizing their children, their possessions, and their motives is standard practice. God has strong words for this sort of misbehavior.

King Saul was out of control. His ego couldn't handle the fact that David was his anointed successor so he chased him all over the kingdom trying to destroy him. Then one day the tables were turned. David's little band caught Saul and Abner sleeping. This was David's opportunity for sweet revenge. "Do him in right now," coached Abishai, "You're justified." David understood God's sacred anointing: *The Lord forbid that I should lay a hand on the Lord's anointed* (I. Sam. 26:11). He was justified in the eyes of men but not in the heart of God.

This message is extremely relevant to the church today. Maybe your pastor has done something wrong in the eyes of God, but usually that's not the case. You don't like him or what he did, or he usurped your family traditions. You just want to get rid of him and start over. God anoints our pastors and leaders, and God disciplines them as well. David set a perfect example. When sweet revenge is within your grasp, resist it. God will take care of your pastor.

Hands off the pastor.

I Samuel 29-31:13
John 19:1-27
Psalm 68:21-27

Seeing is Believing

The world has shrunk immeasurably in the past forty years. When I was a child, my mother said often, "I'll believe that when there's a man on the moon." I recall a day, though, when I sat in my living room and watched Neal Armstrong step onto the moon and take "one small step for man; one giant step for mankind." Seeing is indeed believing.

Jesus made many predictions about His resurrection: "This temple will be destroyed and rebuilt in three days." His disciples and loyal followers were with Him until His last agonizing breath. They heard Him cry out and ask God why He was forsaken. They witnessed His pain and humiliation. They saw the mocking, and they saw Him die. His mortal death was their frame of reference and their reality.

On Sunday morning, they went to the tomb to mourn. Mary Magdalene and Jesus' mother went first, and Peter and John followed a short distance behind. They expected to see what is normal at a cemetery after a recent funeral—a fresh grave with wilted flowers. Perhaps they could arrange things a bit and make certain the situation wasn't compromised. Jesus deserved every iota of respect they could generate.

They saw something they never expected to see. The stone was gone and the tomb was empty. His words never came to their minds. Their thoughts turned to grave robbers and hooligans continuing to desecrate the Holy even after death. Mary Magdalene was panic-stricken; Jesus' mother was broken hearted; Peter was incensed; John believed. When John saw Jesus' folded burial cloth, Christ's words flooded his consciousness. Jesus wasn't dead. The Master was alive. What a liberating realization.

Believe what you see; He's alive!

Reflections on the Word...

June

II Samuel 1-24, I Kings 1-22, and II Kings 1-2
John 20-21, Acts 1-20
Psalms 69-78 and Proverbs 13-15

My Prayer Time for June...

Thanksgiving_____

_____

_____

_____

Intercession_____

_____

_____

_____

Ministry_____

_____

_____

Encouragement_____

_____

_____

_____

_____

If...Then

One of life's earliest lessons is the knowledge that there are predictable consequences to nearly everything we do and say. *If* you cry and pitch a little fit, *then* someone will pick you up and give you whatever you want. *If* you study hard and do your homework, *then* you will make passing grades. *If* you plant an apple seed, *then* you will eventually have an apple tree. It's called the law of reciprocity. In a word, you reap what you sow.

King Solomon—the world's wisest man—reiterated some extremely valuable *if, thens* for those who will pay attention:

- *If* you hang around with wise people, *then* you will be wise.
- *If* you sin, *then* evil will pursue you.
- *If* you're righteous, *then* you will prosper.
- *If* you are a good man, *then* you will leave something of value for your children and grandchildren.
- *If* you spare the rod, *then* you will spoil the child.
- *If* you're wicked, *then* you will go hungry.
- *If* you are a wise woman, *then* you will carefully guide your household.
- *If* you are upright, *then* you will fear the Lord.
- *If* you speak foolishly, *then* it will bring discipline.
- *If* you are wise, *then* your words are your own protection.

When I was growing up, my mother said often, "A word to the wise is sufficient." If only we believed that and could really learn through a word. That would by utopia. Most of us are hard-headed learners; we learn through the school of hard knocks—mostly as a result of our own doubt or disbelief. Solomon's "*if, thens*" are as right as rain. Take heed. Be a quick study.

Ever hearing; never understanding (Isa. 6:9).

The Biggest Fish Story Ever

Fishermen are liars. That's a fact. Everyone has heard about the big one that got away, the humongous fish someone saw but chose not to catch, or the day that the river was so full of fish, our avid angler friend had to throw more back than he brought home. I believe that it's a woman's constitutional right to embellish, and it's the fisherman's right to lie: "This is a moral that runs at large. Take it. You're welcome. No extra charge." (O. W. Holmes)

Jesus' lessons were always relevant to His audience. He taught about the vine to vineyard owners, and He taught lessons about fishing when He was with fishermen. Early one morning, Jesus shouted across the lake to His disciples as they were returning from their night's fishing: "What did you catch?" Every fisherman loves to crow about his catch, but these guys didn't have a thing to brag about. "The fish weren't biting," they hollered back as they began to bring their boat ashore. "It was a fishless night."

Jesus simply told the disciples to cast their nets on the other side of the boat. This was preposterous. First of all, they were out of the deep water near shore; secondly, they had been fishing all night—there weren't any fish. Perhaps to placate Him, but hopefully out of trust, they did what He said. Jesus knew where the fish were. Waulau! 154 fish! Just like that. It was astoundingly unbelievable.

As Christians, we nurture preconceived ideas about what we should do, when we should do it, and where it should happen. We fish in sterile waters while all around us there are plenty of fish for the catching. If your life seems unproductive, look to Him. He will tell you exactly where to cast your net. When He does something "big" in our lives, it is Him that we will be boasting about!

The really BIG stories are His stories.

The Word in Real Time

This Same Jesus

In El Paso, Texas, I made a friend who is one of my precious gifts. Her husband was a chaplain, and since we were all far from home, we became family. We spent holidays together and Friday nights playing table games. One day she called with bad news: They were being transferred. Her news was doubly bad; they were being sent to Taiwan—halfway across the globe. It was devastating to us both.

The day she left El Paso is etched in my mind. I tried to maintain my composure, but I just couldn't. Then she was gone. We wrote often, but things would never, ever be the same. One day out of the blue, she called. Something had to be very wrong, but something was very right. President Carter had normalized relations with Taiwan, and military personnel were coming home. The army had no precedent for this, so they were told to return to their last posts. Unbelievable. Shortly, I found myself back at the airport, but this time was different. My friend was returning just like she left. It was mind-boggling.

Jesus stayed on earth forty short days after His resurrection. Then it was time to go—but not for good. Standing with those He loved, He lifted His arms heavenward and in a flash, He was gone. His disciples were stunned. Not now! After Jesus' humiliating death, and then His miraculous reappearance, why would He leave now? Jesus had prophesied about this day, but they were still speechless. An angel appeared and calmed their agitated spirits: *Why do you stand here looking into the sky? This same Jesus… will come back in the same way you have seen Him go* (Acts. 1:11).

He's coming again just like He left. We don't know when, but we know it's going to happen. One day God is going to normalize His relations with man, and we will be forever with Him in paradise.

He's really coming again!

The Holy Spirit in Residence

Sometimes my husband and I fly seasonal flags from our garage door. It's fun and a bit festive, and our friends like it. But we only fly the flags when we're home. Anyone who knows us knows that if they see one of these banners flying that the Slamps are "In."

King David fought his way all the way into Jerusalem even though the Jebusites announced with bravado that he could be easily over run (II Sam.2). How wrong was that? Safe in Jerusalem at last, David took up residence in the fortress which would forever bear his name, the "City of David." You better believe that the citizens knew when David was "In." The road to Jerusalem was hard-fought and bloody. Now was their time for jubilant celebration. The king was victorious and he was "In."

Hundreds of years later in the same city, the Holy Spirit took up residence in the hearts of Jesus' followers. What a celebration they must have had in that upper room. Jesus promised that He would send the Comforter, and here He was. When the Holy Spirit came on them, they were emboldened and empowered and changed forever.

His promise of a Comforter continued down through generations, and it's just as relevant today as it was the day Jesus vowed that He would send the Holy Spirit. Amazing! I get excited thinking about His power and spirit resting on the church. It's almost too much to comprehend. His blessed Holy Spirit alive in our hearts is the flag that flies above our lives and announces to the world that He is "In." Your heart can be a fortress that will forever bear His name.

Let your banner fly.

A Long Way from Owl Creek

My father was born in a remote area of SE Oklahoma called Owl Creek. To hear Dad tell it, their family defined poor; no running water, no indoor plumbing, no toys, and no amenities. They lived cramped in a three room cottage in the middle of no place. At age nine, Dad's father moved the family across the state by covered wagon to W. Oklahoma. Theirs was a meager existence.

When I was thirteen, our family moved back to Oklahoma from Alaska. Dad thought it would be fun to find the old home place to show us kids. We drove up and down section line roads looking for his old house or school or something to denote that he had been there. To his chagrin, there was no visible evidence of a place called Owl Creek. In a word, my Dad came from no place.

When David was established as king, the prophet Nathan spoke: His name would be greatly remembered, Israel would have a permanent home, but most importantly to David, his children would succeed him. David was humbled and dumbfounded because He knew who he really was. He was the youngest son of Jesse, a shepherd from Bethlehem. *Who am I, O Lord, ... that you have brought me this far?* (II Sam. 7:17b). He was really a nobody from no place.

After retirement, my father and mother spent several months in Europe. Standing by Notre Dame in Paris, Dad turned to Mom and said, "This is a long way from Owl Creek." God has used my father all over this world; his life has been one of impact and influence to hundreds. If God can use the unknown son of a shepherd to be the forerunner of Jesus, and if He can use a poor Oklahoma boy from Owl Creek, He can surely use you. Don't let life or circumstances intimidate you are short circuit the ultimate impact of your life.

God calls from everywhere—even Owl Creek.

Mephibosheth & Rudolph

Y*ou've heard of Dasher and Dancer and Prancer and Vixon...; but do you recall, the most famous reindeer of all? It was Rudolph the Red-Nosed Reindeer.* You've heard of Jacob and Isaac and David and Saul; but do you recall, the least famous grandson of all? It was Mephibosheth, the grandson of Saul.

Some of the sweetest Bible stories are the most remote, yet they deserve attention. After David felled Goliath, neurotic Saul was obsessed with getting rid of him, and he made life miserable for David. David understood the significance of God's anointing, and as long as Saul was the anointed king of Israel, David had a "hands-off" attitude. Ultimately, Saul died in battled along with Jonathan.

David's love ran deep, and He remembered his dear friend, Jonathan, Saul's son. Once in power, King David discovered that Jonathan's crippled son, Mephibosheth, was in hiding. He brought Mephibosheth into the palace to live as his son and returned to him his inheritance—Saul's estate. What a friend. Mephibosheth was blown away. One day he was in hiding; the next day, he was a member of the king's household. What a life change—all a result of the undying friendship between King David and his father, Jonathan.

Have *you* been in hiding, afraid of some past enemy, unsure of your true friends? Are you handicapped by a past failure? Here's good news: Your inheritance is ear-marked just for you. The King is looking for you and has your place in His palace ready. He loves you more than David loved Mephibosheth. We're stunned that He should want us in His house and in His family, but He does. He's not looking for servants; He's looking for family, and *you* are family.

Your place at the table is set.

The Day after "D" Day

Eisenhower was the undisputed inspiration of the Normandy invasion of June 6, 1944. In today's vernacular, we would say to him, "You're the man!" The night before the epic invasion, the general wrote a letter of apology to the troops. No one knew if this massive endeavor would be successful or if it would be a colossal rout. So greatly did Eisenhower feel his responsibility to the world that he went on record to say "Sorry," if (God forbid) he should fail.

David spied Bathsheba from his rooftop. "Kowabunga, I'm king; I can have anything I want, and I want her," he thought. With that, David began his own self-destructive personal "D" Day. While Uriah, her husband, was at battle, David slept with her, and Bathsheba became pregnant. Uh, oh! Got to fix this. David brought Uriah home from battle so he would sleep with Bathsheba and think the baby was his, but Uriah refused to go home and spent the nights with his troops. That certainly complicated things, but a king can get anything done. He sent Uriah to the front line of battle, where he was killed. There you go. Neat and tidy. No one would ever know.

Nathan confronted David with a hypothetical story: A rich man took from a poor man rather than from his own resources. The king was incensed: "This man must die for his injustice against an innocent man." "You're busted, David! You're the man!" Nathan replied. David realized his sin, but it was far too late, and he couldn't undo the mess in which he had so craftily entangled himself.

Eisenhower and David each faced a major test—one passed and one failed. Each of us has defining life moments that reveal our character. Temptation doesn't come from God, but He can help even the weakest man and empower him to resist temptation.

What will the day after your "D" Day be like?

The First Spin Doctors

No one ever seems to be guilty of anything. Routinely, we hear about an unmentionable crime—a crime in which the perpetrator was literally caught in the act. Yet, even when an individual was seen standing in the presence of several eye-witnesses with smoking gun in hand, he is still described as the "alleged" perpetrator. Our prisons and jails are full of *innocent* men and women.

During the '60s and ever since, people have been marching and protesting for their rights. Little is ever mentioned about responsibility or accountability. People—even good people—manipulate and contrive any situation that might implicate themselves in order to give it a positive spin. Such was the case with Annaias and Sapphira. People in the early church had agreed that they would care for one another. It was a regular thing for one Christian to sell property to help another or aid the church.

Annaias and Sapphira's conspiracy finished them both. First, he lied, and then she endorsed the same lie. Hardly had the ushers carried his lifeless body from the church than they were taking hers to rest with him. What was their sin? They conspired to trick the leaders: *With his wife's full knowledge, he kept back part of the money* (Acts. 5:2). They knew exactly what they were doing; this was no misunderstanding. They hadn't broken man's law; they broke a commandment. Peter said it well: *You have not lied to men but to God* (Acts. 5:4b). They both knew precisely what they were doing. They could fake it in front of men all they wanted, but God knew.

A "smart" kid knows when he or she has gone far enough with Good old Dad. Annaias and Sapphira weren't smart—not at all. Messing with the holy and shifting the blame is a deadly game.

Don't even go there.

God's Steamroller

Asphalt is one big black mess until it is packed down and smoothed. It's common to see road construction with massive machines, one of which is the steamroller. This multi-ton machine is simple—a huge roller that compacts and flattens the asphalt so vehicles can drive smoothly on the roadway. The term "steamroller" is a permanent part of our vocabulary. It connotes one entity rolling over another with no regard, but with assured finality.

The early church was persecuted. Christians were beaten, arrested, wrongly accused of crimes, and ridiculed. The pompous church leaders never enjoyed the apostles' popularity; in a word, they were jealous *and* they had a lot of power. The church, however, wouldn't be stopped. "We must obey God," Peter bravely announced when they ordered him not to preach. This made them furious. How dare this upstart fisherman and Christian contradict their authority!

One Pharisee, Gamaliel, had some common sense and addressed the Sanhedrin: "Our approach with these guys isn't working. Every time we squelch them in one place, they pop up in another. When we throw them in prison, it only heightens their passion for the gospel." *If their purpose or activity is of human origin, it will fail. If it is from God, you will not be able to stop these men; you will only find yourselves fighting against God* (Acts 5:39).

Many weird and off-beat things occur in the name of God and the church. We don't need to fight against the wrong, and we will never defeat the right. God has a steamroller that is smoothing situations as it slowly rolls toward eternity. When He starts to move, get out of the way. Nothing, absolutely nothing, was able to stop Him during the apostles' day, nor will He be stopped today.

Stand back. God's rolling.

Heart Stealers

In youth, our affections turn to the opposite sex as we embark on that God-instilled human search to find life's companion to complement ourselves. When we're fortunate to find that one person, we know it. Many times, we've heard it said, "He or she stole my heart." The human heart is the center of our affections, passions, and loyalties—the things, people, and ideals that we hold most dear and precious.

Tampering with people's affections and loyalties is insidious, self-seeking, and evil. God abhors it. We are angered when an individual deliberately disrupts a marriage or any relationship for that matter. It's wrong for one parent to turn a child against the other or sibling against sibling. We are incensed and feel violated: The audacity of it all. How dare they! Yet, this thoughtless robbery of affections happens every day in our world and in our lives.

Absolom was a "tamperer of affections." Deliberately, he manipulated the people against his father, King David. In due course, he "stole the hearts" of David's constituents. Things got so unbearable for David that eventually he was forced to flee from Jerusalem to escape the belligerent atmosphere among the people that Absolom had contrived through his underhanded and crafty manipulations. How sad is that? A king on the run because of his own son. Who would have thought that could ever happen?

Many things and people in our lives are clamoring and demanding our attention and affections. Don't be tricked and don't be fooled. God is not pleased, nor will He tolerate this forever. He is to be our first and only true love—the center of our affections.

Don't let anyone or anything steal your heart.

II Samuel 16:15-18:18
Acts 7:20-43
Psalm 72

Long May He Live

We were shocked when we heard it back in 1965 and even more surprised when the world celebrated the arrogance: "I am the greatest!" Could one person really be so audacious? It's exciting to be in the presence of someone "important," although few would be as braggadocios as Clay. In a way, it colors the mundane of our lives to associate with someone important. We travel long distances to visit the homes and palaces of the rich and famous, take pictures, and get autographs which we treasure. In short, we celebrate them.

The Christian world has long been compared to a kingdom, and *we* have a king. He is one with whom we have easy access, and His availability is constant and non-preferential. It's not necessary to make reservations and stand in line to be meet Him, shake His hand, or get His autograph. We can move boldly and regularly into His presence for a personal audience. Why is He the greatest?

He judges righteously and protects the afflicted. He will last as long as any stars or planets—and even longer. He rules the entire world, from sea to shining sea. His autograph is visible wherever we travel. All kings from all nations will eventually honor Him. His hand will welcome some while it banishes others. When the needy cry out to Him, He *always* answers, for He is the God who takes pity on the weak, and He delivers the oppressed. Everyone is precious to Him.

He is the big "omni:" powerful, wise, ever-present. He deserves our offerings, our prayers, *and* our blessings. Mr. Clay bragged that he was "the greatest." Not so. *He* is greater than the great; stronger than the strong, more faithful than the seasons. He's from everlasting to everlasting. He is always there, regardless. *Praise His glorious name forever, may the whole earth be filled with his glory* (Psalm 72:19).

Let's Celebrate! Amen and Amen.

JUNE

12

II Samuel 18:19-19
Acts 7:44-8:3
Psalm 73:1-14

The Lone Runner

We got the call after midnight: a young man in our church was dead in a car crash. Would my husband deliver the sad news to his parents? This difficult task must be done with delicacy and in person. We called the parents, but no one was home. My husband knew that the young man's father worked as night clerk at a local motel, so together we set out on a painful midnight mission. As we entered the lobby, our parishioner greeted us: "Hello, pastor; how nice to see you." As quickly as the words passed his lips, his countenance dropped; you could see alarm on his face. What was his pastor doing there in the middle of the night? It must be bad news.

Joab defeated Absolom, David's rebellious son, underminer of the kingdom and stealer of the people's hearts. Still, David loved him. Paternal love runs deep for even the most wayward son. David's instructions: "Whatever happens, spare my naughty boy." David awaited news of the battle. A single runner meant good news; he knew that. In the distance he saw just one runner. His heart sang. The battle was won! He saw a second runner; Absolom must be alive as well. This was a terrific day. Perhaps now he would have an opportunity to reconcile with his son. Joab, however, disobeyed the king and killed Absolom. The battle was won; the kingdom was restored; but it was a bitter victory. David mourned his beloved son.

It hurts deeply to lose someone we love—especially when it's a senseless loss. After that night in the motel lobby, I know first hand how extremely difficult it is to break bad news. There's a big lesson here to the church: We dare not be like Joab and slay the son of the king. We aren't the judge! Each of us has disappointed the Father, and yet He loves *all* His kids. God still yearns to restore relationship between Himself and His children whatever they have done.

We're restorers; not killers of the king's sons.

The Word in Real Time

Start Where They Are

Since I began teaching in the '60s, I've taught thousands of students, kindergarten through college. To be effective, a teacher must know where a student is when they begin—regardless of age or subject matter. It doesn't help to talk about what kids "should" know at a certain age, go on and on about other teachers' failures, or try to teach a concept without the student having prior knowledge of the basics. A good teacher knows instinctively that he or she must ascertain where a student is, remediate if necessary, create a solid base, and teach from that point. That's good teaching.

Philip obeyed an angel who appeared to him. Not knowing where or why God was directing him, he headed south from Samaria across the desert toward Gaza. On the road he met the treasurer of Queen Candace of Ethiopia—an important man. He was studying Isaiah as he headed home from Jerusalem where he had gone to worship. The angel spoke to Philip, "Go talk to that man." Philip obeyed again. Delighted to see him reading scripture, Philip asked if he understood it. The Ethiopian's response was to the point: "No, I don't; how will I ever make sense of this word unless someone teaches me?"

Any good teacher would thrill to those words. Philip didn't lecture the Ethiopian on what he "should" know, nor did he go down some other pre-described "plan of salvation." He took the scriptures the Ethiopian was reading and used Isaiah to lead him to Christ. So effective was Philip's approach that they stopped by the side of the road, and the Ethiopian was baptized. What a teacher. Philip saw a man searching, built on his knowledge base and experience, and led him to Christ. There you have it: evangelism in a nutshell. Respect the individual, understand what he or she already knows, and build on that. That's good teaching and effective soul-winning.

Meet your neighbor where he is.

Cataract Surgery

Both of my parents and many of their friends have had cataract surgery, a routine outpatient surgery. Just a few years ago, when old age or disease began to work on the body, and when that slight film began to grow and blur the eyesight, people simply had to endure it. A few, in fact, eventually went blind. Today cataract surgery is routine, rather painless, and highly effective.

Saul of Tarsus was a persecutor of the Jews. Roman citizenship coupled with membership in the Sanhedrin created a deadly blend. With a word, he ordered Christians killed or beaten. He was heartless, ruthless, and sadistically evil; Christians feared Saul. They did not try to witness to him; they tried to avoid him. But, God was not afraid of him. He made Saul and had a "wonderful plan for his life."

Saul's story is a familiar one: On the Damascus road, God blinded him and literally—not figuratively—brought him to his knees. Blind, humbled, and out of control, Saul had to be led to Damascus. Saul was the classic "Type A" individual, and it took an incident of major proportions to get his attention. When God restored his eyesight after three days of total blindness, Saul—AKA Paul—was forever a different man. The former persecutor became the most effective missionary the church has ever known.

It's easy to let the film of life and its pressures grow over our spiritual eyes. When we don't take careful precautions, it's even possible to grow spiritually blind. Only you truly know what your situation is. If you need cataract surgery, make a voluntary appointment with the great physician. Things may grow out of control, and it could be necessary for Him to humble you and bring you to your knees to get your attention.

Do you need spiritual cataract surgery?

15

Apples & Oranges

In teaching writing or oral expression, teachers emphasize the technique called *compare and contrast*. We all use this technique regularly to show differences and similarities between or among any number of different things or circumstances. When two things can't be compared, we often conclude by saying, "It's like comparing apples and oranges." In other words, there are some things that can't be compared—just contrasted.

Giving and generosity can be identical or they can be diametrically opposed—it's a heart issue. You can give without a generous heart, but a generous heart is always a giving one: It's a matter of apples and oranges. A gift is something that costs—either in dollars, time, or talent.

David felt personally responsible for all the bloodshed in Israel so he was building an altar to offer atonement. He approached Araunah to buy his threshing floor to build the altar. Araunah offered to give the land to the king, but David refused: *I will not sacrifice to the Lord my God burnt offerings that cost me nothing.* (II Sam. 24:24). It was crucial to David that his offering be accepted. David knew that God would not recognize an offering as a true sacrifice if it were not something that David himself owned and returned to Him.

During the time of the apostle Paul, Cornelius was a spontaneous giver to the poor, and the angel blessed him for his generosity: *Your prayers and gifts to the poor have come up as a memorial offering before God* (Acts. 10:4). There it is—recorded in both the Old and the New Testament. God requires that our gifts cost us something. When we willingly relinquish something near or dear to us, God accepts our gift as from a generous heart. What will it be?

Apples or Orange? It's not an "either or."

Saint Katherine

My brother pastored an inner city church on the East Coast when he was in grad school. That area of the city had once been a fine middleclass neighborhood. Now, the old church stood on a totally different street corner, and the population had dramatically changed since the days of the church's hey day. Middleclass nuclear families were long ago replaced by subcultures that brought to the area all the pride of their individual ethnicity.

The leadership of the church, though, had lost sight of its mission and overlooked the obvious. Their actions implied that this was still a predominantly middleclass white neighborhood. One lady specifically frustrated my brother. She thought she owned the church and knew what was best. If he didn't watch her each Sunday and beat her to the door, she placed herself there as the guard—not greeter—of the church. When anyone attempted to enter who did not fit her pre-determined specifications as to status, nationality, or skin color, she suggested that they go elsewhere to worship. Jokingly, my brother referred to her as Saint Katherine.

Deplorable actions, we say. Not today in 21st Century America. This problem isn't new. Discrimination was prevalent in the early church. Peter reminded the crowd at Caesarea that it was against their law for a Jew to associate with a Gentile, but God revealed to Cornelius in a dream that he *should not call any man impure or unclean.* He continued: *God does not show favoritism, but accepts men from every nation who fear him and do what is right* (Acts. 10:34).

Favoritism is not of God. There can be a place in our fellowships for anyone and everyone who chooses to worship and be a part. God help us all to be open-minded and open-armed.

It's not about Saint Katherine, it's about Jesus.

God's Heart Wants to Sing

W e've all played the "what if" game. It is fun: What if I won the lottery? What if I had been born rich? What if my parents had lived in a different town? Here's a good one: What if I could have anything in the world I wanted? Anything? Our minds instantly begin to swirl and turn in temporal directions. I'd pay off all my debts and take an around-the-world safari. I'd buy a big house and two or three luxury automobiles. I'd send my kids to the best universities in the country. I'd take care of my aged parents in a style that they deserve. I'd buy a yacht and live in a penthouse. I, I, I.

God told King Solomon that he would grant a wish—the ultimate "what if" circumstance. Kings seem to have it all anyway, but to have God Himself come to a man and offer him his ultimate wish had to be a tantalizing temptation. Solomon wasn't tempted; he didn't miss a beat. He knew that he had a daunting task to build the temple and his palace and calm the people after his father's bloody reign. *Give your servant a discerning heart to govern your people and to distinguish between right and wrong* (I Kings 3:9), Solomon replied to God.

God heard his request, and He felt Solomon's heart. God's heart must have been singing that day. "He gets it. This king really understands that He needs my help to lead and govern wisely. He is a blessing both to me and to his people." And then God spoke to Solomon, and His heart sang: *I will give you a wise and discerning heart, so that there will never have been anyone like you* (I Kings 3:12). What a stimulating and challenging interchange between God and man.

Would you like to make God's heart sing? Ask Him for His wisdom and guidance. In so doing, you will bless the Lord and make His heart sing.

You can make His heart sing.

"Ohi! Ohi!"

Those are Greek fighting words. The closest analogous expression we understand is *Remember the Alamo*. In World War II the fascist dictator, Benito Mussolini, assumed that Greece would side with the Axis powers. In 1940 he sent a message to the Greek Prime Minister, John Metaxes. In a word, the message invited the Greeks to quietly capitulate and become a satellite to his regime. Mussolini underestimated the Greeks. Metaxes' response was terse: "We will have war." Oct. 28 is now a Greek holiday.

The words "ohi, ohi" (no, no) were instantly picked up by the Greeks. Outmanned one to fifty and worn from earlier battles, they rallied against an adversary that was sure to overwhelm them, but their national pride would not be overrun by a pompous dictator. And they fought. So valiant were they that Winston Churchill later commented, "Greeks don't fight like heroes; heroes fight like Greeks." To the world's amazement, the Greeks held the fascist invaders back long enough for the Russians in the east to regroup, and this became a major turning point in the war.

Paul and Barnabas were accosted by a false prophet on Cyprus who opposed them and tried to confuse people and turn them away from the gospel. Paul didn't pussy-foot around or circumvent the issue; he went straight to its core: *You are a child of the devil and an enemy of everything that is right… Will you never stop perverting the right ways of the Lord* (Acts 13:10)? There are times and circumstances that demand and command an immediate, emphatic "Ohi! Ohi!" Circumstances and people arise within and against the church that we absolutely should not tolerate—even for one day. You may feel out-manned, but with God you never are. Just say "Ohi! Ohi!" and let God work.

Fight like a Greek: Make war against the wrong.

Constructive Criticism

Now there's an oxymoron—constructive criticism. What in the world does it mean? We humans are such fragile animals that criticism can crush the strongest, most virile warrior. Even when we ask for constructive criticism or a critique, we really don't mean it. It's frightening and debilitating to be laid bare by even the kindest, most gentle, well-meaning friend. Almost before the words are out of their mouth, we're defending ourselves, explaining our actions. It's a truism: "You catch more flies with honey than you do with vinegar." If only we practiced that idiom.

What good is our message if people feel judged and criticized by us or by the Church? Paul was the absolute master in meeting people where they were, identifying with them, and then soliciting their attention to the message. Perhaps he was the first "great communicator." In Pisidian Antioch Paul followed this routine when he went first to the synagogue to dialogue with the religious leaders. These men were full of themselves, their knowledge, and endless religious palaver. When they invited Paul to speak, they recognized his customary manner: *Brothers, if you have a message of encouragement for the people, please speak* (Acts 13:15b).

That's what the world is still asking the Church: "Do you have any encouraging words for my weary life? I am so beaten down by my job and my finances and my kids and my.... Do you have any news that will lift my spirits and take me through another day? I don't want to hear a laundry list of "do's and don'ts." Can you tell me something good?" You bet! Avoid arguments and meandering dialogues about theology. Ours is a message of love and encouragement and uplift. That's what the world is seeking.

Give a word of encouragement today.

And Heaven and Nature Sing

We love to ski. My husband is pretty good. On the other hand, I'm proud to say I can ski down a mountain without falling—forget about form or grace. I still love it. There's nothing like the quiet beauty of a winter mountain as you glide through snow laden trees and see nature's unspeakable wonders. We live in Kansas, yet try to get to the slopes at least once a year for a "ski fix."

One winter, we coupled our ski trip with a visit to my parents in Idaho. On a day when the Treasure Valley was blanketed with dark, heavy "inverted" air, we set off for Bogus Basin near Boise. As we began ascending the foothills, nothing was visible. At 5,000 feet we were in a virtual cloud; 6,000 feet, the same story. At 6,500 feet, we discussed heading home, but we just couldn't quit. At 7,200 feet we began to see a break in the clouds; by 7,500 feet we were in the most beautiful, pristine day we have ever experienced on any mountain.

All day long we skied in unspeakable weather. The sky was a bright, robin's egg blue; there was no wind, and the runs were spectacular. What a day. As we skied in our unbelievable wonderland, below was the valley's inversion with its murky skies and dismal atmosphere. Not so on the mountain. That day heaven and nature sang with such harmony that a composer could score it into a rhapsody.

It's so easy to get bogged down in life's clouds and think that we will never see the sun again. When we persevere despite the odds, He is there: *The priests could not perform their service because of the cloud, for the glory of the Lord filled His temple* (I Kings 8:11). Do you want heaven and nature to sing in your life? Stick it out through life's inversions. One day you'll pass 7,000 feet; the sun will begin to break through, and you'll bask in His glory and presence.

Hang in there past 7,000 feet.

The School of Hard Knocks

We've all joked about it; we have it printed on T-shirts; but oh how true is this thing called the "school of hard knocks." Our first classes begin in the nursery, and sadly follow us to the grave. Some have more "hard knocks" than others, and some seem destined to repeat their own mistakes. Whatever the cause, and whether it is our fault or not, life knocks us around and bruises us a bit.

The Christian walk is not exempt from "hard knocks." In fact, we sometimes experience even more hard knocks when we take a stand and defend our testimony. Paul knew about hard knocks; his words are prophetic: *We must go through many hardships to enter the kingdom of God* (Acts 14: 22b). Rats! Why did Paul have to include that? We want a life of ease and comfort—painless. News flash! That's not going to happen—not in this life!

Ours isn't a gospel of "works." So, why did Paul say that we won't enter the kingdom without them? The world is looking for people who have triumphed over adversity. As I write this, I am sitting in a cruise ship heading to Alaska where I go each summer and lecture on the beauty of this great land. It's impossible for my husband to accompany me on all these trips, so often I take along friends.

One of my companions was amazing. A number of years ago she had lunch with her husband, told him "good bye" and planned to see him that night for supper. It never happened. That very afternoon he was killed instantly in a plane crash. What an inspiration she is. Her optimistic attitude and clear Christian testimony is evidence that hard knocks only serve to strengthen us. Would she have chosen this path? Of course not! But God is faithful. She has a smile on her face, a song in her heart, and she is a blessing to us all.

Are your hard knocks a testimony?

The General Assembly

The denomination of my heritage has a quadrennial meeting in which people gather from around the globe for services of inspiration. Simultaneously, they conduct business sessions. Most denominations have similar global meetings. Whatever the tradition, these are beautiful times of fellowship and worship. I haven't missed a "general assembly" since 1956. Wouldn't even consider missing.

Church meetings aren't new, and sometimes they aren't pretty. They began with the apostles, and some are very significant in church history. Like "Vatican II" is important in recent church history, the "Council of Jerusalem" is equally noteworthy. The bone of contention between the new Christian Pharisees and the apostles was that the Gentile converts had not been circumcised. That's a "No, No." Tradition was broken, and a church fight was looming.

Tradition is valuable and should be cherished. Yet, forcing someone from another culture to follow traditions that have no intrinsic value in their culture is pharasitical. My father called this the "letter of the law," not to the "spirit of the law." Bold Peter was the spokesman in Jerusalem: "What are you talking about? His message is for Jew and Gentile, heathen and sophisticated—it's all inclusive. It's a heart issue, not one of outward symbolism:" *He made no distinction between us and them, for he purified their hearts by faith* (Acts 15:9).

Just like we are all born alike physically, there is only one way to come to Him. It's not through an outward sign that we superimpose over someone's culture, rather it's through personal faith that results in a purified heart. What are the topics at your church meetings? Are they external issues, or are you focusing on the one thing that really matters—the persons He died to save?

Let's keep our meetings focused on Him.

His Mighty Deeds

Each summer I have an unspeakable privilege to cruise through Southeast Alaska and speak for cruise ship passengers. It's a non-paid job that is rewarding in ways larger than money and fringe benefits. There are some amazing "perks." First of all, I meet people from all over the globe—people of all races, religions, and backgrounds. It's enlightening, educational, and challenging to meet such a human collage.

A bigger perk and thrill, though, is the awesome nature that I am privileged to observe day after day: Grandiose mountains that scrape the sky—many of which have never to this day been traversed by man. The list continues: ancient glaciers, pristine fjords, icy mountain streams, a plethora of wildflowers too numerous to name, the midnight sun, giant creatures of the sea—whales, and the lord of the sky, the eagle. Each Alaska summer day is crowned with new glory and witness to the splendor and radiance of God's incredible nature. The Psalmist said it well: *I will meditate on all your works and consider all your mighty deeds* (Psalm 77:12).

When my summer sojourn in Alaska is finished each year, I return to the daily routines of life. Ever so quickly, I find myself once more absorbed with deadlines and traffic and situations and issues. The fact remains, though, that while I'm bogged down with the routine and mundane of living, Alaska's brilliance remains. There's so much to meditate on in God's splendid world—whether it be the desert or the Arctic or the coastal regions or the vast Midwest. Are you searching for a surefire remedy to the pressures of your life and your situation? Are you looking for a path to purge yourself from the ordinary? Take a moment to meditate on the beauty of the nature and the wonderful people around you.

There's peace and healing in His magnificent world.

Compelled to Help

I met her totally by "accident." Standing in a coffee line at a job orientation, there she was. She didn't fit the mold of my church friends or even my neighbors, for that matter. She was an angry divorcee with three daughters—mad at the whole world. She never told me she wasn't a Christian, but I surmised that she wasn't even though she used His name rather colorfully in conversation. There was something compelling about my new friend. I found myself strangely drawn to her as if she were pleading for help of any kind.

Within a year of our happenstance meeting that was choreographed by God Himself, my friend was gone—one more victim to that dreaded thief of life we know and abhor called cancer. The day I met her, I was drawn to her with an undeniable magnetism. Our friendship flourished and bloomed rapidly. She had one year and six days left on earth, didn't know the Lord, and didn't know anyone who could introduce her. My friends and I loved her and cared for her and her children. Somewhere during that unbelievable year, Rose accepted Christ. Compelling? I should say. Life-changing for all of us actually.

Paul had a compelling vision: *Come over to Macedonia and help us* (Acts 16: 9b). He had no more plans of going to Macedonia to tell the citizens of Philippi about Christ than I had thoughts in that coffee line about witnessing. Philippi (named for the father of Alexander the Great) was a Roman stronghold in Greece—not a likely place for a successful evangelistic campaign. Neither was my friend—the daughter of one of Hitler's storm troopers—a likely person to accept Christ. The compulsion I felt that September day was undeniable. I'm so glad that I listened. In so many ways and circumstances, He's compelling us all to tell our world the good news.

Where is your Macedonia?

Loose Chains and Open Doors

I've been there and it's awesome—the site in ancient Philippi of Paul and Silas' prison. How humbling. These two guys were gutsy. They didn't have to go to Philippi, but God compelled them. And when God compels, we must follow. What's astounding, though, about this sort of obedience is that He never asks us to go anywhere that He will not go with us.

Such was the case of Paul and Silas when they preached in Philippi. One of their converts was a slave girl and fortune teller. When she accepted Christ, this woman renounced her evil ways. Reason for rejoicing? Not so. Distraught by their sudden loss of revenue, her owners knew something had to be done about these religious fanatics—these interlopers from the East. They accused Paul of anti-Roman practices, but the bottom line was first and always money.

A riot ensued and straightway Paul and Silas were stripped, beaten, and thrown in prison, each one chained to guards. Not an easily overcome predicament. But God was in charge of this whole deal. During the night an earthquake struck that tipped the Richter scale. Prison doors flew open; guards and prisoners alike were set as free as birds. This made an instant believer of one guard who begged Paul to tell him how he could be saved.

As Christians we still experience situations where we feel bound, persecuted, and beaten down. When you are in the center of His will, there is never anything to really fear. When we least expect it and in ways that baffle common sense or logic, He still loosens people's chains and opens prison doors, setting captives free. Perhaps you're not physically chained, but you may be captive to a habit or circumstance that is unbeatable. Never fear.

He loosens chains and opens prison doors.

Worthless Idols

Israel and Judah suffered an endless succession of evil kings: the warring Rehoboam and Jeroboam, Abijah, Nadab, Baasha, Elah, Zimri, and Omri. In this laundry list of wicked leaders, only Asa stands out as God-fearing. These men allowed dastardly things to happen: They continually erected Asherah poles of worship, repeatedly compromised with the enemy, allowed male temple prostitutes, melted sacred temple icons and made bronze shields for protection. In a word, they defied and disobeyed God, dishonoring the kingship entrusted them.

At last God had had enough: *So they provoked the Lord, the God of Israel to anger by their worthless idols* (I Kings 16: 26b). You remember, don't you? Those time when you and your siblings or friends pushed the authority figures to the edge. You knew you should back off, but human nature took over, and you danced a dangerous jig around the edges of their tolerance. You misbehaved in front of company or talked back when you knew there would be repercussions. Mom and Dad loved you; surely, you could get by one more time. There was always the proverbial "straw that broke the camel's back," and Dad and Mom exercised their parental right and authority to rein in their recalcitrant child.

We still are worshipping "worthless idols." One of these days God will get to His breaking point with us as well. Idols vary for each of us, but regardless of what it is or what it isn't, each one of us is responsible to examine our lives—the things and people and places that we honor. Even worthwhile things that interfere with us and our relationship with Him come into play as He evaluates and weighs each and every deed and thought.

What are you worshipping?

Wind, Earthquakes, Fire, & Whispers

Nature can be devastating. I've experienced Santa Ana winds and earthquakes in California. In Kansas, I've seen the results of tornados and felt the anxiety of pending catastrophe. Each summer vast regions of our west are devoured by forest fires. Nature is truly awesome, but its potential for destruction is mighty as well.

In Elijah's tête-à-tête with evil at Mt. Carmel, he challenged Ahab. He was a tower of faith as he taunted and teased the 150 prophets of Baal, and God was the overwhelming victor. After Elijah doused his altar three times, God still answered his prayer: *Let it be known today that you are God in Israel…* (I Kings 18:26). With these words, fire fell from heaven and consumed Elijah's offering.

After a miracle, Satan always gets busy. Jezebel pursued Elijah with all her wicked wiles, determined to finish him off. Elijah should have been pumped from the victory, but he was tired and discouraged. Exhausted, he sat under a broom tree and begged to die. Poor, pathetic Elijah. He obeyed an angel and stood on the mountain, awaiting the Lord's presence, and nature began to perform: First came a mighty wind; he didn't feel the Lord. Then came an earthquake; same result, no feeling of His presence. Fire fell from heaven; Elijah was unmoved. At last, God spoke in a gentle whisper, and Elijah recognized the voice.

We grow discouraged and tired like Elijah and try all sorts of things to resurrect a feeling of closeness. When all our hoopla and noisy endeavors are drained, we're still empty: "Where are you, God? You were there in the big miracle; now I feel so alone. Please show yourself; I need to feel you." And He comes—not in a storm or fire or loud noise, but in a quiet whisper. Don't be discouraged. Listen to the quiet; you'll hear Him in the stillness of your heart.

Listen for His gentle, quiet voice.

"I Shall Return!"

Douglas Macarthur made this prophetic statement during World War II when the US Army was forced to flee the Philippians. The people of the islands loved and trusted him; he wanted them to fully understand that he was not abandoning them. Neither Macarthur nor the Filipinos knew when or if that would ever occur.

Paul sailed from Corinth across the Aegean to Ephesus, a bustling port city in Asia. He left behind dear friends, Aquilla and Priscilla, with these departing words: *I will come back if it is God's will* (Acts 18:21). Aquilla and Priscilla loved Paul as much as the Filipinos loved Macarthur. Parting is indeed "sweet sorrow." We really never know *if or when* we will see the other again. Apparently, both Douglas Macarthur and Paul understood the uncertainty of parting.

As dramatic as the words "I shall return" are, they often don't come to pass. Paul's words have a different twist than Macarthur's—"if it is God's will." I believe there are two major lessens in this brief statement. We may never ever see a person again once we leave them; and secondly, even though we might see a particular individual again, it's possible that in leaving a certain place, we will never pass that way again.

It is easy to get "miffed" and upset, parting in a huff at least, but more often parting in anger. In light of the fragility of life, that's a dangerous position. I've known a few people who have had to live with huge regrets because of a fiery and hasty parting. Make each and every parting as though it were your last, for indeed all of our lives are "in God's will."

God's will is in each parting and each meeting.

Unnecessary Commotion

Some people and/or groups of people seem to live in a state of constant turmoil—something is always awry and a bit off kilter. As onlookers, it's easy to observe and question just "What's the big deal and why such a commotion?" When we take the time to carefully study a situation, it's possible to ascertain that the stated reason for the commotion is not always the *real* reason. People cloak their commotion with concerns about issues, but more times than not, the bottom line of confusion is rooted in selfishness, power struggles, and ambition.

Such a situation arose for Paul in Ephesus. In each city Paul visited his routine was to visit the synagogue and discuss Jesus with the scholars and other listeners. That was his *modus operendi*, and it was effective—too effective for the "powers that be." Demetrius, the silversmith, was upset because the new Ephesian converts weren't buying idols any more. He didn't care if they became Christians; He cared that his business was affected. But to challenge Paul straight out could have been disastrous to his reputation. Demetrius solved his financial dilemma by accusing Paul of offending the goddess, Artemis. This accusation stirred up confusion not only among the craftsmen, but among the general public as well.

Commotion and confusion are contagious, and we easily become involved without even knowing why: *The assembly was in confusion. Some were shouting one thing, some another. Most of the people did not even know why they were there* (Acts 19:32). As mature Christians and adults we can learn to think for ourselves. So much trouble, both in our personal lives and in our churches, could be averted if we asked the Holy Spirit to gives us the spirit of discernment to be able to tell what the "real" motives are in a situation.

Listen to the Spirit—not the noise.

II Kings 1-2:25
Acts 20
Psalm 78:40-55

Extra Helpings

Americans love to eat; too much so, I'm afraid. We've all been to a holiday dinner and gorged ourselves with extra helpings of turkey and dressing and pumpkin pie. We've eaten an extra scoop of home made ice cream. We've felt compelled to do our part at an "all you can eat" place, thereby helping them to adequately live up to their name. We've been on a cruise where food was so plentiful and lavish that it was nearly obscene. After all, what could an extra helping hurt? Physically, that philosophy is destructive.

On the contrary, spiritual extra helpings are beneficial. Elisha understood this well. Elijah was near death, and God had ordained Elisha as his successor. What a responsibility. We could equate it today to someone attempting to pick up Billy Graham's "cloak." Huge shoes. For every Moses, God has a Joshua; and for every Elijah, He has an Elisha. As Elijah took his final earthly steps, he was accompanied by fifty prophets—all stood at a distance except Elisha. Undeterred, he wanted to be with Elisha—this spirit-filled man of God—to the end.

Finally, Elijah turned to young Elisha: "What can I do for you?" Elisha knew that he must have Elijah's spirit if he was going be the prophet: *Let me inherit a double portion of your spirit* (II Kings 2:9b). When Elijah dropped his earthly cloak and ascended heavenward, Elisha grabbed hold of it for all it was worth. This cloak embodied the spirit of the man, and now Elisha would test God. Approaching the Jordan, he took Elijah's cloak and struck the waters. When the river parted, Elisha knew that God had granted his request.

We can ask the Lord for many things, but more than anything else, we need His Spirit to rest on us. There will be tests, and with those tests, we will see His spirit. Do you really want God to bless you?

Ask for a second helping of His spirit.

The Word in Real Time

Reflections on the Word...

Reflections on the Word...

July

II Kings 3-25, Jonah, Amos, Hosea, and I Chronicles 1-10;
Acts 21-28 and Romans 1-14
Psalms 78-89 and Proverbs 16-19

My Prayer Time for July...

T hanksgiving _____
_____
_____
_____
_____

I ntercession _____
_____
_____
_____

M inistry _____
_____
_____
_____
_____

E ncouragement _____
_____
_____
_____
_____

Boom Town, Moab

In the early 50s, places like Pampa, Texas and El Reno, Oklahoma sprang overnight from oblivion to front page news. The reason? Oil. These sleepy little towns were suddenly booming with activity created by the discovery of black gold. After the Great Depression of the 30s, the discovery of oil was a boon. Riggers, drillers, and hardhats of all descriptions rushed to these "barren" regions just like Klondikers had flocked to the Yukon at the turn of the century.

A widow from Moab was feeling her own personal depression. Circumstances grew unbearable, and she appealed to Elisha: *Your servant has nothing at all, except a little oil* (II Kings 4:2b). God gave Elisha an ingenious plan: "Send your sons to your cellar to get all your old canning jars—even get your neighbors' jars. God has a miracle for you. Don't stop with a few; collect all you can find."

When the supply of jars was exhausted, they closed their door. Now they had a bunch of empty jars and a little bit of oil, but they still were depressed. Not much of an improvement. Elisha spoke: *Pour oil into all the jars, and as each is filled, put it to one side* (II Kings 4:4). As long as there was a jar, there was oil. When the jars ran out, so did the oil. They then sold the oil, paid their bills, and lived happily ever after.

Are you so low that you feel like there's nothing left but a tiny bit of God? He's available; He just needs vessels. Recently, my church experienced an old fashioned service in which He poured Himself out on the entire congregation. I was out of town and only heard about it. You have to be present when His spirit is poured out to receive the blessing. I believe that if the widow's sons had known the extent to which God would be blessing them, they would have gone to the next town for vessels. Be prepared for His spirit to come.

Bring your vessels not a few.

On Eating Humble Pie

When we kids got too full of ourselves and thought we knew everything and didn't need help, my mother reminded us that we were 'too big for our own breeches.' "There are just some things," she taught us, "that you have to go through the hard way. Some things just aren't easy, and there are no shortcuts. Eat a little humble pie."

Such was the case with Naaman, a commander of the king's army. He was a high-faluting, important man. If you didn't remember, he would remind you. Naaman had anything he wanted at his fingertips; fine food, nice clothing, servants, and privilege. Naaman had it all, but he still contracted leprosy. Uh Oh! This fatal and devastating disease only happened to the poor and the underprivileged, not him.

In a peck of trouble, Nathan finally turned to a humble servant—an Israeli captive who told him about Elisha's healing powers. When a man's back is against the wall, he'll try anything, so Naaman appealed to Elisha for help. Elisha instructed Naaman to dip seven times in the Jordan: "Let me explain. I'm a general; generals don't dip in muddy rivers. There's got to be a more genteel healing at the ready—one more suited to my status. My healing should be an event worthy of the six o'clock news. I will not dip in that old muddy Jordan River." And so Naaman remained leprous. At last, he was forced to humble himself and obey the prophet or die in exile from the disease. When he obeyed Elisha, Naaman was healed.

Are you too good to follow God's path of humility? Does He not understand how important and valuable and above the rest you truly are? As long as that attitude prevails, God will leave you in your suffering. There's healing and health that follows the humble heart.

Humble pie is good for spiritual indigestion.

Born a Citizen of the Kingdom

"Born in the USA! Born in the USA!" Thank you to 'the boss,' Bruce Springsteen. That song, along with other patriotic tunes, stirs our red, white, and blue blood. This is truly a great country, and despite its flaws, we're blessed to have been born here.

Paul's preaching stirred up such an uproar that ultimately he was arrested and brought before the Sanhedrin. This event began a progression of courts and tribunals in which Paul was "privileged" to testify about his faith. The Roman guard demanded that Paul be flogged and questioned to discover the reason for all the commotion. Paul knew just the right tactic for his situation: *Is it legal for you to flog a Roman citizen who hasn't even been found guilty* (Acts 22:25b)? This question was brilliant, and it was rhetorical. The answer was an unequivocal, "no." Paul knew the law and he knew that they knew it as well. His Roman passport was valid.

The Roman guards got nervous: "Are you really a Roman citizen?" "Yes," answered Paul. Impressed, the commander responded: *I had to pay a big price for my citizenship* (Acts 22:28). Once again, Paul had the perfect comeback: "I was born a citizen."

What encouraging words for us today. Christ has paid the price for our heavenly citizenship. It's done. When we accept Him as our personal Savior, we are born into the Kingdom. Move over Bruce, this is bigger than the USA. This is the Kingdom of God. What bigger, better, or more significant credentials do you need? You're passport is stamped.

Is your passport valid?

Restore Us, O God!

Today is our biggest national holiday. It's our day for parades and picnics and fireworks and speeches and reunions. It's a day when we join with family and friends to celebrate this great country, its blessings and freedoms and privileges. But, for the sober, serious American, it's also a day for reflection and evaluation.

Liberals and conservatives alike can agree that we have wandered far from the concepts and ideals of the founding fathers. These men weren't infallible, but they were wise beyond their years—and they were "God-centered." The guidelines set forth in the early patriotic documents such as the Bill of Rights, the Articles of Confederation, and the Declaration of Independence have been diluted and altered and marred until they are often unrecognizable. On reflection, it's not too difficult or unrealistic to mourn for our country.

King David echoed these feelings when he reflected about Israel: *You have made us a source of contention to our neighbors and our enemies mock us. Restore us, O God Almighty; make your face shine upon us, that we may be saved* (Psalm 80:6-7). No one of us is responsible for others' actions, but we are each one responsible for ourselves. "No man is an island; no man stands alone." Today is the 4th of July—a day to celebrate, and a day to humbly appeal to God to "restore our nation." That restoration may take different forms for each of us, but the bottom line remains the same: This is still "one nation, under God." *God help me to do my part in keeping this a truly Christian nation.*

God bless America!

Repetitive Testimonies

I work at home so daily I experience the annoying interruptions of solicitous phone calls and telemarketers. More annoying than the calls is the series of buttons and numbers that are required if you choose to get in touch with a creditor. They ask for your number and ZIP code, and then after an interminable wait—if you're lucky, a live individual will come on the line. Not necessarily an informed individual, just a live one. The first thing they ask you is to repeat the information you just gave them. Irritating to the "nth" degree!

For Christians the opportunity to repeat our testimony should never be irritating. Paul seems nearly inhuman in his eagerness to travel from one official to the next, repeating his story verbatim. Arrested in Jerusalem, he testified there. When they realized he was a Roman, the authorities had a "problem" on their hands, and Paul used their problem to his advantage. They shipped him to the seaside resort area of Caesarea where he was confined until he was brought before Felix, the Roman consulate: "You mean I have to repeat the whole story one more time?" That might be our response, but Paul nearly shouted, "Whoopee! I get to testify before one more authority figure. Who knows? Perhaps my testimony will influence him to accept Christ." And so, up the chain of authority, Paul went, repeating his testimony anew each time.

Who hasn't read Rick Warren's best seller, *The Purpose Driven Life?* My initial response was rather "Ho hum." Not because I didn't agree, rather the book seemed so basic to me. I was taken up short, though, by a non-Christian reader. He was so excited: "This is good news," he shared. "I never knew any of this before. This is amazing." Do you get it? The story of Jesus is old, and it's new. Never get weary of sharing your testimony and telling the old, old story.

The "old" is new to the non-believer.

Too Little, Too Late

As people who lead by example, we must expend all our energies to do the right thing for those who follow. It's true: "I can't hear what you say; your actions speaker louder than your words." As leaders and parents and Christians and citizens, the world is watching whether we like it or not, and this affords us a matchless privilege and an awesome responsibility.

Jehoash was a king with a great deal of power and prestige who ruled during the last days of Elisha, the prophet. Even though Elisha was an invaluable spiritual asset during his reign, Jehoash saw him more as his personal magician, rather than God's spokesman. Jehoash led his nation without consulting the Lord; he didn't have the spiritual strength to stand when he had the opportunity; he failed to recognize the spiritual significance of Elisha's instructions, and his compliance with the prophet was merely perfunctory. All these qualities created a formula for spiritual failure that angered the ailing old prophet.

Just like Jehoash, we know God's history and His word. But, knowing history and heeding it are two diametrically opposite sets of circumstances. Jehoash appealed to the dying prophet, but it was too late (II Kings 13:14). Elisha gave him one final opportunity to prove himself a righteous man when he told him to strike the ground with the arrows he had shot (vs. 18). Jehoash was half-hearted even in responding to Elisha's last request, and his fate was sealed.

> When good fortune comes tapping at your wee cabin door;
> If it catches you napping, it will come there no more.

Opportunities to be true and consistent are present each and every day. We must be ready for the task, because it may not come again.

The last minute is usually too late.

II Kings 14:23-15
Acts 25:23-26:23
Proverbs 16:18-27

A Word to the Wise...

My parents said it to me; we said it to our kids; and they will most likely say it to their kids: "A word to the wise is sufficient." Translated: "Some things need not be experienced; you can learn from the former generation. Heed my word, and it will save you unmeasured grief and heartache." So, listen to the word:

- A proud and haughty attitude will lead to a fall.
- You're better off to live humbly among the oppressed than to share the booty of the arrogant and proud.
- Paying attention to instruction insures prosperity.
- You will be blessed when you trust the Lord.
- A smart person is discerning and can "read between the lines."
- Others are open to your teaching when your method is pleasant.
- Do you want to experience the "fountain of youth?" Listen to Him and understand His teaching.
- Folly produces punishment and creates fools.
- A wise man watches what he says and people learn from him.
- Kind words are sweet to the body and soul of the listener.
- Some people think they have it all figured out, but they end up totally destroying their lives when they leave God out.
- When a man is hungry enough, he will work.
- A rascal's speech is like a fire to his listeners.

There's nothing that needs to be added, or edited, or augmented to this scripture. It stands alone in its own glory and depth: *This is a moral that runs at large: Take it; your welcome; no extra charge* (Oliver Wendall Holmes).

Listen. Heed. Learn.

Monkey See; Monkey Do.

Imitation is one of the best methods of learning. It's cute when a little boy walks in his dad's shoes or a girl dresses up in mother's clothes. We're not surprised when middle schoolers want to dress and look just like everyone else; in fact, looking different at that age is a mark of conformity. We expect adolescents to be secretive and attempt to keep things from their parents. We expect them not to listen. We don't like it, but it's predictable, and somehow we endure it. But adults? We're abashed: "Grow up and think for your self."

One after the other, the kings of Israel followed idolatrous ways, mimicking the habits of the countries they overcame and trying to hide their actions from God; they were predictably wicked: *The Israelites secretly did things against the Lord their God that were not right* (II Kings 17:9). Just like we get exasperated with our kids, the Israelites' actions "provoked the Lord to anger." Even when God warned them, they chose not to listen: *They would not listen and were as stiff-necked as their fathers…* (17:14).

God will ultimately put His foot down against intolerable behavior: *He afflicted them and gave them into the hands of plunderers, until he thrust them from his presence* (17:20b). One would think that being cast away from God would make a person "wake up and fly right." The Israelites were slow learners and continued to compromise: *… they also served their own gods in accordance with the customs of the nations…* (17:37). Monkey see; monkey do.

God expects Christians to follow His word and "think for themselves" accordingly. We are not to look like, sound like, or act like the worldly people around us. Rather, we are to be living testimonies of His righteousness and loving kindness in our lives.

Think for your self: God expects it.

I Told You So

Every modern tourist visits the *Red Dog Saloon* in Juneau, Alaska for a taste of the gold rush. Inside the saloon, it's a flash back to a bygone era with a tin pan piano player, guitarist, and a music leader. There's organized rowdiness today, but years ago, this was a place for hard drinkers. Lives and reputations were won and lost at the *Red Dog*, and some of its tales are local legends.

The Gastineau Channel isn't deep enough to sail through, so ships visiting Juneau sail around Admiralty Island between the mainland and Douglas Island. They leave the same way they came; every good Alaskan sailor has known that for years. In 1952 the crew of the *Princess Kathleen* visited the saloon, drinking until departure. They sailed south along Douglas Island—the wrong direction. At low tide they ran aground at Lena Point. The passengers and crew stayed with the ship and were rescued. The *Kathleen* wasn't so lucky. The tide rolled in, she sank, and was lost forever. The captain knew better. There's a corporate "I told you so" attitude in Juneau about the *Kathleen*. It shouldn't have happened; everyone knows it.

Paul was in a similar situation on his journey to Rome when his ship was trapped in a huge storm. Never at a loss for words, Paul spoke: *You should have taken my advice not to sail from Crete; then you would have spared yourselves this damage and loss* (Acts 27:21b). In other words, "I told you so." He continued: *Unless these men stay with the ship, you cannot be saved* (27:31b).

The church is referred to as the *Old Ship of Zion*. This old ship gets into some major storms, we get tossed about, and sometimes a captain steers us in the wrong direction. That's not the time to jump ship. He's in control of all the storms, and He will see you through.

Stay with the ship.

10

And So We Came to Rome

My husband and I have been married for many years, and we've lived many places—Idaho, Kansas, California, Texas, Washington, Oklahoma, Tennessee, and back to Kansas. At times the road's been rough; yet, "His ways we'd not change, if even we could." All the same, sometimes we say to each other, "How did we get *here*?" Perhaps we've all said that in one way or another. "How did I get to this town, this marriage, this job, or even this church?"

God's ways are mysterious and beyond human understanding. In our youth we have dreams and plans and hopes. There's an old saying that says it well: "Life is what happens while we're making other plans." Life is packed with interruptions, surprises, and disappointments. If we could see them all at the outset, we'd probably be so petrified that we would never even begin. But we strike out, and as Christians, we have the blessed comfort of knowing that wherever we go or whatever happens, the Lord goes with us and before us.

Young Paul chose a life mission: To persecute Christians. But God had other plans for Paul. God led him across the known world as a missionary, even as far as Rome: *And so we came to Rome* (Acts 28: 14b). How in the world did he get to the very center of his world—Rome? Paul never backed away from an opportunity to speak to anyone— lowly or high—about his faith in Jesus. Testifying was his passion. He made it to Rome as a prisoner, not with pomp or glory, but he had an opportunity to testify to Caesar himself.

Where has life taken you? Are you some place you never expected? Did you arrive at a goal from a completely different direction than you ever would have expected? God has been in your life all along, and He will continue to be with you whenever and wherever.

All the way, my Savior leads me...

No Reprieve for Believers

A reprieve? What is it? The dictionary describes it as *the act of giving temporary relief to.* So, what does that mean? Good question. It could mean several different things: temporary relief from an illness; shortening or canceling of a sentence; or just a break in the day-to-day stress of living. Maybe, it means a short breather, like a vacation or a weekend away. Whatever it means, it's refreshing to stop what we're doing, and take a reprieve from the action. Unless, of course, we're talking about our Christian walk.

Paul had persistent tenacity when it came to sharing his testimony. Nothing stopped him; he was undaunted. When you study Paul's life, it's evident that in *every* situation and *every* person Paul saw an opportunity to testify about Jesus. He was so drastically changed on the road to Damascus that he was afraid of no one. Everything in life created another opportunity for the gospel.

After Paul survived the treacherous sea voyage, he was put in house arrest in Rome—not a little ninety-day "Martha Stewart-type" house arrest. His house arrest lasted two years. Anywhere along the judicial conduit to Rome, he could have short-circuited the process. Several legal doors were available, but he persevered in his own defense and in the defense of the gospel—all the way to Caesar: *...they wanted to release me, because I was not guilty of any crime deserving death. When the Jews objected, I was compelled to appeal to Caesar* (Acts 28:18-19). In other words, he refused his own reprieve.

We're arrested and held captive by grace. Sometimes we simply want "off the hook" or "out of the situation." A vacation from work and daily pressures is one thing, but a reprieve from our Christian testimony isn't even an option. We're in this for the long haul.

You're "under arrest" until the end.

Divine Credentials

By education and training, by practice and experience, and, yes, by calling, I am a teacher. Since I was a 5th grader, teaching has been my life's goal and passion. Perhaps the ability to teach is God's greatest gift to me. Coupled with that, though, the responsibility of teaching is even greater. A good teacher must have training and ability, but he or she must also have credentials. The responsibility of the charge demands it.

Because we've moved a lot, I've become an expert of sorts at meeting credential requirements. Each state has its own credentialing quirks, and I've learned to "jump through the hoops" so to speak in order to be hired. As silly as some of this seems at times, it's necessary. No city or state would allow just "anyone" to walk into a classroom of vulnerable and impressionable students and teach. Nor do parents care to send their children into schools where individuals are just "flying by the seat of their pants" when it comes to their child's education. It's just too critical.

And so it is with Christianity. The world demands validity and credentials for our testimony. Guess what? They're available; you can go through the application process and obtain them. Paul understood this: *...through him and for his name's sake, we received grace and apostleship to call people from among the Gentiles to the obedience that comes from faith. And you also are among those who are called to belong to Jesus Christ* (Rom. 1:5-6). The world doesn't care about your "opinion." They can get that any day of the week at the coffee shop or the water cooler. But they care about your credentials. Are you the real deal? You can be. With divine credentials, you can have confidence and strength to go against all sorts of forces and principalities. Divine credentials for your testimony are available.

Take the test and apply today.

That's No Excuse!

Can you remember hearing those words? Honestly, all of us can. We either heard them from parents, teachers, officers of the law, or all three. When one is privy to knowledge, no excuse is acceptable in explaining away disobedience or avoidance of responsibility. Once we're made aware of the rules or regulations or guidelines, "I didn't know" just won't cut it.

Long ago God informed man about right and wrong: *...since what may be known about God is plain to them, because God has made it plain to them* (Rom. 1:19). Can you remember serious talks with your kids that went something like this: "You knew that was wrong when you did it; you've been taught otherwise. What made you do such a thing?" We don't like to admit our anger in these situations, so we call it exasperation or disappointment. It may be those things, but in truth, we're "righteously" angry to think that our child would be so openly rebellious and disregard instruction and guidance.

Since the creation of the world God's invisible qualities—his eternal power and divine nature—have been clearly seen, being understood from what has been made, so that men are without excuse (1:20). Disregarding God's qualities and the displays of nature and going our own way don't just "disappoint" God; they stir up His anger toward mankind. In a word, He says the same thing to us that we say to our kids: "You knew that was wrong when you did it; you've been taught otherwise. What made you do such a thing?" God's rule book—the Bible—has been around a long time, and it hasn't changed. We're expected to comply.

You've been informed; no excuses are permitted.

A Fish Story

Once upon a time God told Jonah to go to Ninevah and warn them of His coming judgment. Jonah was "chicken-hearted," and fled by sea to a totally different place—Tarshish. A huge storm blew up, and while the sailors frenetically tried to save the boat, Jonah slept. When they found him asleep, they woke Jonah and asked him to "call upon his God." Knowing that his disobedience caused the storm, Jonah begged to be thrown overboard.

When all efforts to save the boat failed, reluctantly they threw old Jonah into the deep. Now, for sure, he wouldn't have to obey God. Poor Jonah! God wasn't finished with him, but rather sent a huge fish to swallow him alive. For three days and nights Jonah sloshed around in the dark, smelly belly of that fish—at last promising God that he would obey. And so the fish tossed Jonah onto dry land.

Jonah commenced the three day walk to Ninevah *post haste;* this was a divine appointment. Boldly, he prophesied: "You have forty days until total destruction. Stop your wickedness now or perish." To Jonah's consternation, the Ninevites repented of their evil ways. Touched by their contriteness, God mercifully spared destruction.

The good news should have pleased Jonah, but it only made him mad. "God, look at all *I* went through to get *your* message of doom to Ninevah. The least *you* could do for all *my* troubles is bring *some* hardship on them. They don't deserve mercy, particularly after what *you* put *me* through. I want to see them writhe; I want to hear them beg for mercy. God, this just isn't fair to *me*." God's mercy is abundant. He longs for us to return to Him. Are you mad because someone in your life didn't get what you knew he or she deserved? Give it up. You're not getting what you deserve either.

Do you have a fish story?

Beauty is only Skin Deep

I can't remember her first name, but I'll never forget her. Friends of my parents spent their honeymoon at a California beach resort, and one afternoon, they both fell sound asleep. She suffered severe and life-changing sunburns over her body—specifically her face. As a result, she endured countless skin grafts on her face and neck. Her mouth was distorted and her eyes were disfigured; her whole face had a reddish, stomach-turning tint. She was difficult to look at.

I still recall the last time I saw her. It was after my husband and I were married, and we were visiting "the folks" at the same time their old friends were there. As I sat at Mom's kitchen table chatting with our friend, it dawned on me that I didn't even "see" her outward appearance because of the inward beauty that shone through. She was indeed one of the most beautiful people I have ever known.

Many people "look good" on the outside but their insides are rotten. Paul addressed this issue straightforwardly "Some of you follow the law and are circumcised, but it hasn't changed your behavior or attitudes one iota. Others of you have never been circumcised, but your lives are pure and in tune with the Spirit." *A man is not a Jew if he is only one outwardly... No, a man is a Jew if he is one inwardly; and circumcision is circumcision of the heart* (Rom. 2:28-29).

My friend had little outward beauty, yet she and her husband came to terms early in their marriage with the plight they were dealt, and they chose the high road of acceptance. She couldn't consider a beauty contest; she wouldn't be accepted. Her husband and friends accepted her, and that was evident. Her beauty was lovely to behold and pleasant to be around. *He* accepts us inside or outside the technicalities of the law because He looks at our heart.

Do you have a circumcised heart?

What Color is God's Face?

Do you remember *Up with People*—a Christian group that toured the world for years? They sang one song consistently:

> What color is God's face? What color is God's face?
> It is black, brown, and yellow. It is red; it is white.
> Every man's the same in the Good Lord's sight.

How true; how true; and how consistent with the Word. On the surface, these words appear to deal with racial issues, but the inference goes much deeper than skin tone.

Paul teaches that we are never righteous when we merely observe the law. That concept is a shortcut that only nullifies His righteousness. If all that were necessary for us to do was to memorize and follow a set of outward "rules," life would be simpler than it is. But, following the "rules" doesn't change the heart. The law is in our lives to reveal sin. Think about it. Speed limits would not be necessary without the danger of accidents. The pending danger precipitates the law. So it is with God's laws.

Many Jews were "self-righteous" in their observances of the law. "After all," they implied, "look what I've done or what I haven't done. I'm pure in the eyes of the law; I'm righteous." Paul cut cross grain to this legal posturing: *This righteousness from God comes through faith in Christ to all who believe. There is no difference, for all have sinned and fall short of the glory of God...* (Rom. 3:22-23).

What color *is* God's face theologically? Answer: We're all the same in His sight. Since we were *all* born in sin, we must come to Christ through faith and believe in Him so that we don't fall short of His glory. Praise the Lord, His grace is available to each and every one.

God's face is "your" color.

Righteous Credit

My husband and I have joked that "good credit is our downfall." When we first married, the credit union was across the street; later in California, our friend owned the credit union. We've been on first name bases with our bankers and have always paid our bills on time—regardless how difficult. Recently, we purchased a new car. Within a matter of two hours, we had the check in hand for the full amount. When the credit union asked if we wanted to see our credit report, we answered, "No." We knew that our credit was excellent.

Good credit is important—financially, ethically, and morally. It's simply something you never want to lose. Other things are negotiable, but reputation and character are not for sale. People do a lot to earn God's favor. We attend church services, teach classes, sing in the choir, visit the sick, go on mission trips, and give our tithes and offerings. As important and vital as all these things are both to the Body of Christ and to us personally, they give us no credit in God's ledger book. Alone, these efforts are a "big fat Zero" with God.

Works come from an overflow of a heart of love born through faith in Him: *...to the man who does not work but trusts God who justifies the wicked, his faith is credited as righteousness* (Rom. 4:4b). Each month we attempt to justify our check books—make the entries equal the withdrawals. There's just not enough good that we can do that will ever "justify" what He has done for us; consequently works alone will never cut it with God. So then, what's needed to be "justified with God?" Faith in Him and His love—pure and simple and unadulterated.

Do you want good credit? Put your faith in Him.

God's Plumb Line

In science classes we teach basic machines: the wheel, the pulley, the lever, the wedge. Perhaps it's not a basic machine, but a plumb line is one of the most ancient tools of man. At least as far back as the prophet Amos, it's mentioned. What's the purpose of this basic, but useful, tool? It "squares" up everything else. When hung strategically, gravity pulls this simple line at a ninety degree angle with its surroundings. From that point of reference, everything else can be squared and evened up.

The people of God had grown complacent: *Woe to you who are complacent in Zion* (Amos 6:1). Both then and now, complacency—the condition of feeling comfortable with the *status quo*—is a dangerous condition. God sent the prophet Amos to warn the Israelites to wake up from their smug and contented ways before it was too late. They didn't catch on, but rather they continued in their self-centered and self-satisfied ways.

Amos spoke for the Lord: *The Lord was standing by a wall that had been built true to plumb, with a plumb line in his hand. The Lord said, "Look, I am setting a plumb line among my people Israel; I will spare them no longer* (Amos 7:7-8). God expects us to be no less than "true to plumb." You can square up anything by Him. He wants our lives to measure up perfectly to His word. In a house that isn't built true to plumb, the doors and windows won't fit, and the walls will be off kilter. Without His basic plumb line, nothing else will fit together smoothly. But with Him as the standard—the plumb line—He allows the pieces of life to meld together smoothly.

Truth is the gravitational pull of righteousness.

Advanced Math

Math came easy for me as a student; it made sense. But, when I had an opportunity to proceed to advanced math classes such as trigonometry and calculus, I chose another route. Why should I continue taking advanced math classes that I would never use? You want to know something? I've never used trig or calculus in my adult life. Why? Not because, I couldn't have mastered them and integrated them into my life, but because I chose not to learn them.

Paul gets into some pretty advanced theology in Romans Chapter Five. We can skip over it, using the excuse that we don't understand it or will never use it. OR, we can dig into the Word, attempt to master it, and then apply it to our lives. I opt for the latter because the results are phenomenal:

Where there is no law, there is no sin, but...
Through *one* man's sin (Adam) judgment entered the world.
Adam's sin, then, equaled death for us all.
Man's many sins caused Jesus to enter the world for all.
One sin (Adam's) equals judgment and condemnation.
Many sins (mankind's) precipitated His gift and justification.
Adam's disobedience made sinners out of all.
Christ's obedience to death made righteousness available for all.
When sin increases, grace increases more.
Sin equals death.
Righteousness through Christ equals eternal life.

What kind of a student are you? This equation seems complex; but in reality, it's extremely simple. All the sins of mankind are outweighed by Jesus' death. We, then, must die to the intrinsic sin nature born in us through Adam and surrender ourselves completely to life in Christ. Now that you grasp it, what will you do with it?

Understanding requires application.

Once—and for All

If you've read many of these devotions, by now you know that my mother raised my brothers and me with clichés. When she really wanted to make a point, she would address all three of us: "I'm only going to say this once—and for all." When Mother spoke like that, there was a sense of seriousness, urgency, and finality. She didn't have plans to repeat herself—at least not verbally.

Some things in life we never intend to repeat. They're either too painful, too difficult, or perhaps too foolish to do again. There wasn't anything foolish about Christ's death; it had to be the most painful and difficult episode ever recorded. Here was the sinless, perfect, Son of God offering His life for the sins of all mankind. You and I are pretty decent people. As difficult as it is for us to comprehend Christ's death, we accept it. What about murderers and mobsters and prostitutes and drug dealers and terrorists? Surely, God doesn't lump them in with you and me and our "nice friends and acquaintances."

Christ's death had all the elements of seriousness and urgency and finality of any great drama. God had no other plan for mankind, and He certainly didn't expect Jesus to come and die a second time for the "really bad people." *The death he died, he died to sin once for all; but the life he lives, he lives to God* (Rom. 6:10). You may think your sins aren't as bad as some other people's sins, and in some twisted sort of way, you may feel you "deserve" this gift of eternal life. You've got it all wrong. "Your" sins and "their" sins are all the same in God's sight, and He died once and for all.

We're all the "bad guys."

Hosea 3-5
Romans 6:15-7:6
Psalm 88:1-9a

Choose Your Master

When my husband was a seminarian, we attended a great Sunday school class taught by a remarkable man. This successful businessman was grounded in the scripture, loved our church, and genuinely cared about us young couples. One summer during my hiatus from teaching, he offered me a temporary job in his office. I learned a lot about him there.

He hadn't been a Christian very long; in fact, his devoted wife had literally "prayed him into the kingdom" after many years. One of his longtime employees shared with me that the Monday after Cal accepted Christ on Sunday, he came into the office and made an announcement: "From today onward this will be a different place. Our parties and swearing and drinking days are over. Yesterday I chose to accept Christ as my personal Savior, and I will never be the same again. I'm the boss and that's the way it will be."

What happened to this man? He made a choice—a conscious, willful act of volition—to follow Christ. From that moment forward he was different. Paul explains: one way or the other, we are all "slave" to something or someone. That being the case, we might as well choose to be a slave to Him: *You are slaves to the one whom you choose to obey— whether you are slaves to sin, which leads to death, or to obedience, which leads to righteousness* (Rom. 6:16b).

The question is not whether you are going to choose, but rather who or what you will choose. Robert Frost, the celebrated people's poet, illustrates *choice* with these famous lines:

> Two roads met in a yellow wood
> I chose the road less traveled,
> and that has made all the difference.

I choose Jesus. How about you?

The Devil Made Me Do It!

Remember Flip Wilson—America's side-splitting 70's comedian who dressed up like a woman and became "Geraldine?" His hysterical antics made the whole country convulse with laughter. Geraldine's catch phrase, "The devil made me do it," became an integral part of our national vernacular. As funny as all that was and still is to recall, there's a world of truth in the statement.

Since the fall of Adam, the devil has been manipulating and maneuvering mankind into disobedience. He's good at it. Paul felt this battle of emotions: *I do not understand what I do. For what I want to do, I do not do, but what I hate to do* (Rom 7:15). You know the feelings: You hear a bit of juicy gossip that you know you shouldn't tell, but you can't contain yourself and tell it just the same. Your eye wanders beyond your spouse, and before you know it, you're skating on the thin ice of infidelity. You are filling out your income taxes; no one knows about the cash payments you received during the year, so you deliberately omit entering them on your return. And on the list goes. You're disappointed and even disgusted with yourself, but you just can't seem to help it. We agonize over our humanness.

Again we turn to Paul, *I have the desire to do what is good, but I cannot carry it out* (Rom. 7:18b). Paul sounds helpless against his own flesh, and we resonate with those feelings. Why do we keep sinning when we yearn to do the right thing? Truly, the devil is making you do those things! News flash: In and of and by yourself, you will never conquer the temptations of the devil and all his evil, sadistic cronies. It's a continual struggle to do right—that is until we fully surrender the essence of our real self to the indwelling power of the blessed Holy Spirit.

Tune in tomorrow; there's good news.

Free at Last

Free at last; free at last
Thank God almighty; I'm free at last.

It was one of the anthems of the 60's freedom marchers, and it's indelibly etched on our corporate brain. In our mind's eye, we can see those marchers even now. They're marching arm in arm through the streets of our Southern cities, flailing their protests in the face of heartless and bigoted neighbors. We see young children attempting to enter public high schools while they're being verbally and physically assaulted by mothers and politicians. We hear the barking dogs and see the police batons and fire hoses. The freedom marchers and their supporters had "a cause:" More than anything else, they wanted to be "free" like the rest of the country.

As vital as those marchers are to our history and to the people they impacted, they pale in significance to the daily battle that is fought in the hearts of man. Paul struggled with this battle just like you and I struggle. He was human and subject to all the temptations of the devil. At last he figured it out: *There is therefore now no condemnation for those who are in Christ Jesus because through Him the law of the Spirit set me free from the law of sin and death* (Rom. 8:1). Thank you for that succinct explanation. It's a relief to hear it.

The key to living a peaceful life is found in one tiny word—*in*. When we are *in* Christ, the battle is over. He fought it and He won. There comes a time in our up and down Christian walk that we can't stand the wishy-washy "on again, off again" existence. When we totally accept Him, we are encircled *in* the character of Christ: *In Him, the mind controlled by the Spirit is life and peace* (Rom. 8:6).

And that's the way it is In *the Spirit.*

24

It Really Will Be Worth It All

In her little book, *O Ye Jigs and Juleps!*, Virginia Hudson discusses heaven: "Heaven sure is far away and hard to get to. You don't hear much talk about Heaven. You just hope you get there. I sure am doing my very best, and I sure hope I make it." Honestly, a lot of us share her thoughts; we're just afraid to say them. We never know from day to day what we're going to face. Forget about heaven! We just hope to make it through today and maybe tomorrow."

This earth with its trials and disappointments, its sadness, and even its happy times is NOT all there is. There's probably not a week that passes that we may think: "I'm ready for this life to be over. I don't want *this* to be everlasting." And it's not. Whatever you're going through may seem eternal, but our finite minds can't even begin to fathom the meaning of eternal. You can measure heaven by all the world's beautiful cities, all the great civilizations that have lived and died, the beautiful architectural marvels created by man, the world's great museums that display man's masterpieces. You can visit every cathedral on the face of the globe and glory in man's efforts to touch the face of God. You can travel from continent to continent, touring all the wonders of God's magnificent nature. But nothing—absolutely nothing—you can see or do can even hold a candle to heaven.

Paul said it eloquently: *I am convinced that neither death nor life, neither angels nor demons, neither the present nor the future, nor any powers, neither height nor depth nor anything else in all creation, will be able to separate us from the love of God that is in Christ Jesus our Lord* (Rom. 8:38). What will heaven really be like? I don't know, but this one thing I do know. Jesus will be there and He will be in the middle of it all—eternally.

Heaven's worth the wait; it's worth the struggle.

Hosea 11:12-14:9
Romans 9:1-21
Psalm 89:9-13

What's Mercy, Anyway?

What's the preacher talking about when he throws around words like *mercy* and *grace* and *propitiation* and *reconciliation?* They're too difficult to understand. Please make it simple for "little ole me?" I don't know about *all* the big words, but I think I've got *mercy* nailed down. Here it is: If your child has survived his third birthday, it's only because of your mercy. *Mercy* is not getting punishment you deserve. There! Does that help?

All of us are children of the promise and regarded as Abraham's offspring; that is, we're heirs with the Son—Jesus. God spoke to Moses: *I will have mercy on whom I have mercy, and I will have compassion on whom I have compassion* (Rom. 9:14b). We have mercy on our children when they don't deserve it because we choose to. They're our kids; we love them. It's the same with God. We don't deserve His mercy, but we're His kids, and He loves us. His heart is moved by compassion, and He forgives the unforgivable.

One year on my birthday, I was driving about ten miles over the speed limit. It was a beautiful day; it was my birthday; my mind was on other things—not the speed limit. Big mistake. You've already guessed what happened. I was stopped by our city's finest, and we had a chat. Finally, I timidly asked the officer, "You're not giving me a ticket on my birthday, are you?" He thought a minute and then tore up the ticket. "I guess not," he said, "Have a happy birthday."

I deserved a ticket, but the officer had mercy on me. I was speeding; there was no defense. You can't talk your way out of a transgression, nor can you talk your way into His mercy: *It does not depend on man's desires or effort, but on God's mercy* (Rom. 9:16). Aren't you glad for that? I surely am!

God wants to tear up your ticket.

God's "Buy-Back" Plan

What a boon it would be if someone who sold you a house said, "Regardless of what you do to this house, when you're ready, just let me know. I'll buy it back—no questions asked—at the going market rate." Wow! I'm promoting that. (Oh well, that was a blip of unrealistic and wishful thinking). It ain't gonna happen.

God told the prophet Hosea to marry an unlikely candidate—a prostitute. Why would God do that? Gomer was a woman of the evening, not a Proverbs 31 "virtuous woman." She and her children became representative of the unfaithfulness of Israel. Unfortunately, it doesn't take a rocket scientist to see the parallels between Gomer and Hosea and mankind in general.

Hosea's words echo through history, and they paralyze us with their prophetic and up-to-date proclamation: *Your sins have been your downfall* (Hosea 14:1b) Boy howdy (as my mother would say), we get that. It's a no-brainer. All your achievements, victories, and successes can be obliterated with one act of careless, selfish sinning. You're doomed; you're done for. There's no hope for you now.

But wait. There's more. Hosea bought Gomer back: *I will call them 'my people' who are not my people; and I will call her 'my loved one' who is not my loved one* (Rom. 9:25). What a portrait of love. Hosea was willing to redeem his wayward wife and bring her back into an upright standing. Few men would even consider it.

You see it. It's not difficult. *All have sinned…* God's buy back program was initiated at the cross, and His blood of redemption flows freely for all who will receive. He wants you back, and He's willing to pay the going rate regardless of your sins.

He wants you back—regardless.

"Saying" Is Receiving

Seeing is believing. That's so true. We must interact with things experientially to sincerely believe them or believe *in* them. A truly good teacher knows that merely telling students about the rudiments of writing or the principles of mathematics won't impart the necessary skills. The student must drill and practice and succeed and fail until he finally "sees" the principles of what is being taught. The same holds true for the arts. Just wanting to be a musician or an artist or anything, for that matter, isn't enough. When we work, we "see" the fruits of our efforts—the results, if you will.

"Saying" is vital also, for every accomplishment begins with a seed of confession. A student may say, "I want to learn the multiplication tables," or "I want to master the piano," or "I want to be an entrepreneur." That's the starting line—confession of the desire— putting yourself on notice that this is something you really aspire to achieve. After confession comes a blending of the application with that confession until desires grow to maturity and fruition. Books don't get written until authors say they are going to write. But saying is only the starting line. A writer must write. You can say anything until you're blue in the face, but until you believe and act accordingly, you're speaking hollow words.

So it is with salvation: *If you confess with your mouth, 'Jesus is Lord,' and believe in your heart that God raised him from the dead, you will be saved…* *For with your heart you believe and are justified and with your mouth you confess and are saved* (Rom. 10:9-10). There is something intrinsically positive about confession. We often equate confession with negative overtones; in reality, confession is a positive entity. Salvation begins with confession and comes to maturity through your belief that He will do what He promises.

Say it. Believe it. Act accordingly.

Enlarge My Life

Our nation was birthed imperialistically. We weren't satisfied with our initial thirteen colonies but pushed our way westward into such distant places as Ohio and created a "new frontier." That didn't satisfy either. As time marched on, we added Florida and then the big one—the Louisiana Purchase. That didn't satiate our desire for new land. We advanced into Texas and the Southwest, finally arriving in the Promised Land—California. And yet, that wasn't enough. We moved into the Great Northwest, and in the 1950s we added Alaska and Hawaii—culminating in fifty United States.

Whatever one thinks about our national westward expansion, we can agree that from the beginning days, we have definitely enlarged our borders. Our current configuration and topography has little similarity to the original thirteen colonies. Enlarging occurs for various reasons—need, lust, ambition, adventure. There's something intrinsic in all of us that wants more. When it comes to possessions, land, and money, that longing can be a person's detriment. Spiritually, it can be the most dazzling event of your life.

Tucked away in an exhaustive genealogy chart, is the prayer of an insignificant Son of Abraham: *Jabez was more honorable than his brothers... He cried out to the God of Israel, 'Oh, that you would bless me and enlarge my territory! Let your hand be with me, and keep me from harm ...And God granted his request* (I Chron.4:9-10). What a prayer. If only we could emulate it in our lives and in our churches. As you sincerely pray this prayer, the configuration of your spiritual life and the results thereof will change so much that they will be unrecognizable. He wants to bless you in a big way.

More of you; more of you
I've had it all, but what I need
Is just more of you.

Living Sacrifices

We think of a sacrifice as something or someone dead. An animal must sacrifice its life, for example, for us to have meat. The concept of "sacrifice" means to give up completely something that is essential for the sake of another. Paul urges us to be "living sacrifices;" pleasing to God. What in the world does that mean? Paul must have heard your questioning heart. He delivers an exhaustive list of behaviors that will create living sacrifices.

Be sincere and hate evil; be devoted to one another in love; honor others above yourself; remain zealous in serving the Lord, and the beat goes on with at least thirteen more spiritual injunctions. You can read them yourself; it would be redundant and a bit boring to continue listing them. But… There is something else in this passage that is critical to the follower of Christ that we must examine.

Listen to Paul's poignant and relevant words: *I urge you, brothers, in view of God's mercy, to offer your bodies as living sacrifices, holy and pleasing to God—this is your spiritual act of worship* (Rom. 12:1). It's a divine comparison. Since He has been so merciful by laying down His life for undeserving and unworthy mankind, the very least we can do for Him, is to lay down our lives daily as living sacrifices. The next time you're persecuted unjustly, for example, don't fight against it. It's your "reasonable service" as His living sacrifice.

To me, Romans Chapter 12 list reeks of death—death to myself and my selfish feelings and my agendas. There's some pretty difficult and nearly impossible stuff in it. When our lives are "living sacrifices," we conform no longer to the patterns of the world, but we are changed in our minds because Christ is alive in our hearts.

Lord, prepare me: a living sacrifice.

God's Riddle

Do you like riddles? Here's one: In which equation is the sum less than its parts? Some things in life just don't add up; they don't make any sense. Occasionally, we walk away from an experience or an encounter scratching our head, "What happened just now?" we're thinking; "That didn't add up." The things that don't "add up" often make the most sense in the long haul and the hindsight of retrospect. In our Christian walk, there are things that don't add up either. This is where God's riddle comes into play.

The Ten Commandments have proven the test of time—impossible to improve and unnecessary to edit. They work. And yet, obeying all the commandments can still leave a person empty, and sooner or later the bitterness and anger in his soul will reveal itself. A "Romans Chapter 12 Event" will occur in his life, and he'll erupt with black, hideous venom instead of responding like a Christian. He's obeyed all the laws—the ten original ones and any added along the way. He's been a good boy, but something is plainly missing.

We have a moral and ethical obligation to pay our debts. So it is with the commandments: *...whatever other commandments there may be are summed up in this one rule: Love your neighbor as yourself. Love does no harm... Therefore, love is the fulfillment of the law* (Rom. 13:9b-10). What's the answer to God's riddle: To fulfill the law, you must *love.* Everything we do; every thought we have; every interaction with friend or enemy reveals our true self. Obeying all the laws proves only that we can obey the law. Humanly, it doesn't "make sense" to love the unlovely, but love dictates a "loving" response. The riddle can be explained in this simple equation:

Ten is the equivalent of one.

Here Comes da Judge

The era of the 70s was a weird time in our history; things were just a little off beam, and people were experiencing new techniques in all arenas. One of those arenas, of course, was television. Who will ever forget *Laugh-In*? It was a total new departure into primetime humor that stimulated conversation, launched a whole new stable of comedians, and coined phrases that became a part of our national vocabulary: *velly interesting, Is this the person to whom I'm speaking?*, and the ever popular, *Here comes da judge.*

Judging is inherent to man; we might as well admit it. Consciously or unconsciously, we set up ourselves or our families or our traditions and cultures as *the* standard—a measuring stick. Against this standard, we "judge" or measure every other person and situation. If a person or situation "measures up" to our standards, then they're okay. But, if they deviate in any way, we're abashed and aghast that someone or some organization could "do such a thing." If we're not careful, we spend a lifetime judging anything and everything. Now, that's down right scary.

Paul admonishes us in this arena: *Therefore let us stop passing judgment on one another. Instead, make up your mind not to put any stumbling block in your brother's way. The kingdom of God is not a matter of eating and drinking, but of righteousness, peace and joy in the Holy Spirit* (Rom. 14:13 & 17). We can literally wear ourselves and others out with our judging. A person may measure up one day and fail the next. They never know where they stand with us when we continually sit in the judgment seat. What a better and more peaceful world it could be if we listened to what God is telling us and allowed Him to deal with our neighbor. He's pretty good at convicting and exposing the open heart to His standards.

He's da real deal when it comes to judges.

Reflections on the Word...

August

I Chronicles 11-29, II Chronicles, Ecclesiastes, and Micah
Romans 14-18, I Corinthians, II Corinthians 1-4
Psalms 89-114 and Proverbs 21-23

My Prayer Time for August...

Thanksgiving_____

_____

_____

_____

Intercession_____

_____

_____

_____

Ministry_____

_____

_____

_____

Encouragement_____

_____

_____

_____

_____

The Word in Real Time

The Color of the Carpet

In our churches and our homes we "fight" about the most insignificant things. In the church, one camp may feel God leading them to lay blue carpet, one group may "know" that God's will is for brown carpet, and a third group may feel that tile is better altogether. We disagree about music and worship styles, and we argue over service times.

News Alert: God doesn't care what color the carpet is. It's more imperative *to* praise Him than to quarrel over *how* to praise Him. What are we talking about? We're talking about compromise and concession for the good of the body—Christ's church. As long as we quarrel and fight and disagree over insignificant things like carpet color and worship styles, our attentions are diverted from the central issue. Genuinely worshipping and adoring Him and living in harmony one with another get left behind in the dust of self. If Satan can't get us to blatantly sin, he'll manipulate us to disagree and go after one another over inconsequential and trivial issues.

Here's another news alert: Quarreling behaviors do not attract the world to Christ or to the church; in fact, they drive them away. People have enough conflict in their own lives; they don't need to take on yours or those of your church. Listen to Paul: *May the God who gives endurance and encouragement give you a spirit of unity… as you follow Christ Jesus, so that with one heart and mouth you may glorify the God and Father of our Lord Jesus Christ* (Rom. 15:5-6). Do you want your church and your life to be attractive and winsome to the lost? Surrender your own petty concerns and opinions to Him in the interest of unity. Give it up!

Some things don't amount to a hill of beans!

Don't Mess with the Sacred

I love Texas; I like its people with their open honesty, and I *love* their little phrase: "Don't Mess with Texas!" If you've ever lived in Texas as I have four different times in four different places, that phrase says it all. Texans are proud; they're expansive; and they're convinced that Texas is the best place on earth. A wise Gentile knows not to contradict their conviction.

God's word gives clear and explicit instructions about how we are to handle and honor sacred things and the sacraments. In God's eyes, certain things are non-negotiable and are not to be "messed with." In the Old Testament, the Ark of the Covenant embodied His promise and the epitome of His holiness—the physical representation of all that was sacred and holy. The Ark led as the Israelites crossed the desert, the Red Sea, and the Jordan River, and God protected it. It came with easily understood handling instructions—one of which was that no man should ever touch it.

During the reign of Saul, the Ark was kept in the home of Abinadab. With David in power, it was time to bring the Ark back home to its place of prominence. The Ark's homecoming was accompanied with rejoicing; it was a good thing. But the oxen that were carrying the ark stumbled. When Uzzah reached out his hand to steady the Ark, God struck him dead on the spot. That doesn't seem fair; he was just helping God out. But God didn't need Uzzah's help; He wanted his obedience. God said "Don't touch," and that's what He meant. We will never know what God could have done that day to steady the cart because of the hasty act of one man. God's instructions about the sacred are not to be messed with or tampered or watered down or compromised. He has a reason for everything He asks. The sacred is His territory.

Keep your hands off the sacred.

He Deserves It

Sometimes we say rather tongue-in-cheek, "He deserves it." It may not be a good thing that happens to an individual, but because of their behavior or because of our poor relationship with them, we're glad when they "get what they deserve." All too seldom, though, we genuinely express to another the fact that they *really* do deserve an honor or recognition, or something else good that happens to them. Why is that? A rhetorical question, I would venture to answer. We enjoy seeing a person get what they deserve when its discipline, but we have a bit of difficulty praising them for something good. Human nature, I guess.

After the Ark was successfully returned to Jerusalem, and after David had defeated a host of enemies, he began to contemplate on God's goodness. He might have agreed with Johnny Appleseed: "Oh, the Lord's been good to me, and so I thank the Lord; the Lord's been good to me." Has he *ever* been good to each one of us? David commenced to sing a song of praise for all of God's amazing goodness: *Great is the Lord and most worthy of praise… Splendor and majesty are before him; strength and joy in his dwelling place; ascribe to the Lord the glory due His name* (I Chron. 16:25, 27, &29).

Stop and think about it: All the good that's happened to you; all the difficult situations in which He's been right beside you; all the joy and blessings of nature. They all come from Him. He is worthy; He deserves our praise and our adoration and our celebration. He is truly greater than the greatest. He is more worthy than the godliest person you know. His splendor and majesty are spelled out daily through the beauty of His world. You are His dwelling place and there is joy in dwelling in Him. I just get blessed thinking about it. Praise the Lord!

He deserves all the glory and all the praise.

A Strong Finish

Races of all sorts—relays, auto races, horse races—are exciting and can take the most bizarre and unsuspected turns. The front runner is an envied position, but it never guarantees a winner. Approaching the finish line, a runner can stumble. On the final lap of a 500 mile race, a car can crash or permanently break down. A prize winning horse can break his leg and forever be disqualified from the race. It's the winning position that counts—the one who crosses the tape first. In order to finish, it's necessary to conserve strength and pace yourself to the very end.

So it is with the Christian "race." Yes, we're in a race, but we're not racing against one another. Our race is against the forces of evil—both within and without ourselves. We have a finish line as well, and that isn't death. There's no victory in death; the victory exists in what lies beyond death—heaven and eternity with Him. Our challenge in this race of life is to stay strong and true until we break the finish tape: *He will keep you strong to the end, so that you will be blameless on the day of our Lord Jesus Christ* (I Cor. 1:8).

No one likes a quitter, and no one wants to be a quitter. Quitting is for the weak, the sissy, and the faint of heart. You're not in this race alone. Just like an Olympic winner has a coach, so we have Him with us: *God, who has called you into fellowship with his Son Jesus Christ our Lord, is faithful* (I Cor. 1:9). Every step you take, He is right there with you—He's faithful. He will never abandon you. You may feel as though you're on the back stretch all alone. Not so. He is there, and He will be with you when you cross the finish line. One of these days you will be the front runner, and your race will be finished. Don't give up; don't quit. He's with you.

Finish strong!

August Resolutions

The year is a little over half spent, and we wonder where it has gone. January begins, and before we know it, the days have flown by until it's nearly fall. January is a time of renewal and retrospection—a time when we make resolutions for change in the upcoming year. I think, perhaps, that a year is too long. Would you like to make an August Resolution? You would? Okay; let's do it.

We could focus on weight. That's always good for a resolution. Or we could zero in on our finances. That's another popular resolution topic. What about relationships? Always a winner in the resolution category. Oh, I know. What about our relationship with Christ and others? Let's go for it: *I am resolved to know nothing while I was with you except Jesus Christ and him crucified* (I Cor. 2:2). Now, there's a resolution and a half!

That's too big for a yearly resolution; it's proposes a life time of challenge. What is Paul testifying about in his own life, and how can it apply to you and me? How easy it is to get our eyes away from Him and begin to look at others' faults and shortcomings. Or, how easy it is to become critical of our spouse or our pastor or of the way the church is run. Here's what I think Paul is saying: "If it's not about Him, just don't tell me. I'm so into Him that I neither have time for the petty trivialities of daily life nor do I want to taint my relationship with Him with the gossip." Thanks, Paul, we need that reminder:

> Let's talk about Jesus; the king of kings is He;
> The Lord of Lords to me throughout eternity.
> The great "I am the way;" the truth, the life, the door.
> Let's talk about Jesus more and more

He's my August resolution.

An Old Man Stopped...

My father often quoted *The Bridge Builder* by W.A. Dromgoole. This poem tells about an old man who stops at the end of a long day and builds a bridge across a wide chasm. An onlooker chides him: "You will most likely never pass this way again. Why bother with so much trouble?" The old man's response is haunting:

> The builder lifted his old gray head,
> "Good friend, on the path I have come," he said
> "There followeth after me today
> A youth whose feet must pass this way.
>
> This chasm that has been naught to me,
> To the fair haired youth may a pitfall be;
> He, too, must pass in the twilight dim;
> Good friend, I'm building this bridge for him"

God anointed Solomon to build the temple in Jerusalem. King David recognized the possible hazards that could accompany such a massive building project. Like the old man in Dad's poem, David didn't want his son to fail: *My son Solomon is young and inexperienced... Therefore, I will make preparations for it (the temple)* (I Chron. 22:5). David wanted more than anything else for Solomon to succeed, and he appreciated his personal responsibility in his son's success.

We know that our children are following us. Although we have no control over their adult actions or decisions, in their formative years, we have an awesome obligation to do everything we can to equip them with skills to overcome the chasms that appear along the way. David's prayer could be ours also: *Now, my son, the Lord be with you, and may you have success. May the Lord give you discretion and understanding when he puts you in command* (I Chron. 22:11).

God, bless our adult children.

AUGUST

7

I Chronicles 24:1-26:19
I Corinthians 3
Psalm 92

Who Can Make the Sun Shine?

O, who can make the sun shine; I'm sure I can't, can you?
O, who can make the grass grow; No one, but God, 'tis true.

Do you remember that little children's chorus? It had several verses, some neat hand motions, and we sang it often. We loved it. The questions were rhetorical, but they were theologically sound. There was no answer to any of them except, "God."

The Early Church was having one big fight over who each new convert was following. Some advocated Apollos; others promoted Paul; still others supported Cephas (I Cor. 1:12). Paul called them spiritual babies: *I gave you milk, not solid food, for you were not yet ready for it* (I Cor. 3:2). These immature Christians were following men instead of God. Until the early church understood, Paul had no choice but to continue spoon feeding them.

"What's so big about Apollos?" Paul asked. "Or, what is Paul? We are mere men—God's chosen representatives—that's all. Here, maybe this will help:" *I planted seed, Apollos watered it, but God made it grow. So neither he who plants nor he who waters is anything, but only God, who makes things grow* (I Cor. 3:6-7). How very appealing it is to assume that spiritual growth occurs because of us or our efforts. Not so! True spiritual growth is only precipitated by the watering of the Holy Spirit and the study and application of His Word.

Love your pastor. That's a good thing. Enjoy the fellowship and growth stimulated by your small group. That's a fertile place for growth. But never forget; God is the one who generates growth and maturity in Him.

Can you make the sun shine? I don't think so.

August

245

Modern Parables for Living

Some things can't be improved. They stand alone in the strength of their own reality. King Solomon asked the Lord for one thing—wisdom—and God gave it to him in abundant proportions. Sometimes it does us good to stop, read, and digest some of the short, pithy sayings of this wise man:

- Do you want your life to be ruined? Then, allow your children to run wild; this will make them irresponsible.
- A "quarrelsome" wife will drive you to distraction just like a dripping water faucet.
- You inherit houses and lands; but you choose an inappropriate life partner.
- Couch potatoes are lazy people; if you don't work, you'll go hungry.
- When you follow instruction, you are protecting your life; when you laugh at instruction, you're inviting disaster.
- Giving to the poor is really giving to the Lord; He sees it.
- When you discipline your son, you're creating hope for him. But, when you allow him to do "whatever," you're inviting death and danger into his life.
- When you fly off the handle, there is recompense. If you come to this guy's rescue, he'll just do it again.
- Do you want to be wise? Listen to instruction and obey it.
- All our plans are nothing unless the Lord is in them.
- The deepest desire of any man is to have unfailing love.
- You're better off poor than to lie and become "successful."

O, God, give me wisdom like Solomon.

Unswerving Justice

The concept of *straightness* has positive and serious connotations. We refer to an honest person as being "straight as an arrow;" we walk the "straight and narrow;" we ask someone who appears intoxicated to "walk the straight yellow line." *Straightness* is indicative of honesty and uprightness; *swerving* implies the opposite. We might say that a person is "dodging the truth" or "circling the issue." It's critical to "toe the mark," as my mother often said.

When God established Solomon as the king of Israel, He recognized his upright character: *I will establish his kingdom forever if he is unswerving in carrying out my commands and laws* (I Chron. 28:7). Solomon was promised spectacular leadership *if* he adhered to God's laws and commands: *Be careful to follow all the commands of the Lord your God, that you may possess this good land and pass it on as an inheritance to your descendents forever* (I Chron. 28:8b). That's a pretty amazing proposition, but it's conditional.

What are you passing on to your children and grandchildren? Sure, you've got some "stuff" and maybe a little money. That's nice. Solomon sure had a lot more stuff and money than you, but God didn't mention his stuff or his money. When it's all said and done, "stuff" is irrelevant. What counts big time are character and uprightness and living a consistent life in front of our kids.

David made a pledge to Solomon that I would like to pass on to my kids: *Do not be afraid or discouraged, for the Lord God, my God, is with you. He will not fail you or forsake you until all the work... is finished* (I Chron. 28:20b). When God is with you, and when you are following His laws—the straight and narrow—you have nothing to fear. His laws are true, and He is faithful.

Follow God; you will never need to swerve.

The Family Rule Book

Every family has an unwritten "rule book." It's not published, but to survive in that family one had better know what's in it—and adhere to it religiously. Family rule books have some commonalities: The people we don't talk politics with; those with whom we don't discuss religion; or those with whom you never, ever as long as you live discuss the Christmas of 1988. Some of these topics may be inconsequential to you, but they aren't with someone else in the family. It's a matter of wisdom and maturity to avoid a certain subject rather than kick off World War III. Knowing and following the family rule book is a vital and basic component of family survival.

The Corinthian Church was problematic—they seemed to quarrel over just about everything. People who had been sexually immoral, idolaters, adulterers, prostitutes, homosexuals, thieves, drunkards, and slanderers were all converted and had become a part of the Corinthian church. They each carried a whole bunch of baggage with them. Many were taking one another to court over the other person's "sin," forgetting that they, too, had been a sinner until they *were washed, sanctified, and justified in the name of the Lord Jesus Christ and by the Spirit of God* (I Cor. 6:11)

Exasperated to his last very nerve, Paul used himself as an example: *Everything is permissible for me, but not everything is beneficial. Everything is permissible for me—but I will not be mastered by anything* (I Cor. 6:12). Paul is pointing them to the family rule book. "We're in this together," he's saying. "Each one of you has a past deserving of a law suit. It's permissible by law for you to sue one another, but it isn't beneficial to the church—and it isn't necessary in Christ." When we are truly "sanctified and justified" we avoid certain things that seem benign to us for the sake of the body.

What's permissible is often not beneficial.

When My Ship Comes In...

My husband's stepfather was one of the most unique and colorful individuals I've ever known. Born in poverty during the depression, he suffered polio as a boy. The disease affected his speech, and he was a life time stutterer; he couldn't say three words in a row correctly. He was unique in more ways than his speech. Extremely excitable, he was always just a few steps behind the current trends—but he tried. Joe Slamp was both entertaining and winsome. He was subject to bouts of depression which he did his best to laugh off. He loved to describe his plight: "When my ship comes in, there'll be a dock strike."

Boy, we know that feeling. Sometimes our timing just seems all wrong. We all love the story of the person who was "at the right place at the right time." He or she got in on the ground floor of a major business that ultimately soared to the top of the Dow Jones Industrials. We take secret pleasure in identifying with those successful people who testify on the infomercials in the middle of the night. I wish my timing was as good as theirs; I, too, could be talking about my multi-million dollar net worth.

You know what? God has a time and place prearranged for every detail of your life, and it's always perfect. Solomon spelled it all out in black and white: *There is a time for everything, and a season for every activity under heaven: a time to be born and a time to die...* (Ecc. 3:1-8). You don't have to worry about when your ship is coming in. God's tidal charts are in order, and He's got your life all charted. And it's all good: *He has made everything beautiful in its time* (Ecc. 3:10). Enjoy your life; He designed it specifically with you in mind.

His timing is always perfect.

Free To Be a Slave

After the Emancipation Proclamation, many slaves chose to stay on the plantations of their former owners and continue working for a wage. You could argue that many had no choice, that they had no preparation for the "real world," and that they were tricked into staying on once they were free. A lot of that is true, but it begs the question. Many of the slaves truly loved their former masters and could think of doing none other than to stay there and work for them.

This is not a lesson in American history, but the parallel is obvious. The Corinthian Church was having yet another disagreement. Ever the intermediary for Christ, Paul attempts to explain how to handle their dilemma. Some were purporting that if you weren't circumcised, you must be circumcised at once. Others said circumcision wasn't necessary. Paul nails them both: *Circumcision is nothing and uncircumcision is nothing. Keeping God's commands is what counts* (I Cor. 7:19). In other words: Let's focus on essentials.

Once we come to Christ, we continue being the same person, yet transformed by His spirit. If you come to Christ a teacher, you will probably remain a teacher. If you're a plumber before you know the Lord, you will most likely still be a plumber. I've known people who felt that to be a Christian they must become a pastor or a foreign missionary. Changing a vocation doesn't make a person a Christian; He changes our hearts, and then we answer when He calls: *For he who was a slave when he was called by the Lord is the Lord's freedman; similarly, he was a free man when he was called is Christ's slave* (I Cor. 7:22). When we truly love Him, we can think of nothing else than to be His "love slave."

Choose to be His slave.

Leave a Long Shadow

I've known a few giants in my life. Not really physical giants like Goliath and not famous by the world's standards, but giants nevertheless. There was Earl, a layman in Spokane, WA. He's been gone for years, but he was a giant—always the eternal optimist, the constant supporter of my dad (his pastor), a believer in people, and a practical joker. He was unforgettable.

There was Cordelia, an elderly lady in El Paso, TX—a member of my husband's church. She was remarkable. During the war, every Sunday she cooked a meal for any servicemen who came through the church door in that military dominated city. Her generous spirit was not dampened by arthritis or the plagues of old age. She was a delight and an encourager *par excellence*. You get the picture. Their shadows were long and shed joy across every person they met.

Solomon says that if we are reverent, our "days will lengthen like a shadow." What a promise. My two friends never met each other, yet they had a lot in common. One had a lot of money and the other had little; yet, they both were generous with everything and anything they had. They were both optimistic and enjoyed life, consequently, making them a joy to be around: *So I commend the enjoyment of life, because nothing is better for a man under the sun than to eat and drink and be glad* (Ecc. 8:15). They were both workers who enjoyed their work: *Whatever your hand finds to do, do it with all your might…* (Ecc. 9:10a).

These two "giant" friends of mine figured it out. The Christian life can be fun. Yes, there's work to be done, but it can be done in such a way that we enjoy it and others enjoy being around us at the same time. Christian, lighten up. Enjoy life. You too are casting a shadow.

Do people enjoy standing in your shadow?

14

Bread and Water

Our home is on a pond that attracts many geese and ducks. They're beautiful to watch as they glide across the surface of the lake with their entourage of ducklings or goslings in tow. But, they can be a mess if you feed them. One of our neighbors gets a big kick out of throwing seed along the water's edge. Bring on the birds! When they come out of the water and start eating their way across our lawn, they aren't so beautiful. They're a nuisance. The moral: When you cast bread crumbs along the water's edge, you will always get geese and ducks in your yard. Geese follow bread.

There's a spiritual application here as well. When we sow seeds of kindness or generosity, they return to us sooner or later. Solomon said it this way: *Cast your bread upon the waters, for after many days you will find it again* (Ecc. 11:1). We've heard the popular phrase, "no good deed goes unpunished." There's a bit of humor in that phrase, but the good we do comes back to bless us, while the evil returns to haunt us. We don't "do" so that we "get," but good deeds have a way of coming back to us.

My husband and I once helped a friend who was in a difficult predicament. Since then things have gotten much better for her. Now, she is in a position to bless us, and she does. We didn't help her because we wanted something from her; we helped because she needed help, and she needed a friend. But she didn't forget. "Our bread has come back a hundred fold." It's true; you can't out give God. Some of our most valuable gifts to God are made to His people. What a blessing it is when someone says, "You were there when I needed you, and now I want to bless you." Truly, the only safe place for anyone is in the heart of another. Give and it shall be given unto you.

Bread cast on water is never wasted.

The Word in Real Time

Quiet Desperations

Philosophers have said that most men live their lives in "quiet desperation." We begin life with high aspirations, goals, and ambitions, but somewhere along the way, living interrupts our plans. Stuff happens that we neither planned nor anticipated—divorce and death and disappointment. Middle age approaches and passes us by. We wonder what happened; we feel adrift in the vast ocean of life. The plans of our youth seem as distant as the far away shoreline: the old rhyme says it well: *Some men pick the high road, and some men pick the low. And in between on the misty flats, the rest drift to and fro.*

Regardless of what occurs in life, though, the Christian doesn't need to experience this quiet desperation. Paul portrays the Christian life as a race vastly different than, say, the New York City Marathon. In a marathon there is one winner, but in *our* race each participant can be a winner. To successfully complete a marathon, the athlete must undergo rigorous, consistent, and determined training. Just to finish such a race implies endurance and perseverance; marathons aren't finished by sissies. There's a goal, and it's the finish line.

To start out haphazardly in a race guarantees failure: *Therefore I do not run like a man running aimlessly; I do not fight like a man beating the air* (I Cor. 9:26). Do you want to finish the Christian race and win the prize—life eternally with Him? I believe we all want that more than anything else. You may feel as though your life has been aimless and that you are just beating the air. Cheer up. Qualification for the prize is the finish line—pure and simple. With His help, you can make it. Paul articulates the feelings of us all: *I myself will not be disqualified for the prize* (I Cor. 9:27b).

Run to win.

Permissible but not Constructive

If we lived in a total vacuum, it really wouldn't matter "a hill of beans" what we did or said, or where we went or didn't go. We are, however, social creatures, and your actions and mine impact one another whether we like it or not. I don't like it necessarily, for example, but I've learned to live with the fact that since my husband is a pastor, people expect certain things from me that they don't expect from themselves and others.

Whether I admit it or deny it, the very fact that he is a pastor and has a high profile in the church creates a higher standard for me; people watch me. (Oh, how I wish they didn't, but they do)! And so, some things I might do or say or places I might go are governed by their standard. Don't feel sorry for me; I don't feel boxed in; this is only a point of Christian maturity. By the way, this is *not* a double standard. You're not off the hook if your husband isn't the pastor. We live by a higher standard when we profess Christ. Certain things that would never faze us are simply not constructive to the Body.

Ever the artist of word pictures, Paul says it vividly: *"Everything is permissible"—but not everything is constructive. Nobody should seek his own good, but the good of others* (I Cor. 10:23-24). There are times when I wish I could honestly say that I don't understand that. There certainly are times when I don't like it. But I do understand it, and you probably do as well. Alone on a desert island or isolated in Alaska it might not matter so much what you said or did, but it matters—and it matters big! We know that people should keep their eyes on God and not on others, yet we know that they are watching us as well. This should never be a hindrance, but it can be a guiding principle, making our lives constructive to others. God, help my life to never be a stumbling block to one who is watching.

It's not for you; it's for others.

The Word in Real Time

If My People...

The tiny word *if* is really the biggest little word in the English language. It implies a condition; something must happen to make the original statement a true one. *If* signifies the largest cause and effect sequences imaginable: *If* you study the right material for the test; then you will pass. *If* you properly guard your diet; then you will not be overweight. *If* you deposit money into a retirement fund; then you will have means in your old age. And on we could go.

God has a huge *if* for His church: *...if my people, who are called by my name, will humble themselves and pray and seek my face and turn from their wicked ways, then will I hear from heaven and will forgive their sin and will heal their land* (II Chron. 7:14). This is truly huge; actually, it's three *ifs* jam-packed together followed by three consequential results.

Do you want to hear from heaven? That sounds great. "Just a word, Lord, just give me a word." Do you want your sin forgiven and healing in your land? Those two sound pretty terrific also. Well, here's God's formula for that type of "success" in your life: (1) We must earnestly call on Him. That doesn't mean a simple little "now I lay me down to sleep" prayer. No, it connotes intercession and pleading our case before His face. (2) We must humble ourselves when we pray—not with righteous robes pulled around us like the Pharisees. No, not that. We come on our face, completely and totally unworthy. And, (3) We must quit our wicked ways. Ouch! That hurt. That's what the Book says, though: "turn from your wicked ways." Doesn't need much amplification, does it? And the results of this divine *if, then* proposal? Who can even begin to predict what might happen for good in the world and in the church *if* and *when* God's people obey this injunction?

If...Then...When?

All for One – One for All

Alexander Dumas incorporated the concept of single-mindedness in effort for the good of the whole many years ago in his masterpiece, *The Three Musketeers*. The four musketeers (that's right; there were really four of them) were each one unique and different from the others. Yet, their battle cry, "All for one and one for all" has survived the literary test of time.

Gifts and talents and passions: These are all contemporary terms being applied in educational circles and in the business arena. They imply "team building" and oneness, but they aren't "new." Not at all. They're scriptural! *There are different kinds of gifts, but the same Spirit. There are different kinds of service, but the same Lord. There are different kinds of working, but the same God works all of them in all men* (I Cor. 12:4-6). It's comfortable to focus on *our* gift or *our* area of service, but the Word is clear. The source of each and every gift is the same, and the use of each and every gift is all for the common good of the Body: *...the manifestation of the Spirit is given for the common good* (I Cor. 12:7).

What's your "gift?" What is your area of service to the Lord and His church? When Christians fully understand the "all for one and one for all" concept, then the Body is liberated to grow accordingly. Service and gifts and passions don't require "by-lines." Your life is not an editorial for God's heavenly newspaper; it is a testimonial sacrifice to Him as a result of your love for Him. Everyone is important—the pastor, the pianist, the custodian, the parking lot attendant. There are no big or small servants in this kingdom: *God has combined the members of the body ...so that there should be no division in the body... If one part suffers, every part suffers with it; if one part is honored, every part rejoices with it* (I Cor. 12:24-26).

We are "one" in the bond of love.

Heat and Power

In my office there is a recliner that we've had for years. It's old; it's not very pretty; but it sure is comfortable. On that old chair we have a portable massage and heat attachment. Perhaps that's what makes the chair so comfortable. Occasionally, I retreat to "the chair" with my Bible or current project, recline it to its full length, and flip the power switch for the massage. I must be careful, though, for there are two switches: power and heat. Heat is nice, but it only gets hotter and hotter when left on alone. It's the "power" switch that commences the massaging and brings me true relief.

The Corinthian Church was having so much trouble. Paul spends an inordinate amount of time tediously addressing all the issues that were plaguing them—the heated topics, if you will: immorality, idolatry, selfishness, lack of understanding of the Body, and more. Continuing to center on heated topics is cyclical and redundant and non-productive. After a while, it's necessary to move on down the road and focus our attention on the truly basic issues; Paul understood this concept. He concludes Chapter 12 with a brilliant introduction to Chapter 13: *But eagerly desire the greater gifts, and now I will show you the most excellent way* (I Cor. 12:31).

Paul follows his plea with one of the most beautiful, poetic pieces of literature every penned by man—the love chapter of the Bible. Love is the "power" behind all the heated things we say and do: *The Lord is good and his love endures forever* (Ps. 100:5a). We can get all heated up and passionate about this issue or that circumstance, but we must continually be drawn back to the center of it all—the Love of God: *And now these three remain: faith, hope, and love. But the greatest of these is love* (I Cor. 13:13).

Love is truly the "most excellent" way.

No Discouraging Words

Brewster Higley had it right: "O, give me a home… where never is heard a discouraging word…" Wouldn't that be nice? I should say it would, but encouragement is pretty rare and almost nonexistent. Yet, we crave it. From the most successful business man to the smallest child we yearn for positive strokes. Let's face it; encouragement is nearly a lost commodity. Everywhere we go—at home, on the job, at church, on sports teams—we're being evaluated or rated. Evaluation is meant to be constructive, but for some unknown reason, we equate "constructive" with explaining how a person could improve.

Here's my idea for a new praise chorus: "O, give me a church… where never is heard a discouraging word." I'm promoting that. The Word has something to say here: *Everyone who prophesies speaks to men for their strengthening, encouragement and comfort* (I Cor. 14:3). We equate prophesying with the mystical, but Paul explains it as a way of edifying (building up) the church. There are many spiritual gifts enumerated in I Corinthians, and each of them has its place in the Body. But prophesying is progressive: prophesying encourages; encouragement strengthens, and strength leads to comfort. I say; let's prophesy!

Listen to Solomon: *Gold there is, and rubies in abundance, but lips that speak knowledge are a rare jewel* (Pro. 20:15). We can have a wealth of this world's goods, but if our words are harmful to others, they only tear down His body—the church. *Dear God, bless my lips and make them your instrument of encouragement to my brother and foe alike. Keep them still when they could harm, and open them when they can bless. Amen.*

And the skies are not cloudy all day.

Rest on Every Side

Lately, I've been overwhelmed with a nearly 100% response from friends, acquaintances, and business associates: Almost to a person, I receive the same response when I ask people how things are going: "Oh my," they sigh, "I'm just so busy." Despite, or in spite of, all our computers and palm pilots and fancy cars and microwaves and gadgets, we're still too busy. What's going on? It shouldn't be this way. We need some "down time" somewhere along the journey. Rest. That's what we need. Not just a good night's sleep (although some of us would opt for that), but genuine, refreshing *rest*.

Asa was a righteous king; from Day One he acknowledged God as the leader: *Lord, there is no one like you to help the powerless against the mighty. Help us, O Lord our God, for we rely on you, and in your name...* (II Chron. 14:11). Because of Asa's humble spirit, God enabled him to reform Israel. With the people's support, he tore down the detestable idols and cleaned up the land. When all of this was completed, Asa held a great celebration before the Lord: *They entered into a covenant to seek the Lord... with all their heart and soul* (II Chron. 15:12).

Have you felt powerless against the mighty "busyness" and demands of your job, your family, your church? Asa and his people felt powerless when he began leadership. Do you rely on God and call on His name? Do you seek the Lord with all your heart and soul? Asa decided early in his reign that He must have the Lord with him or he would be overcome and fail. When the work was done, God gave Asa and the people a promise: *They sought God eagerly, and he was found by them. So the Lord gave them rest on every side* (II Chron 15:15b). Do you want to truly "rest in the Lord?" Then seek His face, rely on Him, and follow His leadership.

"Rest" is a beautiful four-letter word.

Yosemite Sam

Do you remember *Yosemite Sam*? He was a cartoon character who continually made outlandish declarations and then backed them up with this statement of finality: "...or my name's not Yosemite Sam." Perhaps you remember this one:

> I'm glad to be the way I am, who cares if I look funny?
> No matter what the others say, I'm glad that I'm *Bugs Bunny*.

Neither one of these characters is particularly memorable and certainly there's nothing spiritual in them ...or is there?

God created each one of us unique and special and different. Yet, *He* created us, and that's a vital spiritual concept to grasp. There's not a single one of us who doesn't have a past. We err; we sin; we make huge mistakes. Our humanness tempts us to want to be someone else or something different. That's deadly, and it's not possible.

Paul referred to himself as the "chiefest of sinners," yet he made no apology about who he was. He came to terms with his choleric, focused personality. Through grace Paul came to fully understand that he was who he was because God created him that way. And if God created him, surely He could use Him: *But by the grace of God I am what I am, and his grace to me was not without effect. No, I worked harder than all of them—yet not I, but the grace of God that was with me.* (I Cor. 15:10). Even in this testimony, Paul's choleric personality bursts through, yet he is unapologetic.

Spiritual flagellation is futile. Wishing for someone else's personality or temperament is deadly. You may, like Bugs Bunny, think you look funny, but God made you. He can improve you where you need it. He wants to use His unique creation—you—for His service.

Be glad you're "Yosemite Sam."

It's Not Your Fight

In teaching school and serving as an administrator, I've broken up more than my share of fights. I took a loaded gun away from an irate parent one day and even confiscated a long-bladed knife from a despondent young lover. It's true that "fools rush in where angels fear to tread." Fights can escalate quickly and for the dumbest reasons—there's no accounting for them. In the heat of "battle," kids get involved who don't even know what they're fighting about. On more than one occasion, I've looked across my desk at a teenager involved in an altercation and asked, "Why are you even here? This wasn't your fight."

Some people are instigators; some are rabble rousers; some are peacemakers; and some are busybodies—pure and simple. When we get involved in someone else's battle, we create a peck of grief both for ourselves and for those around us. Jehoshaphat defeated Moab and Ammon against overwhelming odds and numbers. How? The king listened to the Lord: *Do not be afraid or discouraged because of this vast army. For the battle is not yours, but God's... Take up your position; stand firm and see the deliverance the Lord will give you* (II Chron. 20:15b & 17). Read the book; Jehoshaphat won.

It may appear as though you and yours are outnumbered and outgunned—never fear and do not be discouraged. This battle we're involved in is against forces and principalities that are not ours; it's a war instigated and waged by Satan against Almighty God. It's not necessary for us to come out slugging and flexing our muscles. We need to take a strong spiritual position against the devil; stand firm in it; and watch to see how God will overcome the wickedness and evil that's rampant all around us. It's not your fight. He's perfectly able to handle it, and He *will* be the victor.

The battle is the Lord's.

II Chronicles 21:4-23:21
I Corinthians 15:50-16:4
Proverbs 20:25-21:4

Hardware and Software

When I was growing up, *hardware* meant hammers and screw-drivers and machines, while *software* wasn't even a part of our vocabulary. But terminology has changed since the early 1970s. When we talk about *hardware* these days, we're referring to computers and palm pilots and electronic gadgets. *Software,* on the other hand, refers to the programs that we download and use on the hardware. Hardware lasts, but software comes and goes and is continually being augmented, enlarged, and improved. One is *perishable* while the other is *imperishable*.

Mysteries and secrets are fun. We love them, but curiosity demands that we understand the mystery and discover the secret. Paul depicts God's heavenly kingdom as a "mystery." The *perishable* (our physical bodies) cannot inherit the *imperishable* (everlasting life). One day we will die and leave our *perishable* bodies. But that won't be the end; we will inherit the *imperishable*—eternity. It all seems backwards; hence, it's a mystery.

Paul describes God's perishable versus imperishable mystery: *For the perishable must clothe itself with the imperishable and the mortal with immortality. When the perishable has been clothed with the imperishable, and the mortal with immortality, then the saying that is written will come true: 'Death has been swallowed up in victory'* (I Cor. 15:53-54). Our bodies are imperfectable, mortal, and amoral. Our souls are perfectable, immortal, and moral. They are not going to ever perish; our souls will live forever. *Oh God, help us Christians to protect and guard our souls—the imperishable that will live forever with or without you.*

Death in Christ leads to eternal victory.

Tension, Pressure, Pain...

We consider tension to be negative. We have tension headaches, tension in our neck, and tension between others and ourselves. We say that we can "feel" tension in a situation. There is, however, a positive component to tension; in fact, tension is a necessary ingredient to physical growth. Muscles can't grow until tension is applied to them, for instance. We become painfully aware of this when we attempt to stretch muscles that have lain dormant too long.

Creatively, tension is critical. It is, in fact, dissatisfaction with the *status quo* that has spurred many an inventor, writer, philosopher, or scientist to stretch beyond the norm and delve into areas yet unresearched or undiscovered. Tension, then, can be a good thing. It is the force that drives creativity. It can be the genesis of greatness. Listen to Paul: *I hope to spend some time with you, if the Lord permits... because a great door for effective work has opened to me, and there are many who oppose me* (I Cor. 16:7 & 9). Is your head spinning? Mine is. Paul doesn't miss a beat. Sure, there's tension; many oppose him. Opposition doesn't slow him down for one millisecond. His statement is one of the "eternal optimist."

I wonder (now this is just me), yet I still wonder; if I had many people opposing me would I remain that positive? Paul's opposition had to be giving him one humongous headache. But, you don't hear him asking for extra strength pills or whining about difficulties. Paul chose to turn an extra tense situation into a glorious opportunity to preach the gospel. He has a boat load of extra strength available through the Holy Spirit. What an example for us in the tense situations of our lives. Instead of viewing opposition as tension, we can choose to see it as an open door of opportunity for witnessing.

Tension can equal opportunity.

Success Breeds Failure

I'm often "afflicted" with insomnia. I've discovered that if I lay in bed my mind runs wild as I attempt to solve all the world's problems before dawn. But, if I slip into the family room and watch TV, I fall back to sleep in short order.

Television takes on a new dimension after midnight. Its entrées consist of sitcom reruns, old movies, evangelists, the history channel, and infomercials. Success has no real definitive explanation; it's elusive and as varied as the millions who are obsessed with it. The core of all the infomercials is the same—success! If you subscribe to their course, a personal "coach" will guide you from the doldrums of your dull life into success, prosperity, and financial freedom.

Uzziah was a mere boy of sixteen when he became king; in fact, he had just received his driver's license. He was still "wet behind the ears." He sought the Lord—with positive results: *As long as he sought the Lord, God gave him success* (II Chron. 26:5b). It's odd; I haven't heard "seeking God" mentioned on my safaris through the desert of late night television. Uzziah was onto something. We could take a lesson from him.

Uh Oh! Uzziah messed up. He was so successful, I'm afraid that he forgot the source of his success: *After Uzziah became powerful, his pride led to his downfall. He was unfaithful to the Lord his God…* (II Chron. 26:16). God cursed Uzziah, and he lived to his dying day in exile as a leper. So, what's the message? Will we get leprosy? Probably not. Leprosy was Uzziah's prescription. But the message is clear; success comes *by* and *through* God. When we become prideful, God jerks our chain and reminds us that He is the author of our successes; we are the creators of our own failures.

Pride leads to a downfall.

The Word in Real Time

II Chronicles 29:1-31:1
II Corinthians 1:12-22
Psalm 103:13-22

Church Cleanup Day

In the spring a church often designates one Saturday as church cleanup day. Everyone joins to clean out a year's worth of accumulation. A dumpster is soon full as the buildup from the building and grounds is transferred to it. Kitchen cupboards are cleaned and dishes stacked for return; classrooms are emptied of an array of Bibles; the organ bench is relieved of the load it has acquired since last year. Trees are trimmed, flowers weeded, windows washed, and minor repairs are made. Dinner is served; it's a good day.

When Hezekiah became king, the temple was in a great big mess. He brought the priests together for a field trip: "Look at what we've inherited: The doors are off their hinges, foreign idols are in the temple; this place reflects a lack of respect for God. His anger will burn against us until we clean it up." *I intend to make a covenant with the Lord... My sons, do not be negligent now...* (II Chron. 29:10-11).

And thus was born the church cleanup day. Our cleanup objective is cosmetic, but theirs was spiritual: *They brought out to the courtyard of the Lord's temple everything unclean that they found in the temple* (II Chron. 29:16b). After the mess was cleaned out of the temple and burned, Hezekiah purified the temple. He called a celebration of sacrifice to the Lord. Things would be different now.

Cleaning out what collects in our buildings is good, but there's a larger message. Little by little messy things accumulate in the church; they clog up spaces intended for God; they stifle worship and service. Call it revival; call it spiritual renewal. Call it what you want; its name is irrelevant, but call for a spiritual cleanup time. Get rid of the trash; clean the windows of your corporate soul so that the light of His love can shine from your church to the world.

Get the dumpster; God's cleaning house.

AUGUST

28

II Chronicles
II Corinthians 1:23-2:11
Proverbs 21:5-16

Hearts and Hands

We are our brother's keeper. A fully devoted follower of Christ feels such thankfulness and overwhelming lack of unworthiness for God's love that from a heart of love, he spontaneously gives to others. Long before the day of the New Testament Church and the apostles' teachings about caring for the needy, God instituted a plan to take care of others. Once again, we turn to Hezekiah.

After the temple was cleaned and the people were back on God's track, they began to amass abundance. So many tithes were dedicated to the Lord that the temple could no longer hold them. Heaps of goods piled up outside the temple. Hezekiah inquired about this surplus. Listen to the answer: *Since the people began to bring their contributions to the temple of the Lord, we have had enough to eat and plenty to spare, because the Lord has blessed his people, and this great amount is left over* (II Chron. 31:10). Hezekiah solved his dilemma by building storerooms. The surplus was used to supply the needs of the priests and the needy within the congregation.

The church where I worship has a wonderful program called "Hearts and Hands." Each family brings a monthly contribution of groceries and non-perishables in addition to tithes. From our abundance we stack heaps at the church. This overflow feeds dozens of families each week in our community. No one misses a thing because most of us have more than we need in the first place.

God has always had a plan. Hearts dedicated to God dictate the work of the hands of His children. This is a New Testament concept. No, it's Old Testament—dating all the way back to Hezekiah. Is your church lacking financially? Begin to tithe and give of your abundance. It will bless you, your pastor, and the world that you serve.

You can never give too much.

Lost and Found in the Temple

Several years ago in the middle of one of our moves, I lost my glasses. My husband and I looked high and low—in the car, the closets, in boxes—everywhere. No glasses. At last, I bought another pair. We were building a new house that year so it was two years before we decorated for the holidays. As I began to unpack lights and Christmas bulbs and memories, there they were—my glasses. I had them all along. For two long years my prescription glasses lay buried among the Christmas decorations.

After the wicked rules of Manasseh and Amon, Josiah, the boy king, purged Judah and Jerusalem. He tore down the Asherah poles, destroyed idols, and broke the altars to Baal. Again they began to repair the temple, and once more the people gave generous offerings. One day as the Levites brought the offering from the temple, they accidentally found the tablets of Moses with the Ten Commandments inscribed on them. Here was God's prescription for man totally buried and lost right in the temple. Not only was it lost, but the people had forsaken the law. Josiah was fearful at what God's response would be, but God had mercy on them.

Can you imagine? Here's a modern scenario; read the headline: "Church cleanup day reveals lost Bible. It's been at least two years since anyone has read it, referred to it, or heeded its commandments. No one even missed it." How unlikely is that? A lot of things go on in our churches and congregations. Most of these things are good, and yet most of them can go on without missing a beat whether we have the Word or not. The Word is His prescription for a healthy spiritual life. We can't live successfully without it.

Don't lose the essentials.

The Glory Hole

If you go out Basin Rd. in Juneau, Alaska on the backside of Mt. Roberts, you will find things in almost the same condition they have been for over a hundred years. Once, this area was buzzing with activity and high hopes. A hotel clung precariously to the mountainside; today there are no visible remains of that hotel. There are only abandoned mine shafts. If you know where to look, you can turn to the right of the road and hike through the underbrush for several hundred yards. When you do, you will witness a sight that tourists today never even hear about—a huge, gaping cavern in the side of the mountain about the size of a half city block. Rotten, rickety shafts descend hundreds of feet into the hole.

During the gold rush, this region was teaming with miners and profiteers hoping to make it big and strike it rich. Now, the "glory hole" is abandoned, neglected, dangerous, and long forgotten—even to the locals. What was once the scene of glory and abundance of gold is now only an overgrown mass of underbrush that you must know your way around just to find. You have to shimmy across water pipes, battle mosquitoes the size of a Volkswagen Beetle, fight through brush, and endure rain to even catch a glimpse of it.

And what for? This is no longer a place of excitement and glory, but now a forgotten and exaggerated memory. There is no glory here: It can't be found; it can't be resurrected; and it can't be reconstructed. The glory is elsewhere. And so it is spiritually. We dare not rely on the spiritual glories of our past—as wonderful as they might have been. Each day we must seek His face for "new glory:" *For what was glorious has no glory now in comparison with the surpassing glory. And what was fading away came with glory, how much greater is the glory of that which lasts* (II Cor. 3:10-11)!

From glory to glory, He's changing me.

The Tennessee Vase

You know *The Tennessee Waltz;* you've sung about a *Tennessee Christmas,* but this is the story of my Tennessee vase. In Nashville, we built a home that had a small recessed alcove inside the front door. This area was about two and a half feet high and a foot deep. It was perfect for "something." We purchased some silk magnolias for that spot and then went on a search for the perfect vase.

My vase had to be tall, angular, and rose-colored to match my carpet; it had to be perfect. Nashville has numerous malls, and I visited them all. But, no luck; no one had just the right vase. I shelved my vase search and went about life, knowing that sooner or later my vase would turn up. At a retreat in Jackson, TN some ladies invited me to go antiquing with them. Somewhere in our shopping, we turned a corner. We were no longer antiquing; we were "junkin."

In a tiny junk store that was cluttered and crusty and dirty, I spied my vase. It was dirty; but it was tall; it was rose-colored; it was angular; it was perfect. The proprietor saw the glimmer in my eye, for when I asked the cost, she named an exorbitant price. I didn't quibble but wrote the check and carried my treasure home. I washed and shined the vase, and my husband arranged the flowers perfectly. The whole effect was stunning. We had numerous visitors after that, and many commented: "My, what pretty magnolias." To my chagrin, not even once did *anyone* comment on my vase.

My friends, the Christian walk isn't about you. It's about the treasure you contain: *We have this treasure in jars of clay to show that this all-surpassing power is from God and not from us.* (II Cor. 4:7). A crystal vase, a clay pot, a Styrofoam cup, a canteen, a wet rag. Any vessel surrendered to Him is suitable to carry His love.

You are His vessel and you have the treasure.

Reflections on the Word...

The Word in Real Time

September

Micah 5-7, Isaiah, Nahum, Zephanian, Jeremiah 1-2
II Corinthians 5-13, Galatians, Ephesians, Philippians 1
Psalms 78-114 and Proverbs 21-23

My Prayer Time for September...

Thanksgiving_____

_____

_____

_____

Intercession_____

_____

_____

_____

Ministry_____

_____

_____

_____

Encouragement_____

_____

_____

_____

_____

The "Favorite Son"

Every state has someone who came from humble beginnings, attended the local schools, and then went on to accomplish great things. In so doing, this individual inadvertently put the name of his state or town "on the map." We live in Kansas, and although this is a small population state, we have our fair share of "favorite sons." But the most renowned is Dwight David Eisenhower. Born in Texas but raised in the small Kansas town of Abilene, he went on to be the commander of the Allied invasion of Europe in 1944 and later the 34th president of the United States.

The prophet Micah foretold that the Messiah would come from the small tribe of Benjamin: *But you, Bethlehem Ephrathah, though you are small among the clans of Judah, out of you will come for me one who will be ruler over Israel, whose origins are from of old, from ancient times* (Micah 5:2). Who would have thought? God's messiah surely should have come from New York or California. He'd be off to a better start that way since more people would know him. He'd have more electoral votes. But God doesn't work that way.

My husband came from a small church in a small town in Southwest Washington. Unless you are from that area, you have probably never heard of Camas. Locals call it "smelly valley" because of its pulp mill. No one of significance could come from a little church like that. God goes to the big "First Church" to get his next crop of ministers. Isn't that the way it works? Not in Camas. During the time my husband was growing up, God called at least five full time Christian workers from his church. Where are you today? Does it seem as insignificant as Camas or Abilene? Look around; God may have one of His "favorite sons" right there in your local church teen group.

Small churches can grow big men.

Making Up Is Hard To Do

Like many Americans of the 1970s, we loved Karen and Richard Carpenter's music, especially one of their biggest hits, *Breaking Up Is Hard to Do*. You probably remember the song, and you probably remember those high school "break ups" with your steady. They were nearly catastrophic. You didn't know how you would survive another day after the big break up.

As difficult as breaking up is, *making up* is harder. Break ups are usually heated and emotional. One party or the other walks away. When you make up, someone must take the first step back toward the other. Someone has to swallow his or her pride and admit that he or she was wrong; compromise is required for making up to be successful. Theologians give this a big name: *reconciliation*.

Our churches offer many different ministries, and they're all good, but reconciliation? That's novel. It's what the church is all about anyway. Christ's death reconciled God and man and forever bridged the gulf of man's sin: *God reconciled us to himself though Christ and gave us the ministry of reconciliation…, not counting man's sins against them* (I Cor. 5:18-19). Talk about compromise. Christ willingly laid down His blameless life in order to bring us back into fellowship with the Father. How amazing is that?

We get "up miff tree;" someone didn't see it our way; so we walk away. Compared to making up, breaking up is easy. Oh, what a tremendous relief when we swallow our pride, compromise, and admit that we just might have been wrong. Christians don't act like the world: *If anyone is in Christ, he is a new creature; the old has gone, the new has come* (I Cor. 5:13). Our homes, churches, neighborhoods, and our world need reconciliation more than any other ministry.

Reconciliation is a six syllable word.

The Rejoicing Sorrowful

Have you ever attended a funeral where people wept and rejoiced at the same time? Sure, they were going to miss the departed loved one and friend, but they knew that he or she had gone to a better place. They knew that he or she was ready for eternity. They knew that their loved one wanted to be with Jesus. Such services become celebrations for a life well-lived and an eternal reward well-deserved.

Paul endured troubles, hardships, distresses, beatings, imprisonments, riots, hard work, sleepless nights, and hunger. Those are his words (not mine) and what a list it is. Can any of us say we have suffered like Paul? I live in the same area as Gracia Burnham. She and her husband, Martin, were held captive by gorillas in the Philippians for over a year. In a final gun battle, her husband was killed, and she returned home a missionary widow. Gracia is an unbelievable testimony of God's joy in sorrow. You know what? I think Gracia could apply Paul's list to her life. But not me!

Paul's list of comparisons and contrasts continues and crescendos in this statement, *we were sorrowful, yet always rejoicing* (I Cor. 6:10a). What is Paul saying to us and to the church? Life as a fully devoted follower isn't always a bed of ease. You may lose your job—even at the hands of Christians. You may suffer all kinds of hardships—even death like Martin Burnham. We're human and these things make us sad. Guess what? They sadden the heart of God as well. We will never be sorrowful and rejoice at the same time without the infilling love of Christ and the power of His Holy Spirit. Cheer up. This world isn't all there is.

He's joy in the midst of a storm-tossed life.

Me! Me! Pick Me!

School teachers recognize that statement. We've all taught the exuberant, sanguine little girl or the effervescent little boy who always wanted to be "picked." When you ask a question, his or her hand is the first one up, and although they don't always have the right answer, they never seem intimidated. They love and thrive on attention. They want to be the line leader and the hall monitor and the lunch ticket collector and the teacher's helper. We're fond of these kids, but they sometimes drive us to distraction. "After all," we attempt to explain to them, "other children deserve a turn." If only we had that "problem" in the church.

The prophet, Isaiah, came face to face with the Lord, and he was never again the same; in fact, he wrote it down and dated it: *In the year that King Uzziah died, I saw the Lord seated on a throne, high and exalted... above Him were the seraphs, and they were calling to one another: "Holy, holy, holy is the Lord Almighty"* (Isa. 6:2-3). The sight of the Lord made him feel unworthy; he couldn't imagine that God could use him. He certainly wasn't about to volunteer. But God pursued him, *Whom shall I send? And who will go for us* (Isa. 6:8b).

In one fell swoop, Isaiah realized his place in God's grand scheme, and his hand went up: "Here am I, Send me!" Unworthy? Yes. Called and anointed? Yes to that as well. God's church always needs willing volunteers. He may not be calling you to be a prophet; that's incidental. But He's calling you. When you see Him and when you hear Him, like Isaiah, you'll recognize His face and His voice. When He calls, raise your hand; write it down and date it. God is choosing you for service.

Raise your hand if you're sure.

The Word in Real Time

Special Privileges

At one time or another we've all enjoyed "special privileges." When you behaved yourself, your parents entrusted some freedoms to you that were a privilege at the time. Perhaps you were sick, and a friend cleaned your house and cooked. You feel privileged to have the help and the friends. Or, maybe a friend has a lovely home in the Colorado Rockies that he offered to you, free of charge, for a week's vacation. That's a privilege.

Mature adults accept responsibilities, but we don't always enjoy them or consider them a privilege. Washing clothes, paying for groceries, and a thousand other things are examples of responsibilities that we willingly accept when we take on a family. We do them, but we don't always relish the opportunities. There are spiritual opportunities— church attendance, tithes and offerings, and attending the needs of others—that we can began to consider responsibilities rather than privileges. That's dangerous territory; the next logical step is to turn those acts of worship into objects of resentment.

Paul used the Macedonian church to teach the Corinthians a vital lesson. The Macedonians were poor, but they were overflowing with joy. This joy spilled over into all they did—including giving. They begged to support Paul out of their meager means: *Entirely on their own, they urgently pleaded with us for the privilege of sharing in this service to the saints* (II Cor. 8:4). Whoa! What's wrong with these people? Nothing. Paul continues: *For if the willingness is there, the gift is acceptable…* (II Cor. 8:12a). I've known some generous poor people and some miserly rich folks. It's not what we have or how much we give; rather it's our willingness to give from our means that turns spiritual responsibility into an unspeakable privilege.

Gifts accepted from willing hearts.

The Nursery Stump

Because the great Alaskan forests flourish where glaciers have deposited their residue of moraine and silt, their root systems are shallow. These shallow systems cause the giant Sitka spruce and western hemlock and other indigenous trees to be highly susceptible to wind and weather. When the winters come and the winds began to surge across the vast glacial expanses, many of these trees cannot sustain the force and fall silently. But that's not the end of the tree.

The stump of the tree still contains life, and little by little it begins to replenish itself by nurturing and hosting a miniature forest. First come lichens, then ferns, then tiny forest flowers. Given enough time, the seed of a new tree will find sustenance on that "nursery stump" and begin to shoot heavenward from it. A Sitka spruce stump, for example, can give birth to a brand new tree—not necessarily a Sitka spruce.

The prophet Isaiah draws a beautiful word picture for our reading and contemplating pleasure: *A shoot will come up from the stump of Jesse; from his roots a Branch will bear fruit* (Isa. 11:1). Do you see what I see? Out in the woods there's an old stump—useless to most of us—but from that stump begins to grow a brand new tree. And if the tree isn't remarkable enough, this tree will bear fruit. Amazing. God is creating something new from "next to nothing."

How fitting that a nursery stump should illustrate the coming King. Circumstances will be entirely different when the Messiah comes—lions will lay down with lambs, and "a little child will lead them." Who is this little child leader? Hundreds of years before Christ's appearance, Isaiah foretold His birth and leadership. Check the nursery. God may have some amazing leaders there.

Death nurtures life.

On Having Your Sufficiency

When I was a college student, we had a wonderful pastor whose mother-in-law lived with the family. Apparently, she was a remarkable spiritual giant—and a unique individual. He shared one Sunday in a message that when she had had enough to eat, she would push her plate away and remark, "I've had my sufficiency." His illustration has stayed with me for decades. *Sufficiency*: the awareness that you've had enough. Now, there's a novel concept.

We live in a society where *enough* is never enough. Madison Avenue has so conditioned us that from pre-school to the grave, we seem to always want more. Infants have more gadgets and clothes than they can ever wear or use; children have more toys than they know what to do with; adolescents have more liberties and spare time than is healthy; adults buy more things than they can afford; and many seniors amass more wealth than they will ever spend. Rarely, do we see someone turn down something just because they have enough. But those who do refuse more than they need have learned an important life lesson *and* a significant spiritual principal.

On the flip side of abundance and "more than enough," there are times when we really do lack funds or time or some other essential commodity. That's where Paul's amazing spiritual principal comes to play: *God is able to make all grace abound to you, so that in all things at all times, having all you need, you will abound in every good work* (II Cor. 9:8). God's amazing grace is available some of the time. No! You read it incorrectly: *All* grace, *all* the time, *all* you need, for *every* good work. Do you long to make a difference and be effective as a Christian? He is sufficient for *all* your needs, *all* the time—spiritual and physical.

All that you need He will always be.

Loretta Young and Carla Tortelli

Are you old enough to remember the *Loretta Young Show*? If not, let me introduce you to Loretta. She was a glamorous, elegant actress who hosted a television show in the 1950s that bore her name. Each program began with Loretta's dramatic entrance in a graceful, flowing floor-length chiffon dress. She spoke eloquently as she greeted the audience in her soft raspy voice and welcomed us. What a contrast to Carla, the unfeeling, abrupt, crass, loud, uncouth, waitress from the 1980s hit show, *Cheers*.

What these two women were like in real life begs the question, but on stage they were completely different characters. They are as different as night and day, as young and old, as black and white. Not even in the same ball park. There is, we would say, no comparison between the two. How in the world does this all fit into a devotional book? Here goes: Paul admonishes the Corinthians to look deeper than the surface. The surface reveals only an outward, human comparison. If we knew these two women personally, for instance, our conception of either of them could drastically change. But all we know of them is two-dimensional—what is seen on a small screen.

Paul explains: *We do not dare to compare ourselves with some who commend themselves. When they measure themselves by themselves and compare themselves with themselves, they are not wise* (II Cor. 9:12). Human comparisons within the Body are deadly; we "dare not" do it. But, we do. Someone is flashy and "appears" spiritual, and we begin to measure our lives by theirs. Christ is the only safe standard with which to compare and contrast our lives. His standard is higher than any person you'll ever meet; He will always be consistent; He will never have a lapse and let you down or disappoint you.

Be wise; make Him your standard.

Swift Action with Instigators

Teaching and work in the church have been my life. When my kids were at home, I chose not to have a contract. I substituted so that I could be available for my kids. This subbing took me into hundreds of different classrooms of all ages. In addition to regular classes of math and language arts, I've taught some crazy things—swimming (I don't swim well), calculus, foreign languages, computers, even wood shop. In every classroom I've entered, I have crossed the threshold with the knowledge and keen awareness that there will be at least one instigator—and maybe more.

A good teacher—especially a sub—learns early on how to spot, isolate, employ as your "helper," or evict the instigator. You simply cannot maintain order with them there and acting out—forget about teaching. It does not matter whose child they are, if they're disrupting the learning environment, they must be dealt with. Why must we deal with these kids? For the sake of the others. Perhaps you help them learn self-discipline and respect for others, but that's not your primary concern in a classroom. Each student deserves the right to quality "time on task," and if one or two students rob the others of that right, they must be handled swiftly.

Acting out happens in the church as well. We've all seen it. The church isn't always as wise as a good school teacher. Rather, we dance a little jig around the instigator, excusing their behavior and explaining it away, or dodging it because of "who" they are or "who" they are related to. Not! *Drive out the mocker, and out goes strife; quarrels and insults are ended* (Pro 22:10). There are many creative ways within the Church that problems can be handled before we "drive someone out." The key is that we have the courage to deal with instigators for the sake of the others within the Body.

Consider the entire Body—not just one person.

A Shelter in Storm

The Lord's our rock; in Him we hide
A shelter in the time of storm.
Secure whatever ill betide,
A shelter in the time of storm.

How lustily and with what fervor we've sung that old hymn. And we meant it, didn't we? Storms are overwhelming and destructive; they can come out of nowhere at any time. On Oct. 25, 1918, in the world's longest and deepest fjord (the Lynn Canal) between Skagway and Juneau, Alaska's worst maritime disaster occurred. *The Princess Sophia*, a Canadian Pacific Railroad ship, struck Alexander Reef in the midst of a blinding snowstorm. The ship had no where to go for shelter; it was stranded "high, but not dry." While rescue ships circled them in the storm, a strong wind caught the *Sophia's* stern, and as onlookers watched in horror, 353people slipped instantly to an icy grave.

Tomorrow we commemorate September 11—a day when our country was caught off guard in a blinding storm. Without a doubt, it was our second national "day of infamy." We had no where to turn for shelter; together we watched in horror while the unspeakable played out in graphic color before our eyes. A storm? I should say. One with monumental ramifications that have impacted the entire world.

Paul addresses storms and sufferings: *I have been in danger in the city, in danger in the country, in danger at sea; in danger from false brothers* (II Cor. 11:26). Yet, his writings continually express joy and his delight in service to Christ. A day never begins that we are not in some kind of danger. When we concentrate on it, we paralyze our very existence. We have no answers at times to our storms, yet we look to Him who is our shelter in the time of any storm.

He truly is a rock in a weary land.

SEPTEMBER

11

Isaiah 27-28
II Corinthians 12:1-10
Psalm 106:40-48

Holy Compensation

Compensation is expected. When we're hired to do a job, it is with full understanding that we will be compensated; we will be paid in dollars and benefits for time and effort expended on that job. When we pay car insurance premiums, we expect to be compensated if there is an accident. It is extremely frustrating to beg an insurance company for benefits that are rightfully ours. If you have ever worked somewhere when the corporate funds ran low, you know the fear that overwhelms you around payday. Will I be compensated this week? Few of us could or would continue to stay on a job where compensation was not fairly and regularly given.

On a job, we're compensated for our talents and strengths. With an insurance company, we are compensated if we pay the premiums. Compensation in these cases is the monetary replenishment for time and effort expended. Compensation (according to Slamp) could mean "picking up the slack." God has a pretty nifty compensation program for His followers. He "picks up the slack" where we are weak: *My grace is sufficient for you, for my power is made perfect in weakness. Therefore I will boast all the more gladly about my weaknesses, so that Christ's power may rest on me* (II Cor. 12:9).

In the deep recesses of our hearts, we are all aware of our weaknesses. They're undeniable and blatantly obvious. Paul said it: "What I want to do I do not." But His grace—oh, His grace. It is sufficient to compensate for all our weaknesses. Where you are weak; He is strong. When you are tempted; He's your conscience. When you're discouraged; He's there to lift you up. When you're abandoned; He's a friend that "sticks closer than a brother." He wants to compensate—pick up the slack—for your deficiencies and weaknesses, but it can only happen as you surrender and apply His grace to your life.

Amazing grace is His compensation plan.

September

283

I Can't Hear You!

That sounds reminiscent of a drill sergeant, doesn't it? Many of us have heard that sing-song, in-your-face command on television and in movies, but those who have survived boot camp have "lived" those words. This is my understanding: When the drill sergeant shouts, "I can't hear you" in the hearing of a recruit, it's in his best interest to speak up—pronto! If you're in "this man's army," the drill sergeant wants you to speak up and admit it. Be proud of it.

God has similar feelings for those of us in His service, and although He's not a drill sergeant, His words are clear: *Let the redeemed of the Lord say this… Let them give thanks to the Lord for his unfailing love and his wonderful deeds, for he satisfies the thirsty and fills the hungry with good things* (Psalm 107:2 & 8-9). We have so much to be thankful for: His everlasting love, His deeds reflected in nature and in our lives, His provisions for us, and *all* the good things He sends our way. "Speak up," He's saying to us, "let the world know what a great and loving and protective and tender God I am to my people."

This is a "throw away" society. It seems that just about everything we have is made to last only a short time. When we go to a fast food restaurant, all our utensils are disposable. Cars and appliances are built to last for just a few years, or so it seems. Life is tough and sometimes it seems unbearable. Things happen that nearly flatten us both physically and emotionally. His love is *in* and *over* and *through* it all. And it lasts. When all your gadgets are broken; when your friends turn their backs on you; when disappointment overwhelms you; His love endures. He longs to hear you shout from the highest mountain and the lowest valley of your life:

His love endures forever.

Over Here! Follow This Way

In the Portland, Oregon Airport located near security, there is a full scale mock-up of an airplane. This mock-up is an interactive "toy" for children to play on. It's complete with a nose and captain's seat, followed by a large accompaniment of passenger seats. Early one morning my husband and I were standing in an interminable security line. Suddenly, an extremely precocious four-year-old little girl spotted the mock airplane. Spontaneously, she ran to it and began to motion and shout to all of us uninformed public, "Over here, over here; here's the plane. Let's go, everybody. Over here."

Our cute little friend was wrong about the plane, but she certainly thought she was right. It looked like a plane to her. Why were we all standing so close and not boarding with her? If we would have followed her, we would have been wrong. It doesn't take much to see a spiritual implication here. Every day we are being beckoned and motioned and pulled to follow this way or that. Some of the voices calling us aren't legitimate—merely a mock-up of the real thing.

God's voice is real. He's always there speaking through the noise and confusion and den of life: *Whether you turn to the right or to the left, your ears will hear a voice behind you saying, 'This is the way; walk in it,"* (Isa. 30:21). You can't get away from Him. His voice is not loud and it isn't demanding; it's still and small. Yet, His voice is consistent. My friend's son hired on to a fishing boat in the Gulf of Alaska to get away from the influence of his godly mother. Guess what? Out on the Gulf of Alaska with a bunch of rough fishermen, he had a Christian Captain. This young man was part of a captive audience because the captain played Christian music night and day. "Though I go to the ends of the earth, there you will be with me." You can never run away from His voice.

He has a path for you; walk in it.

A Modulation in "D"

Depressed and down-hearted with deep-seated feelings of despondency, the desperados dwelt in dim darkness, dreading death and destruction. Dramatically, they disparaged directions and denounced the decrees of their deity. In disapproving disappointment, the deity dispersed them to degrading duties; they dithered about, and there was no one to deliver them from their own disaster.

Then they deliberately demanded that the Lord dissolve their difficulties, and He delivered them from their defaming doom and distress. He denounced and diminished their dark deeds, and they laid down their chains of demonic depression. Endorse devotion to the deity for His dependable deliverance, and His delightful deeds for the detainees of darkness. He disengages doors of disruption and disintegrates dividing walls.

Some developed into dummies through their disparaging deeds, and were doomed because of their denial and self-damnation. Duh! They detested digestive dietary delicacies divinely designed; they drew near the doorway of disaster and death. In their deep despair they demanded that the Lord drop their disabilities, and He delivered them from their dire dilemma.

Drum roll. He dispatched them with His declaration and demolished their degradation. He delivered them from the dirt of the grave. Declare that they determinedly delight in the Lord for His devotion and deliberate dedication to these despicable down-trodden disciples. His deeds are dependable to men. Declare that they devote daily to the deity, and declare His enduring demonstrations with ditties of joy and delight.

A modulation from minor to major.
Derived from Psalm 107

A Tête-à-Tête at Washerman's Field

After King Sennacherib of Assyria captured all the fortified cities of Judah, he dispatched his field commander to Washerman's Field to meet Hezekiah's representatives. The commander gloated about Sennacherib's overwhelming victory against the people of Israel and offered Hezekiah's men a bribe: "The King of Assyria will give Hezekiah 2,000 horses if he will capitulate. After all, there's no way that Judah can win against Assyria. It is prudent and in your best interest to accept Sennacherib's final offer." It was a face-off if there ever was one.

Ridiculing the leader and mocking God is a dance on thin ice. These brash men were undeterred in their effort to secure Israel's allegiance by downplaying Hezekiah's faith in God's deliverance. After all, Israel didn't stand a chance. And so the men of Judah delivered the Assyrian ultimatum to Hezekiah, but he refused to be intimidated or surrender. But he did consult the prophet, Isaiah: *Now, O Lord our God, deliver us from his hand, so that all kingdoms on earth may know that you alone, O Lord, are God* (Isa. 37:20). And Assyria fell.

Once or twice (or more) in my life I've met one of God's enemies at my own Washerman's Field. The delegation that has met me there speaks manipulative, deceitful, and self-serving words that are direct from the enemy himself. They seem to take pleasure in explanations built on half-truth. They always arrive when I'm discouraged or tired—or both. Washerman's Field could have been Hezekiah's "Waterloo," but he knew whose he was and who He was. Rather than capitulate, Hezekiah had his own tête-à-tête with God, and God delivered him. We can have the same courage in the head to head battles we fight against the enemy of our soul.

You can be victorious at Washerman's Field.

Isaiah 38-40
Galatians 2:11-39
Psalm 107:33-43

Say, "Calf Rope"

When our dad "rough housed" with us, he'd pin one of us down or get us in a playful headlock until we couldn't move. Then, as we'd beg to be let loose, he'd say, "Say, calf rope." No one ever explained to us what "calf rope" meant; we knew. It meant, "I surrender." We're born in a struggle, and all of life perpetuates that pattern. Surrender? Not me. No way. I'm tough; leave me alone.

Surrender, though, is at the fulcrum—the crux and the heart—of the fully devoted follower. We must give up; we must die; we must surrender self so that we can live in Him: *I have been crucified in Christ and no longer live, but Christ lives in me. The life I live in the body, I live by faith in the Son, who loved me and gave himself for me (Gal. 2:20).* What a word picture—a metaphor *par excellence*.

Christ was physically and literally crucified—put to death—in His body. If we choose to live *in* him, we must first be crucified *with* Him. When I die to my ambitions and my selfish pride, then there is an empty place in my heart for Him to take up residence. Christ has some place to live—on the throne of my heart. Death to self implies that I am no longer alive in myself, but I'm alive in Him. Once I am dead to myself and Christ's life is living in me, then my physical body becomes a vessel to hold Him. How beautiful is that?

Our lives will be a continual struggle between us and the Father until we surrender. In one way or another, He will lock us in and pin us down. My dad simply would not let us go until we surrendered with the words, "Calf rope." Between us and Dad this was a game, but between mankind and God, this surrender thing is an issue of life and death. You might as well say the words and enjoy His presence in your life, for He will not let you go until you surrender.

"Calf Rope" is more than a game.

17

The Ragged Rich

You heard it growing up, and so did I. When Mom was tired and exhausted, and when we had finally driven her to distraction, she would say, "You kids are wearing me ragged." That paints a pretty clear picture, doesn't it? I visualize a tattered, worn garment with raveled edges, torn spots, and holes—virtually useless. A considerate person wouldn't even think of donating that garment to the Good Will or Salvation Army. Once a piece of clothing reaches the ragged category, it's useless except as a cleaning rag. Nothing outstanding to aspire toward; that's for sure.

Riches are elusive and fickle. Have you ever tried to pick up the white of an unboiled egg? Pretty difficult, actually impossible, wasn't it? Riches are just as difficult to keep a hold of, and in many ways just as insignificant. Solomon throws up a huge warning sign about riches: *Do not wear yourself out to get rich; have the wisdom to show restraint. Cast but a glance at riches; they are gone, for they will surely sprout wings and fly off to the sky like an eagle* (Pro. 23:4-5). I've watched an eagle swoop down from the sky, snatch a salmon from a rushing river, and soar instantly to his or her nest. Just like that: the salmon was swimming contentedly in the river, minding his own business, and then he was gone. So it is with riches. Here one minute; gone the next.

We enjoy the fruits of wealth, but riches demand care and attention. Everything you "own," ultimately owns a little bit of you. Family and friends and memories—those are the things we cherish in our golden years. Jesus echoes Solomon's words, "lay up for yourself treasures in heaven, where neither moth nor rust doth corrupt, and where thieves do not break through nor steal: For where your treasure is, there will your heart be also."

"True riches" keep the edges smooth.

Daddy

Of all the tender and endearing names given among family members, "Daddy" is one of the sweetest. To me, it conjures up precious memories of a distant childhood. We can call him, "Father," or "Dad," or "Hey, you," but "Daddy" implies a relationship that runs deep. It's a carry-over from childhood that we take with us even when our fathers are gone. "Daddy" is one of the first words we learn; we know it all our lives. It's not a vocabulary building word. It's abundantly more than that. It's fundamental.

I know extremely successful adults who have outstanding careers and high-profile positions in the community, and yet they speak of their "Daddy." No one thinks they're being childish or immature when they refer to "Daddy," rather those who weren't so fortunate to have a good relationship with their father are envious. I was blessed with a beautiful relationship with my "Daddy," but what about the people who did not have a good relationship with their earthly "Daddy?" What about people like my husband who was abandoned in infancy by his earthly father? I'm glad you asked.

Whether your father treated you well or not, or whether you even knew your father, you still have a "Daddy" in heaven. This is not a flippant or disrespectful statement. Not at all. We are His sons and heirs. When I talk with my "Daddy" on the phone, I sense his spirit even though I'm not with him physically. The same holds true for us and God: *Because you are sons, God sent the Spirit of his Son into our hearts, the Spirit who calls out, "Abba—Daddy—Father"* (Gal. 4:6). Do you feel like you missed out somewhere along the line in the "Daddy" realm. Consider this: Since Jesus recognized God as His "Daddy," and since you are a son or daughter of God and His joint heir, then He is your "Daddy" in Heaven. You can sense His spirit.

I love you, Daddy.

That Doesn't Count

Children are such fun to watch; they profile a microcosm of the adult world, even from infancy. Have you ever stood at the door of a nursery and watched toddlers interact? It's pretty educational. It doesn't take long to spot the leaders, the followers, the nurturers, the instigators. They're all there in miniature—just waiting to blast their way into classrooms, workplaces, and the world at large. And, of course, there's always the whiner—the cry baby. They learn young, and whining follows them for a lifetime if they don't curb it. It's their incessant whine, "That doesn't count," and "that's not fair" that grates us when we deal with whiners.

We've seen it repeatedly; we've done it, too. In playing a game, we jokingly say, "That doesn't count." Games are games, but life is serious. A careless word can be dismissed by the one who said it as something that "didn't count." Kidding or not, careless words aren't easily forgotten by the one spoken to or the one spoken about. Perhaps we do something that we know is a bad influence or go somewhere that's marginal. Internally, we dismiss it as an event that "doesn't count." God is not a heavenly scorekeeper, but all our acts and actions and thoughts matter both to Him and to our witness.

Paul enumerates the freedom we have in Christ. "Well, then," you might say, "if I'm free in Christ to be circumcised or uncircumcised, Gentile or Jew, then what difference does it make what I do or what I say? God knows my heart, and that's all that counts." Wrong! *The only thing that counts is faith expressing itself through love* (Gal. 5:6b). All the "things" you do that you think count for God and make you look good in front of others are worthless until and unless they are expressions of your love through your faith in Him. Your actions, words, and thoughts always count.

Are you counting the cost?

The Plural Singular

Many of my friends think I'm weird, but I love teaching English grammar. It makes sense to me, and I find it fascinating. If that makes me strange, then so be it. In grammar we learn that a plural noun always employs a plural verb while a singular noun uses a singular verb. It's easy to remember. Singular verbs end in "s," i.e. the boys eat (pl.); and visa versa the boy eats (sing). Aren't you glad you're reading a devotional to learn this? In addition to singular and plural nouns, there is a hybrid called the "collective" noun. This noun has parts but functions as one, i.e. "a" crowd, "a" collection, "a" body.

There's much teaching about the many "gifts" of the spirit. One person may be a teacher; another may be an encourager, and so on. With the "fruit" of the spirit, however, you are not allowed to pick and choose; spiritual fruit is an all or nothing commodity. "Fruit" is our spiritual collective noun. It is one, yet its many parts function as a whole: *The fruit of the Spirit is love, joy, peace, patience, kindness, goodness, faithfulness, gentleness, and self-control. Against such there is no law* (Gal. 5:22-23). Notice the singular verb "is" in that verse. Paul did not say, the fruit(s) of the spirit "are."

So what! Are you blessed yet? Here goes: Paul is teaching an intrinsically basic truth in this passage. We can't hide behind anything. I can't say, for instance, "By nature I'm impatient, so that "fruit" isn't for me." Not so. The fruit of the spirit that we are producing is what gives the spirit-filled person an "edge" in all situations—even sticky wickets. Just as it's impossible to be "a little married," it's equally impossible to possess part of the fruit of the Spirit. It's all or nothing at all. As His Spirit dwells in us, we begin to see fruit that even *we* find surprising. "Fruit" is His collective gift to us in the Body; we merely pass it on through our lives.

The "plural" fruit is "singular."

A Note on God's Hand

Everyone has done it at one time or another. What's that? You remember, don't you? Someone gave you an important address or a phone number that you really needed and could not afford to lose. You rummaged through your pockets or purse with no luck. When you couldn't find a scrap of paper, you wrote it on the palm of your hand. After all, if it's on your body, you can't lose it.

We are immensely significant to God; we really matter to Him. As much as you may love your spouse or your children or your grandchildren, God loves you more. There is no comparison between our earthly love and how much He loves His children or to what lengths He will go to save one of us. He longs to fulfill our needs and comfort us in our despair: *In the time of my favor I will answer you, and in the day of salvation I will help you; I will keep you...* (Isa. 49:8).

His covenants promises that He will help us and keep us. That sounds terrific, and I really want to believe it. But what if God forgets? What if I get out in the ocean of life and start to go down for last time? Will His rescue boat arrive in time? What if I'm stranded in the desert of desperation? Will He reach me with the water bucket of hope before I perish? God won't forget you. How can I be so sure of that? Because, He has your name written on the palm of His hand: *See, I have engraved you on the palms of my hands* (Isa. 49:16). That's the most comforting news yet. My name is a part of Him; wherever He goes, my name goes with Him. You can't beat that.

> *I will never leave thee or forsake thee,*
> *In my hand I'll hold thee; with my arms enfold thee.*
> *I will never leave thee or forsake thee,*
> *You are my beloved; I will comfort you.*

We're in His hands and on His palms.

Adopted!

Each summer my husband and I host a cookout at our home for our Sunday school class. It's a yearly highlight and dozens attend. This year's cookout was pretty typical with one exception: We always have several "new" people attend, but this year's special guest was a little sixteen month old named Abby. Who is this little doll, and why is she so special? Abby is the brand new Chinese daughter of a couple in the class.

Abby's parents have been arranging her adoption for months, and they recently traveled to China to claim their treasure. And did they ever receive a gift. This little girl is perfect; she has no diseases, no deficiencies, and no apparent signs of neglect. They are blessed, but the one who is truly blessed is the one who as yet doesn't even realize her good fortune—Abby. In China, because she is a female child and was abandoned, her future was bleak. Now all the assets and resources of her new adoring parents are hers for the asking.

Many of us feel as though we're in the same position as this little orphan. We've been left behind it seems with no real future. Take heart, my friend: *For he chose us in him before the creation of the world... In love he predestined us to be adopted as his sons through Jesus Christ in accordance with his pleasure and will...* (Eph. 1:4). Before the world was even created, God chose you as His adopted son or daughter. He has been arranging your adoption for years; He'll travel to the farthest corners of the earth to bring you back into His home. All His assets and riches and resources are totally at your disposal, *We have redemption in accordance with the riches of God's grace that he lavished on us...* (Eph. 1:7). You've been adopted as His son or daughter. Come home and begin enjoying the rights and privileges of the Father's house because you're His.

You're adopted into one amazing family.

Isaiah 55:1-57:13
Ephesians 2
Psalm 110

Abundant Pardon

The word *abundant* conjures up varied images: We think of it as "more than enough," plenty, or even bounty. We might say, for example, "The harvest was abundant." Instantly, we identify this as a good thing. *Abundant* always falls on the positive side of any equation. *Pardon* is a different word entirely; it, too, implies a good thing. When a person is pardoned, he or she is set free from a duly deserved sentence received for a committed crime. These two words juxtaposed present a curious picture. You are either free or you're not; there is no such thing as "set free more." It's an oxymoron.

Isaiah implores us to "seek the Lord while He may be found." Because of Adam's fall, we are all born in sin; no man is good enough to face God until he is forgiven. Each man errs and sins causing him to need this undeserved pardon. Listen to the ancient's words: *Let the wicked forsake his way and the evil man his thoughts. Let him turn to the Lord, and he will have mercy on him, and to our God for he will freely pardon* (Isa. 55:7). There it is; God's oxymoron: He longs to pardon us abundantly. Yet, we must come to Him as a repentant sinner—repenting not just of our evil ways but of our evil thoughts. He won't force Himself on us or break our will.

How than can man be saved and receive this abundant, undeserved pardon? One way and one way only: *For it is by grace you have been saved, through faith—and this not from yourselves. It is the gift of God* (Eph.2:8). We've been taught that grace is "unmerited favor." In light of Isaiah's words, that computes. His pardon is abundant; it's free; it's unmerited; it's more than enough. Praise His name for His unfailing love and undeserved and abundant pardon for your sins and for mine and for the sins of the world.

His gift isn't an oxymoron; it's a miracle.

How Big is God?

Toddlers love the "so big game." Remember it? You hold out a baby's arms as wide as he or she can reach and ask, "How big is Baby?" While the chubby little infant coos and laughs and gurgles, our answer is always the same, "So big!" He loves it. It's a rudimentary self-realization teaching technique. The little one is beginning to comprehend that he or she is somebody with dimensions and possibilities. Whatever you may think about the existential philosophy of Edna St. Vincent Millay, her words beautifully portray man's effort to comprehend the magnitude of God:

> The world stands out on either side
> No wider that the soul is wide.
> Above the earth is stretched the sky
> No higher than the soul is high.

God has limits and boundaries that far surpass human cognition. In his efforts to explain God's vast love and power to the Ephesians, Paul says it even better than Millay: *And I pray, that you, being rooted and established in love, may have power… to grasp how wide and long and high and deep is the love of Christ, and to know this love that surpasses knowledge—that you may be filled to the measure of all the fullness of God* (Eph. 3:18-19).

How can we discover God's vastness, His power, and His majesty? Those dimensions won't come to a shallow Christian. To discover and know Him in His fullness, we must dig into His word. He is bigger than your biggest problem. He has more love than you need—even for the vilest people in your life. His healing surpasses the knowledge in all the medical schools of the country. The beauty of His creation is more than the beauty of all the art and architecture ever created by man. He is more than more.

God is Soooo Big!

A Worthy Life

We have a strong internal gauge that indexes "worthiness." We are often severely agitated because someone got a promotion or a raise who we don't feel is worthy. We think we know them, and they "don't deserve it." Those of us who grew up scratching for everything, looked wistfully at those more privileged—those who were given a new car in high school or whose college education was underwritten by a financially able family. Even the most generous individuals who don't resent a friend's windfall find themselves wishing that such a blessing would come their way now and then.

Who can really gauge "worthiness?" It's subjective and intangible. Everyone has his or her own opinion on whether another is worthy or unworthy. When it comes to living the Christian life, however, all who seriously consider the price paid for our salvation are plagued with personal feelings of "unworthiness." We don't deserve His love and forgiveness; it's truly humbling to know that Christ physically died for our salvation. In a word, it's overwhelming.

Paul was so weighted down with his personal sense of unworthiness that he called himself a "prisoner of the Lord." Sure, he was in prison in Thessalonica, but this reference goes beyond bars and chains. Paul was irresistibly drawn into Christ's service. He didn't want to do *anything* that would defame or mar the name of the one who died for him. And, he implores us: *I urge you to live a life worthy of the calling you have received* (Eph. 4:1). What's the apostle teaching? We have been called; Christ died for us; it's an awesome thing to bear His name. Everything in my life and yours—every thought, every word, every action—must be worthy of His matchless name.

Don't do anything to mar the name of Christ.

The Foot in the Door

If you don't want them inside your house, don't let the salesman or whoever is knocking get a foot in your door. Once their foot is wedged in your door, it's physically impossible—short of being downright rude—to get them off your doorstep. Everyone has been there. We've been there relationally, also. We knew, for instance, that a certain individual wasn't right for us, but we entertained them nevertheless—often to our own dismay and demise. This can lead to frustration and anger.

Anger is an emotion of considerable significance. Many crucial social reforms have evolved because a righteous person couldn't tolerate an injustice any longer. They got so "mad" that their anger became the impetus that propagated change. Nursing anger and allowing it to fester, though, is deadly: *In your anger, do not sin. Do not let the sun go down while you are still angry* (Eph. 4:26). This passion called *anger* is double-sided. It can work for good; yet more often than not, it is disastrous. Anger must be dealt with immediately for it to have positive effects. Paul says, "Deal with it now—today!"

Anger is the "devil's foothold." *And do not give the devil a foothold* (Eph. 4:27). If old "split-foot" can get any wedge of anger in the door of your heart, he is thrilled. Anger does destructive things to lives and relationships. Perhaps we could even say that all sin is birthed in anger. The papers are full of "crimes of passion." A husband sees his wife with another and kills the perpetrator. Now, because of anger, the husband is the perpetrator, and everyone suffers—the killer, the victim, his family, and society in general. We could list one example after another, but that begs the question. The message is clear. Curb your anger; ask the Holy Spirit to help you with it today!

Keep Satan's foot out of your door.

Heavenly Forgetfulness

When I was a girl, every Sunday morning while we ate breakfast our family listened to "The Old Fashion Revival Hour," from the Long Beach Municipal Auditorium with the Rev. Charles E. Fuller. It all sounded so big and important and impressive—almost like heaven. But even more arresting than the imposing sounding auditorium and "the reverend," was his pianist, Rudy Atwood. Each Sunday he excited this child's heart as he danced across the keys with arpeggios and embellishments, playing the gospel song, "Heavenly Sunshine." I can hear it today. Oh, how I longed to be there and enjoy some of that "heavenly sunshine, flooding my soul with glory divine."

As enticing as "heavenly sunshine" was to my Alaska-bound life, God promises us something much more appealing and lasting than sunshine: *Behold, I will create new heavens and a new earth. The former things will not be remembered, nor will they come to mind* (Isa. 65:17). That's "heavenly forgetfulness." Pretty incredible, isn't it? His plans are to make everything brand new in your life and mine. And in addition, He promises to forget all the bad stuff; it won't even be a fleeting memory to Him. That's liberating news. What did you or I do to deserve such love? Nothing. But, we're His children, and He forgives, and then (Praise the Lord!), He forgets!

Not only will He forget, but then His joy will be fixed on us, His people: *I will rejoice over Jerusalem and take delight in my people; the sound of weeping and of crying will be heard in it no more* (Isa. 65:19). This is all too good to be true, but you better believe it. It's true. He forgives; He forgets; and He delights in His children. Sunshine is good; it warms us and cheers our hearts. But, forgetfulness, what can be said?

Heavenly forgetfulness: Such a deal.

If Dr. Powers Were Here

Dr. Powers was a key individual in my childhood. He was the church superintendent who appointed my dad to leave Texas and travel to Alaska as a missionary. Periodically, the mission board sent Dr. Powers to Alaska to visit the mission. To my childish mind, Dr. Powers was like God himself; he was to be respected, and he was due special treatment. But, in an humble one bedroom parsonage, it was impossible to give anyone "special treatment."

Because of limited budget, my parents had to keep Dr. Powers in our home. In truth, he was a warm, loving man of God; still Mom and Dad did everything possible to make his stays special for him—and us. Mom and Dad moved to the fold down couch (no hide-a-bed) in the living room and Dr. Powers got their bed. And, yes, all of us shared the same tiny bathroom. After three or four such visits, our family coined an evocative phrase, "Would you do that if Dr. Powers were here?" If someone spoke out of turn or did something inappropriate at the table, then the proverbial question about Dr. Powers was forthcoming. It's a great family memory.

Relationally, Paul teaches about this. Where is your heart when it comes to service? Do you do things because someone important is watching, or do you do them because they're right? *Obey your earthly masters with respect and fear... Obey them not only to win their favor when their eye is on you, but like slaves of Christ* (Eph. 6:5-6). Mom and Dad wanted us to *always* behave like we would if the good doctor were in our home. So it is with us Christians in our relationships. We work out of a loving, giving heart—whether someone special is watching or not; for indeed He is always there.

What if the Lord were here?

Blessed Insurance

*I*nsurance is an expensive necessity. By definition it is an official guarantee against loss. *If*, for whatever reason, something or someone is lost, and *if* you own insurance, then compensation is yours. My husband and I have joked that we are "insurance poor;" we can't afford the insurance we have, but we can't afford to be without it. If we need it, we're blessed that we own it. *Assurance*, on the other hand, has a different connotation. By definition it is confidence in an outcome. We often refer to this as a "gut level feeling."

There's a common, unspoken notion that God provides some sort of heavenly insurance—somehow we're protected against tribulations troubles, and trials. How quickly we learn that this idea is nothing but a trick of the devil and a spiritual misnomer. Have you ever sung the old hymn?

> Blessed insurance, security is mine.
> Oh, what great knowledge of safety divine.

No; you probably never will. We have no such insurance. But, oh my dear friend, we have something vastly better—divine assurance.

As difficult or heartbreaking or disappointing as your life may be at times, you can know—that means have full knowledge—that there is something better: *I always pray with joy... being confident of this, that he who began a good work in you will carry it on to the day of completion in Christ Jesus* (Phil. 1:4 & 6). God is a gentleman—true to His word. He never begins something that He's not willing to finish. Another scripture gives this promise, "These things are written that you may know that you have eternal life." As long as you are obedient and faithful, you can know that you know that you know—without a shadow of any doubt.

That's blessed assurance.

Put Words in My Mouth

No one appreciates being trapped or manipulated by another's self-serving motives. We've all said it: "Please, don't put words in my mouth," or "He put words in my mouth that I didn't even think—must less say." It's a miserable feeling of betrayal to be misquoted or misrepresented. Words begin to fly around, and before we know it, someone is dreadfully hurt by another's carelessness.

What if God is the one who puts the words in your mouth? Would that be different? Jeremiah, the "weeping prophet," pled with the Lord, *Ah, Sovereign Lord, I do not know how to speak: I am only a child* (Jer. 1:6). He wasn't really a child, but we identify with his feeling of inadequacies. We've been there: "God, I don't know what to say." God had an answer for Jeremiah, and He has one for us: *Then the Lord reached out his hand and touched my mouth and said to me, 'Now I have put words in your mouth'* (Jer. 1:9). What a promise. When we don't know what to say, we can be so close to Him, that He can put just the right words in our mouth.

Hundreds of years after Jeremiah, Paul spoke to the Philippians about the eternal significance of words: *At the name of Jesus every knee should bow, in heaven and on earth and under the earth, and every tongue confess that Jesus Christ is Lord, to the glory of God the Father* (Phil. 2:10-11). There is coming a reckoning day when God will put words of praise in people's mouths who have never spoken such words. One way or the other, we will confess that He is Lord. Everyone will say the words, and everyone will glorify Him. For some, though, their first praise will be their last. They will confess, alright, but sadly, it will be far too late. *God, please put words in my mouth to influence people so that their words of confession will not be too late.*

Let the words of my mouth be acceptable.

Reflections on the Word...

Reflections on the Word...

October

Jeremiah 2-51, Habakkuk, Lamentations, Obadiah
Philippians 2-4, Colossians, I and II Thessalonians,
I and II Timothy, Titus, Philemon, and Hebrews 1-2
Psalms 115-119 and Proverbs 23-26

Thanksgiving_____
_____
_____
_____

Intercession_____
_____
_____

Ministry_____
_____
_____
_____

Encouragement_____
_____
_____
_____
_____

Looking for a Great Pastor?

October is "Pastor's Appreciation Month," and how long overdue this gesture is. For far too long, pastors and their families have been overworked and under appreciated. Those called by God into full time service are indeed blessed. Despite all the difficulties, criticisms, and sacrifices none of them would want to change their life—that is, unless it's Monday morning. And yet, the "called out life" is often one of isolation and loneliness. Pastors are people, too, and they appreciate expressions of love and thanks.

A good pastor is a gift; not necessarily a great preacher, or a cracker-jack administrator, or a humorist, but a gift. Pastors come in many sizes, colors, ages, and shapes. Cherish him or her; don't attempt to remake or replace them: *I will give you shepherds after my own heart, who will lead you with knowledge and understanding* (Jer. 3:15). When your pastor has a heart for God, he's worth a hundred flashes in the pan. Be willing to overlook his faults and personality quirks, because God says, he is the one who will lead your congregation wisely. You, though, must allow him to lead.

Paul commends Timothy as an example of a true spiritual leader: *I have no one else like him who takes genuine concern in your welfare. Timothy has proved himself, because… he has served with me in the work of the gospel* (Phil. 2:20 & 22). Like Timothy, most full time pastors take genuine interest in their congregation's welfare. They have proved themselves well in the work of the gospel.

It's October. Make an opportunity to show some sort of sincere appreciation for your pastor and his family. It's been said that great men build great churches, but the converse is just as true as well: Great churches build great pastors.

It's October; help build a great pastor.

Joy beneath the Pain

When I was a high school student in Spokane, WA, one of the summer highlights was the hydroplane races on Lake Coeur 'd Alene. These boats are constructed in such a manner that they sail across the surface of the lake at incredibly hazardous speeds. This is the scientific principal known as *hydrofoil*. You may experience it on an extremely rainy day. If your car is traveling at the right speed, and if there is enough water standing on the road, hydrofoil will virtually lift your car, and it will sail—out of your control—across the lanes on the surface of the water.

Suffering of all sorts visits believers. Initially, suffering was born because of Adam and Eve's sin. Don't be too hard on Adam and Eve, though, for if it hadn't been them, it might have been you. God created man as a "free moral agent" and gave him the right to make his own choices. Unfortunately, some of our choices are poor—and they produce suffering and pain. Other forms of suffering, though, are not designed or orchestrated by us in any way. We are helpless to control or resist senseless disasters, thorns in the flesh, rejection and abuse, other peoples' sins, and life's seasons. They enter our lives with astounding predictability and sure fire destructibility.

It's possible to be victorious in life's sufferings. The Spirit is the believer's spiritual hydrofoil; He lifts above even the most agonizing conditions and gives a joy beyond human reason. In spite of persecutions and beatings and jail time, Paul makes this bold pronouncement: *Forgetting what is behind and straining toward what is ahead, I press on toward the goal to win the prize for which God has called me heavenward in Christ Jesus* (Phil. 3:12). If God's grace was available to Paul in all his suffering and persecution, it can be there for you as well.

Joy is the Christian's hydrofoil.

A Penny for Your Thoughts

You've been lost and far away in deep contemplation when you heard the voice of a friend, "A penny for your thoughts;" or "What are you thinking about?" It's easy to wander down aimless mental trails—lost in a crowd. Some mental meanderings become the genesis of creative discovery; one thought leads to another until eventually, we have the solution to a dilemma or the seed thought for a great invention. Some mental journeys are benign and harmless, but some can be the kernel of ultimate destruction and personal disaster. If certain sins were never entertained in thought, for instance, they would have never become reality. It's that simple.

If some thoughts are harmful and potentially destructive, what are we to do? Paul admonishes the Philippians to "guard their hearts." Deeds born in thought and nurtured in the heart are birthed through actions. So, what's the answer? Here goes: *Finally, brothers, whatever is true, whatever is noble, whatever is right, whatever is pure, whatever is lovely, whatever is admirable—think about such things* (Phil. 4:8). Since these are the things we should be thinking about, it stands to reason that there are some thoughts that are "off limits."

When your thoughts are wrong, ask God to help you focus on the truth; when you're tempted to think about man's sleazy affairs, pick up God's word and think about His goodness. When evil and wicked thoughts play tag through your consciousness; plead the blood to cleanse your heart. When people share the "dirt" about someone, talk about and concentrate on their God-given attributes. "As a man thinks in his heart, that is the way he will be." More than anything in the world, man is searching for peace. Evil and wicked thought patterns stir up animosity and dissension, but when your thoughts are pure, Paul says, "The God of peace will be with you."

Good thoughts are worth a million dollars.

The Colosee Cafeteria

Cafeterias can be fun; a patron can pick and choose—a little of this and a little of that. The early Colossian church was a virtual spiritual cafeteria. Reminiscent of today's popular religious climate, the Colossians threw all the current spiritual offerings into the mix. They then chose the religious thought or philosophy that was convenient or expedient for the occasion.

Colosee First Church was advocating a little Gnosticism, a little asceticism, a little of the Greek gods, a little of the Roman gods, a little pantheism, a little astrology, a little Christianity, a little of anything spiritual. This made sense and was convenient for the Colossians; at least in their pre-Christian mindset they thought so. Paul was righteously incensed by their lack of knowledge regarding the supremacy of Christ; he had to speak up. These people just did not comprehend; they demanded his teaching.

And teach he did: *He is the image of the invisible God.... For by him all things were created: things in heaven and on earth, visible and invisible; all things were created by him and for him* (Col. 1:15-16). It's disquieting to know that little has changed since Paul wrote to Colosee. The general public at large (and some in the church) have the notion that if there is anything good in a certain teaching, then whatever philosophy is being purported by whatever evangelist or politician or TV talk show host must be acceptable.

God was pleased to have all his fullness dwell in him, and through him to reconcile to himself all things, by making peace through his shed blood (Col. 1:19-20). There it is, folks. None of the isms or talk show hosts or politicians or television evangelists is enough. Jesus is all that is enough. He is all we need. He is sufficient.

Jesus is enough; He's all-sufficient.

Picked for the Team

If you were a cheerleader, then you won't understand this. In truth, the rest of us didn't like you in high school. Just kidding! If you were an athletic klutz like me, you know what I'm talking about. When the gym teacher chose the two most athletic kids in the class as team captains, we all lined up and waited in sheer torture. I knew without a doubt that I would be the last one chosen. You could hear the team members whispering to the popular captain, "Don't pick her; we'll lose. She's good at math; make her the scorekeeper." These experiences were so agonizing that it's a small wonder we "athletically challenged" survived.

We cart our adolescent feelings of angst into our adult years: "Will I get the job? Will we qualify for the loan? Will the church ladies let me into their group?" And on and on it continues—sadly, sometimes into the senior years. Being chosen is a big deal. There is one place, though, where everyone qualifies—everyone gets picked. *God has chosen to make known among the Gentiles the glorious riches of this mystery, which is Christ in you, the hope of glory* (Col. 1:27).

Do you hear it? You got picked! In a deliberate, volitional act, God chose you as a part of His forever family. Such a deal. For years it was a secret, but Jesus changed all that. All His glorious riches—every attribute of His holiness—all the resources of the creator—are at your disposal because you're in. You're a member of the team. All His glory lives in you; that's your vertical relationship with Him. Now you have a horizontal responsibility to your family and neighbors; you become the channel—the vessel—that is their "hope of glory." You are worthy to carry this amazing treasure to a broken and bleeding world.

You made the cut; you're on the team.

Footmen or Horses

Have you ever seen small things get blown out of proportion or big things appear to be overlooked entirely? It happens. When we observe it in ourselves or in others, we shake our heads in disbelief: "Get a grip; you're making a mountain out of a mole hill. This, too, will pass." It's easy, but potentially disastrous, to get our attention diverted from the essentials and begin to major on minors.

As a college student, a verse captured my attention. At the time, I had no idea of its significant implications in my life; but I felt God saying, "This is critical; take note:" *If you have raced with men on foot and they have worn you out, how can you compete with horses? If you stumble in safe country, how will you manage in the thickets by the Jordan* (Jer. 12:5)? Jeremiah states the obvious: "If you're losing when you're racing with mere men, do you think you stand a chance when you run with horses? If a little rain depresses you, what will you do when there's a big flood?"

Since that day, I have mentally tabulated events in my life as either footmen (ordinary events) or horses (crises). It's been an amazing process. Often my first reaction is, "This is a horse." A reality check tells me differently, "No, this is just daily living; it's no real big deal." As I followed this pattern, there were NO horses for a number of years. None! Eventually, though, some very big things in my life occurred that I honestly had to label "horses." Perspective is the central element of life in Him. If we get strung out over a tonsillectomy, for instance, how will we deal with cancer? The beauty is that He is with us in all life's situations and circumstances—routine or difficult. The grace that is available for the footmen is accessible when horses come thundering around the track.

Beat the odds—run with horses.

The Smithsonian Chair

Ten years ago our daughter had delicate surgery at a large university hospital. Her father and I waited anxiously as the surgeon did his magic. When she returned from recovery, my husband went to our hotel to rest. One of us needed to be with her, so I chose to stay to tend any of our daughter's needs. I settled in for the night; the nurse dimmed the lights and promised to return with a bed. Alas, a bed was not forthcoming.

The nurse brought me two pillows, a sheet, and an ancient chair—my Smithsonian chair. (It truly belonged in a museum). Its upholstery was a dirty, cracked vinyl with a "reclining lever" on the right side. After our daughter was comfortable, I tackled the chair. What a hoot! With a pillow behind my head, and the other at my back, I pulled a sheet over me with my left hand, simultaneously reaching for the reclining lever with my right. I was a "Lucy" show, but no one was watching. At an unidentified point, the chair became an ejection seat, shooting me upward. With the help of two more pillows, I finally devised a way to defeat the chair. Inevitably, each time I successfully reclined and began to nap, my daughter moaned or turned, forcing me to disengage the chair and tend her needs. After all, she was the reason I was there.

I was so absorbed in manipulating and conquering the chair that I began to resent the interruptions. Didn't our daughter understand how much trouble this chair was? How easy it is to get our attention on to things as inconsequential as a stupid old chair: *Set your hearts on things above, where Christ is seated at the right hand of God. Set your minds on things above, not on earthly things* (Col. 3:1-2). *God, help me to keep in mind why I'm here and focus on you and your purposes, rather than unimportant matters with no eternal value.*

It's about people, not chairs.

This is the Day...

In 1971 on their way to Boston, my parents suffered a severe and debilitating car accident. We lived in San Diego then, and I was the only family member who could get to Albany, NY where they were taken for care. The first two or three weeks were touch and go for them both, and they ultimately were hospitalized in Albany six months. For ten days I conducted my own lonely vigil as my parents labored past the first critical days and survived surgeries. Ultimately, they were placed on the "recuperation list."

Early one morning in a semiconscious state, my father was awakened by a nurse. As he took notice of his surroundings, he told me later that he was painfully aware of his condition—a broken back, severe internal injuries, and hundreds of miles away from home and friends. Yet his response was classic: *This is the day the Lord has made; let us rejoice and be glad in it* (Psalm 118:24). The nurse was speechless: "Who *are* you?" she queried. My father then began to witness to her as he explained that he was a child of God and how good God is, regardless of the circumstances.

What a heritage! Each day is a blessing in which we have occasion to rejoice. Like my father, we may find ourselves flat on our backs in a strange place among strangers, yet we're alive and His spirit is with us. Rejoicing and being glad aren't conditional responses; they are purposeful decisions of the will that we have the privilege to act on if we so choose. Too many of us treat this word as though it were provisional. "God I'll rejoice and be glad when you do something good for me; God I'll rejoice when everything is going my way for me and my family." The operative word here is found in the verb *is*. It won't *be* the day. It hasn't *been* the day. No. This *is* the day.

God is good—all the time.

1989

Has your family had a 1989? It was a dilly for us—a year we'd like to forget. You know what I'm talking about. 1989—or whatever year it was for you—was our year when everything went south in a big fat hurry. Nothing went right; in fact, things went from bad to worse. My husband was unemployed and finishing a doctorate; I was in a master's program; both of our children were in college. We had house payments, car payments, higher education payments up the kazoo, and NO income. It was distressing, depressing, and debilitating. Where was God?

Guess what? God was smack-dab in the center of 1989. Miracles happened in '89 that hadn't happened before or haven't since. In ways we still can't grasp, bills were paid on time. When we were at our lowest, God picked us up and remade us. Jeremiah describes 1989 to a "t:" *The pot he was shaping from the clay was marred in his hands; so the potter formed it into another pot, shaping it as seemed best to him* (Jer. 18:4). I can't say that our "pot was marred," but it was sure broken. Because of 1989, God has reshaped the direction of our lives. Since that fateful year, He has led us in good paths and opened doors that may never have opened had we not been broken and totally dependent on Him by the events of an unforgettable year.

Do we want to repeat 1989? Never! We don't even like to remember it most of the time. But there is something healthy that comes with the painful recollections of '89: Our lives are totally and completely under His control—good times and bad. They're under His control when people deliberately do us wrong and dismiss us with a shrug. He's still working, and He's working on us through it all: *Like clay in the hand of the potter, so are you in my hand* (Jer. 18: 6b). When you are completely broken, you are in His hands.

He's at work in your 1989.

Paul and Nelson Eddy

There's an innate characteristic in mankind that desires to have someone stand with him. With few exceptions, we are social creatures; we long—even yearn—for approval, acceptance, and support. Nelson Eddy sang about it and we all know the words:

> Give us some men, who are stout-hearted men
> Who will fight for the right they adore.
> Start me with ten who are stout-hearted men,
> And I'll give you ten thousand more.
>
> Shoulder to shoulder, and bolder and bolder,
> They grow as they go to the fore
> Then there's nothing in the world can halt or mar a plan
> When stout-hearted men can stick together—man to man.

Paul loved the church at Thessalonica; they were good to him, and he longed—even yearned—to visit them again. Dire circumstances beyond his control forced him to remain in Athens, but he was so concerned about his northern friends that he sent young Timothy to check on them. Timothy's report was good; the people stood with him: *In all our distress and persecution we were encouraged about you because of your faith. For now we really live, since you are standing firm in the Lord* (I Thes. 3:7-8).

It's an inexpressible comfort to have someone stand with you—not just in the good times, but when your plans are thwarted. The church could do well to heed Eddy's words: "Give us some men who are stout-hearted men." The world longs—even yearns—to witness a church that stands bolder and bolder against evil and sin. There's nothing that can stop or mar the plan of a "shoulder to shoulder church," empowered by His grace.

Stand firm: Shoulder to shoulder.

Rock, Paper, Scissors

Do you remember this kid's game? Believe it or not, there is international adult competition in this game of wits. The clenched fist represents rock; the open fingers are the scissors; and the flat, salute-like palm represents paper. Paper covers rock; scissors cuts paper; rock smashes scissors. The best two out of three is the winner.

People experiment with many different things in their search for truth. A friend of ours named Bob sold everything and moved to a distant city to follow a man who promised him peace and happiness. He didn't find either, but Bob did lose his home and his financial security. Misguided and betrayed? I should say! Today, Bob is a shell of his former self—enslaved by drugs and forced to panhandle on the streets to eek out a day-to-day existence. Another friend, Dan, went the opposite direction and sought wealth, prestige, and power. He was successful in his search, but ended up alone and bitter.

God's word is the real pathway to peace: *"Is not my word like fire,"* *declares the Lord, "and like a hammer that breaks a rock in pieces? Therefore…* *I am against the prophets who steal from one another words supposedly* *from me* (Jer. 23:29-30)." Bob and Dan were misled when they listened to someone or something that "sounded" good but was counterfeit: *They tell false dreams and lead my people astray with their reckless lies,* *yet I did not send them or appoint them* (Jer. 23: 32b). Bob's life was cut apart by a false prophet with a false doctrine who didn't come from God. God's word is true; it won't fail. It is His paper over rock; His scissors over paper; His rock over scissors. It is the fire that burns the palaver and dross of phony prophets. It's the hammer that smashes false doctrines and delivers us into a life of peace.

God's word is hammer and fire.

The Sunday Roast

Nearly every Sunday as I was growing up Mother cooked a roast while we were at church—including potatoes, carrots, and onions. A mouth-watering aroma greeted us as we came into the house from church. We all have pleasant memories of those Sundays around the dinner table with the good china and the good silver— and Mom's delectable pot roast. Good food; good company; good conversation. At least that's the way it should be. Unfortunately, a lot of Sunday dinners aren't that ideal.

Sunday dinner conversations of "church people" can be a roast of another variety: The preacher's sermon was too long, or it was too deep, or it was too simplistic. He used too much scripture, or he hardly used any scripture. The music was too loud or it was too soft; it was too contemporary, or it was too traditional. There was too much music or not enough. The sanctuary was too hot, or it was far too cold. The preacher's entire sermon was about money. The teenagers who sat behind us disturbed so much that we couldn't worship. The words on the screen are distracting; what's wrong with the hymnal? And on and on and on. The "silent listener" to our conversations must have a broken heart.

Paul has some suggestions for Pastor Appreciation Month: *Respect those who work hard among you, who are over you in the Lord and who admonish you. Hold them in the highest regard in love because of their work.* (I Thes. 5:12-13). Dear, dear friends: What are we thinking, and what are we teaching our children with such conversation? Again and again the scripture says that we can be a "sweet aroma" to the Lord. Let's quit roasting the pastor and church leaders and heed Paul's admonition, *Live in peace with each other.*

Respect your pastor; don't roast him.

OCTOBER
13

He's Got Plans for You

I t's exhilarating and stimulating when someone we respect says to us, "I've got some exciting plans, and they include you." This comment could come from your employer, a civic group, someone in your family, or a leader in your church. When another has plans for you, that comment conveys trust. We accept the fact that someone we love and/or respect believes and trusts in us. We're excited to hear the plans, and we want more than anything to please the one who is including us in his or her big plans.

Jeremiah was an unpopular prophet; they were always trying to shut him up because his message was one of exile and captivity. False prophets tried to dispute and undermine him, but he stood firm in prophesying exactly what God told him to say—regardless of its popularity. Jeremiah prophesied that their disobedience against the laws of God would force Israel to be in bondage to the Babylonians for seventy years. It's no wonder he wasn't popular; no one likes bad news even when it's true.

Yet, Jeremiah came to Israel with a word of promise: *For I know the plans I have for you, declares the Lord, plans to prosper you and not to harm you, plans to give you hope and a future* (Jer. 29:11). Are you in some sort of bondage—bondage either of your own making or something outside your control? Take heart, God has plans for His children, and that includes you. He plans for you to do well; He doesn't wish bad luck on you; He wants you to have a good future—both on earth and eternally with Him in heaven. But, you and I have a part in the plan: *You will seek me and find me when you seek me with all your heart. I will be found by you* (Jer. 29:13). When you seek Him earnestly, you will discover Him; in so doing, He will reveal His plan for you. Are you down? Cheer up.

God's got something big in mind for you.

14

A Psalm 119 Prayer

Dear God: It's me; please hear my sincere and earnest prayer. Lord, would you please teach me and make me teachable to follow all your laws. When you teach me, this is my sincere promise to you: "I will keep the laws that I learn to the very end of my days." Sometimes, Lord, I really don't understand the law that I'm attempting to follow. So please Lord, help me to comprehend the reasons for the law. I promise; I will keep the law and obey it—not just in my actions—but in my heart as well.

God, will you guide my life with your holy roadmap? When you do, I feel comfort and delight and protection. When I'm tempted to wander, please nudge my thoughts and my heart back to your laws and away from my selfish agendas. God, often I'm tempted to look at things that are inconsequential and unimportant. This could be my destruction. Save me Lord by helping me redirect my thoughts and attention toward what is pure and what is lovely.

God, I want more than anything in this world to honor and respect you—even fear you for the right reasons. I implore you Lord; complete your promise in me so that I might do this thing I want to do. In your mercy, would you take away the humiliation of my sins that I dread to even remember? In my heart of hearts, I know that your laws are good and for my good. God, do such a work in me that I long for your laws regardless of whether they are instructing or reproving me. And finally, God would you preserve and save my life and hide me in your righteousness. Thank you, God.

Amen and Amen.

Settle Down

Your parents said it; you said it to your kids; and you've said it to others: "Settle down!" In nearly forty years of teaching, I've spoken those words hundreds of times to thousands of kids. Those two words say it all. Nothing constructive can be accomplished when there's a lot of commotion, when everyone is riled up, or when one person is out of control. The first thing an agitated person must do is "settle down" before we can reason with him or her.

In his first Thessalonian letter, Paul warns the church about idleness. When a person isn't busy, he or she can initiate a lot of commotion and agitation wherever he is, but it's devastating in His church. Remember the old adage: "Idle hands are the devil's workshop?" Idleness breeds trouble: *We hear that some among you are idle. They are not busy; they are busybodies. Such people we command and urge in the Lord Jesus Christ to settle down…* (II Thes. 3:11-12). Hold it, Paul, you've quit preaching and gone to meddling. Oh, how I wish that weren't so. I've seen this behavior and so have you.

Someone gets a "burr under his saddle," and everyone hears about it. Paul speaks again: *If anyone does not obey our instruction… take special note of him. Do not associate with him, in order that he may feel ashamed* (I Thes. 3:14). That's strong and to the point. The devil has a field day when we allow a few people or factions within our churches to spin out of control. Corporately, the church has the authority to speak up and say, "Settle down." God's church is too important and the message is too vital not to. If you are the one who needs to "settle down," God can deal with you as well. When a person constantly needs to be petted, promoted, pampered, and pleased, they are dangerous to the Body. Pray for him or her and ask the Holy Spirit to fill your mouth with kind words, "Settle down."

Have courage to deal with busybodies.

Considered Faithful

We form opinions about others according to their behaviors, and (sad to say) they do the same about us. We consider a certain person to be trustworthy because his or her life reveals that characteristic, for example. We might consider another person undependable. Their words may sound right when they make a promise, but when the chips are down, they just don't come through. It's true, "actions really do speak louder than words." Whether it's right or whether it isn't, we make judgments and determinations about others in light of their actions.

Paul—ever the choleric—was avidly fervent in his discipleship of Christ. He knew his past and referred to himself as "the chiefest of sinners" and as a violent man. Yet, after his conversion and his many evangelistic journeys, Paul knew where he stood with God, and he told us precisely what he thought: *I thank Christ Jesus our Lord, who has given me strength, that he considered me faithful, appointing me to his service* (I Tim. 1:12). That bold statement fits Paul's character, yet it has a message for all temperaments. Paul knew himself. He knew that despite his evil past, when God thought of him, He thought of a faithful man.

What does God think about you? Do you even know, or have you ever thought about it? Does He consider you "faithful," or does God know that when the chips are down, He can't really count on you? Some people in my life are so significant that their opinion about me and my life really matters. There's not a single person whose opinion, though, matters more to me than God's opinion. I want Him to think well of me, and I can know what He thinks of me when my behaviors—my life—reflect faithfulness to Him.

Does God consider you faithful?

Is There Any Word?

A crisis rallies everyone. When someone suffers an accident or is lost or critically ill; we care. We call the emergency room or intensive care unit or the family to find out their condition. When my mother suffered a serious stroke, our family was stirred by the overwhelming concern of friends all across the country. Was the last word good or bad? Was she critical? What could they do to help?

Things were dismal for Israel, and God sent Jeremiah to deliver the bad news. Their continual disobedience had worn God's patience thin; the Babylonians would overrun them. Jeremiah's assignment was to deliver the word. He wasn't warning; he was telling: *Do not deceive yourselves, thinking, "The Babylonians will surely leave us," They will not* (Jer. 37:9)! His words enraged Israel. What was wrong with Jeremiah? He must be fabricating this future gloom and despair.

When Jeremiah endeavored to flee Jerusalem and escape to Benjamin, his own people accused him of deserting to the Babylonians. Poor Jeremiah; he couldn't win for losing. Israel beat and arrested its own prophet. After many days in prison, King Zedekiah sent for him privately. He wanted to know what was really going on, and so he appealed to the prophet: *Is there any word from the Lord* (Jer. 37:17b)? Jeremiah stuck with his prophecy; it still wasn't good.

What word is your pastor bringing? We would always choose for it to be an encouraging word, but what if we've disobeyed and the word is a warning word? Then what? Pastors are sent with God's word, regardless of its popularity. The Israelites would have been so much better had they listened to *all* their prophets, but ultimately Jeremiah was the one sent to lower the boom. Listen to your pastor before it's too late; his words are God's words to you and your church.

Hear the word of the Lord.

Stuck in the Mud

Alaskan springs are invigorating after a long winter—that is if you can endure mud. It may be different today, but when I was a girl, mud was so common in spring that we didn't think much of it. Either my father was stuck or helping someone who was. Drivers tested streets with poles to see how deep the water and mud was. Once stuck, it took a concentrated, corporate effort to get "unstuck."

When King Zedekiah received a "bad word" from the prophet, he was done with him. If Jeremiah didn't have good news from God, then he would pay personally. The king handed him over to people who had no mercy whatsoever. They dropped him into a deep empty cistern—empty of water, but full of mud: *and Jeremiah sank down into the mud* (Jer. 38:6b). Reminiscent of Joseph's brothers, they knew that would finish him. Imagine how Jeremiah must have felt?

He was God's prophet, saying God's words to God's people; but they continually and ruthlessly mistreated him. I'm confident that Jeremiah had a pity party down in the mud: "God, what went wrong here? I've spoken your words, but they've done me no good. I'm paying while they're playing. God, why have you allowed this to happen to me? I don't deserve this kind of treatment."

God was working. The Cushite, Ebed-Melech, had compassion and appealed his release. A Cushite was an improbable humanitarian candidate to deliver Jeremiah from his miry pit, but God used the most unlikely person. Where are you? Are you stuck and feel like God has forgotten you? Are you disappointed with God and wonder what He's doing with your life? Leave your situation to Him. Deliverance may come from the most implausible source. Let God work in your life in His way.

He'll deliver you from your miry pit.

Spiritually Fit

This is the day of "fitness." Everyone talks about it; billions of dollars are spent annually getting fit. People have their own personal trainers along with a personalized fitness program. From preschoolers to senior citizens, people flock to gyms and health spas to get in shape. Despite all this hoopla and expenditure, more people are overweight, have flabby muscle tone, and are out of shape than ever. It's a real paradox.

Being fit is more than a craze; it's more than a passing fancy; it's a lifestyle. We love to blame our flabby conditions on genetics, but there are other significant factors that we can personally control: diet, exercise, periodic rest and relaxation, to mention a few. These components, as much as a fitness program, will serve us well in avoiding illness and accidents. As important and critical as it is to be physically fit, it is even more vital that we be spiritually fit.

Temptation confronts us daily. Paul cautions young Timothy about spiritual fitness: *Train yourselves to be godly. For physical training is of some value, but godliness has value for all things* (I Tim. 4:7-8). It's necessary to be spiritually fit, and we must develop a spiritual fitness program. We have a trainer—God; and we have a book of instructions—the Bible. I can pass the spa every single day of my life, but it does me no good until I go into the gym and began to work out. It's the same with spiritual fitness. We can "train ourselves to be godly" by spending time with the trainer and following His guidebook. These components will serve us well when Satan comes against us with all his numerous, creative temptations.

Spiritual fitness is a lifestyle.

Tough Love

People with recalcitrant and defiant teenagers often opt for the "tough love" program as a last resort. This program draws an emotional line in the sand with rebellious kids: "This is it; we're not going to tolerate your inappropriate behavior any longer; things will be completely different until you make a change." Whether we subscribed to the formal tough love program or not, any parent worth his or her salt has been tough with his kids at one time or another. It's necessary to develop maturity and responsibility to have boundaries, expectations, and consequences.

When Babylonia finally overtook Israel as Jeremiah prophesied, many Israelites chose to flee to Egypt where they anticipated better conditions—at least they wouldn't starve. In yet another unpopular prophesy, Jeremiah warned against this: *I swear by my great name, says the Lord, that no one from Judah living anywhere in Egypt will ever again invoke my name...* (Jer. 44:26). "There you go again, Jeremiah, handing out negative advice. Can't you ever say anything uplifting or encouraging?"

Recalcitrant? Disobedient? Defiant? The Israelites were all these. By now the old prophet was accustomed to their hard hearts. They had beaten him, imprisoned him, thrown him into a well, and tried to starve him. What difference did it make? He might as well relay all God's words: *This will be a sign to you that I will punish you in this place... so that you will know that my threats of harm against you will surely stand* (Jer. 44:29b). Christian friend, God means business. He means what He says, and He says what He means. He will not back down on either His promises or His warnings. He loves you more than anything, but He won't tolerate inappropriate behavior forever. Don't cross His line in the sand. Don't even go there.

God's love is tough.

Jeremiah 46:1-47:7
I Timothy 6:3-21
Psalm 119:73-80

The Brass Ring

In high school my friends and I sometimes goofed around at a local amusement park. We loved to ride the merry-go-round. Sure, we were too old for it, but maybe it was our way of saying that we didn't want to grow up and face the real world. As the merry-go-round incessantly revolved to the music of the calliope, there was a spot that if we leaned out far enough, we might catch the "brass ring." The sad thing, though, was that as each revolution brought us closer, we tensed up to catch the ring, thus missing the joy of the ride. We wanted the silly, little free ride that the brass ring insured.

There's something instinctive in mankind; we want the brass ring—something free and easy. I've seen people shove and push and do physical harm to others in their efforts to get to the front of the line and get something free. Paul gives Timothy a whole laundry list of warnings: avoid envy, strife, malicious talk, evil suspicions, constant friction, and ill-gotten financial gain. That's a mouthful, and it takes a lifetime of God's grace to be victorious in all these areas. These are all critical, but he elaborates on one specific "unhealthy interest." What's that? It's greed.

What is ill-gotten gain? It's something that we either stole or accidentally received. It may last; it may not. *But godliness with contentment is great gain* (I Tim. 6:6). I must have read that wrong. That's what it says: "contentment is gain." You mean "stuff" won't give me contentment? That's right! Paul continues: *For we brought nothing into the world, and we can take nothing out of it* (I Tim. 6:7). Now, I'm confused. Everything I've learned in this world—in the schools, the workplace, and sometimes the church—teaches me that the more I have, the happier I will be. Check your notes. Do you really want to be happy and content? Forget about the brass ring.

Enjoy the ride.

Fan the Flame

It's common knowledge; everyone knows it. When you want a fire to grow, you fan the flames. Thousands of dollars in damage have been caused in some of our great Western forests because the wind picked up causing a fire to grow exponentially. Conversely, we've all seen a flame flicker and die when just a small puff of air would have given it rebirth.

Paul was overwhelmed with sentimentality as he wrote to his young protégé, Timothy, about his rich heritage given him by his mother and grandmother. This young man was the perfect candidate to pick up the torch and carry the flame after Paul left the scene. Paul had great hopes for Timothy, and Lois and Eunice were counting on him, too: *For this reason I remind you to fan into flame the gift of God, which is in you...* (II Tim. 1:6). Paul *and* his family believed in him. Can you imagine how Timothy must have felt? Here was the great apostle who not only believed in him but was encouraging him to continue his work. If Paul believed he could do it, he would sure give it a shot. What a birthright!

My husband came from an extremely humble beginning. No one expected him to be one to "fan the flame." His pastor, though, believed in him and saw his giftedness. When his family had nothing, this man came to David's parents' modest home and spoke with them specifically about David. He informed Dave's parents that their family had a "treasure." A treasure? They hardly had money for the next meal. But, based only on the encouraging words and belief that his pastor had in him, David set out for college. He had no money, but someone believed in him, and that's all it took. For years now he's been "fanning the flame." Thank you, Bob Shepherd.

Who are you encouraging to fan the flame?

Play by the Rules

During the 2004 summer Olympics there was a mammoth hoopla over the gymnastics competition. Some encouraged one competitor to give his medal to another; yet he played by the rules. The judges' ruling: the medal would stay with the original winner. Playing by the rules is critical: *If anyone competes as an athlete, he does not receive the victor's crown unless he competes according to the rules* (II Tim. 2:5). When you've played by the rules, then you are comfortable with the decision of the judges. If, however, you skirted the rules or "fudged," then a bushel of trouble awaits you.

Paul is making a significant spiritual point. As important as it is for athletes to play by the rules, it is exceedingly more critical to "play by the rules" spiritually. Okay; what are the rules? You may be sorry you asked. Our rules are different than the world's rules. Theirs is an "eye for an eye," but ours... Well, listen to Solomon (Prov. 25:21):

> If your enemy is hungry, give him food to eat;
> If he is thirsty, give him water to drink.

You're joking. That's not in my rule book. Well, check your book; maybe you're reading the wrong chapter. Christians are even more accountable than Olympians when it comes to playing by the rules. Following the rules is serious business. Every Olympian plays to win a crown and a medal. It's thrilling to see one of our athletes on the victor's dais, wreath on his head, medal around his neck and our flag behind him. That's victory. No, it's just temporary victory. One day you and I will stand with Him in glory. The national anthem won't be playing, but heavenly hosts will be singing such music as we've never heard. We'll be wearing a crown, but it won't be one of olive leaves, it will be the crown of His righteousness.

Play to Win.

OCTOBER
24

Jeremiah 50:11-51:14
II Timothy 3
Psalm 119:89-96

The "Ah" Factor

Abram was a lowly shepherd when God notified him that he would be the father of many nations. This was impossible. He was far too old, and Sarai was nearly one hundred. "God, you've got the wrong couple. May I make a suggestion? Find a young couple; they would groove on this news. But not us, God." God's plans would not be thwarted by Abram's protestations.

Eventually, Abram believed God, but Sarai sure didn't. She laughed: "Old man, I know you've got a lot on the ball; but this dog won't hunt. We aren't having a baby." Convinced that God meant what He said, Abram commenced making preparations. He bought nursery furniture, a car seat, high chair, and a complete layette. Ten years later, Sarai ceased her laughing; wonder of all wonders—she was pregnant.

A curious thing took place in Abram and Sarai at the birth of Isaac. They were old and barren—the perfect nominees for God's miracle of procreation. The Hebrew word for "breath of God" is *ruwach*. To put His everlasting seal on this transaction, God changed their names; Abram became Abraham; Sarai became Sarah. The "ah" factor—the breath of God—was alive and well in their old bodies.

In writing to Timothy, Paul uses this same word in defining His Word: *All Scripture is God-breathed and is useful for teaching, rebuking, correcting, and training in righteousness...* (II Tim. 3:16). Do you hear it? It's the "ah" factor. The literal "breath of God" in the Holy Scriptures gives us divine authority in its use. The Word isn't just another book; it's the breath of God, breathing life and hope into our weary lives.

"Ah!" The word of God.

The Word in Real Time

Sweeter Than Honey

Roses are red; violets are blue; sugar is sweet, and so are you. If I had a dollar for the many times I've heard or said those words, I might be rich. Sugar is sweet, but so is honey. Alone, either sugar or honey can be sickening sweet, but there are still times when we have a "sweet tooth" and demand candy or ice cream or chocolate. Potatoes and gravy won't satisfy; vegetables aren't sufficient; we need just a little something sweet—and the sweeter the better.

Words can be sweet as well. We love it when our spouse whispers "sweet nothings" to us. He or she may not do it often, but when they do, it's refreshing and comforting. We even use endearing pet names such as "Sweetheart," or "Sugar," or "Honey." All of these are indicative of closeness and an intimacy with the other person in the relationship.

Our relationship with the Lord should be the dearest and sweetest of all. Of course, we are close to our spouse—closer than any other living person. Yes, our children are dear, but the closeness we feel with Him supersedes all other human passions. Just like we love for our spouse to speak to us affectionately, so we love to hear His words of endearment: *How sweet are your words to my taste, sweeter than honey to my mouth; I gain understanding from your precepts; therefore, I hate every wrong path* (Psalm 119:103).

Do you want your spiritual soul satisfied and filled? Then listen to the sweetness of His words. It will open doors of understanding and lead you along the right pathway. I can guarantee you this as well; God delights in hearing your sweet words of adoration and praise as much as we enjoy hearing and reading His.

The Word satisfies the spiritual "sweet tooth."

Lamps and Light

Light is a necessary physical element that we need to thrive, and intellectual light and spiritual light are metaphors of physical light. The concept of light implies that we can see. The sun is the physical light of the world; it shines during the day; thus, we use the term *daylight*. But, when the darkness of night falls, we need a lamp. Lamps are dispensers of light into a darkened area.

Both lamps and light have importance. Imagine that you're on a camping trip; during the night you answer nature's call. As you start down a rough, rocky and unfamiliar path, you need light for that path. Your light shines ahead and reveals the way, but just seeing where you need to go isn't enough. You need to know where you are. Therefore, you need a lamp for your feet so you don't trip over a twig or an uneven spot in the ground.

The psalmist described the paradox of lamps and light: *Your word is a lamp to my feet and a light for my path.* (Psalm 119:105). Do you comprehend the spiritual metaphor? The Word shows us where we are—a lamp to our feet; and it shows the way we are to go—a light to our path. Both are necessary. Recently, during a full moon, my husband and I stepped out on our deck and saw it—big and yellow and round, reflecting into the little lake by our house. What a light the moon is when it's full. Sometimes, though, life gets dark and heavy and we wonder if our little light is shining. Like the moon dispels the darkness of night so the Word dispels the darkness in your life and then your little light shines in a darkened world.

This little light of mine; I'm going to let it shine.
Don't let Satan poof it out; I'm going to let it shine.
Let it shine; let it shine; let it shine.

Let it shine 'til Jesus comes.

The Mentorian Society

My high school offered a priceless public speaking opportunity. Members were called mentorians, and each one was assigned a mentor. With the help of a local businessman or professional, each mentorian prepared a speech on a current topic; the speech was then honed and practiced. One day a month mentorians presented their speeches to a home room class in the school. I was a Mentorian; my mentor was a dentist; my topic was Civil Defense.

It was an honor to be a part of the "Mentorian Society." Years before peer tutoring or community involvement were vogue; it was just a great idea orchestrated by a progressive high school—a way for citizens to "reproduce" themselves through students. Hands of assistance and mutual interest reached generationally in both directions. An older public citizen mentored a student; and in turn, the student taught his or her peers. What a creative concept.

As novel as this idea sounds, it's not new. Paul wrote about it to the early church. Life experiences are not just for personal benefit; they are highly significant for the next generation: *Then they can train the younger women to love their husbands and children, to be self-controlled and pure...* (Titus 2:4). In all arenas—relationally, physically, emotionally, or spiritually—every life experience has value for another. You have amassed invaluable wisdom, discernment, and experience that can be "the" saving factor for a young Christian. Many are not blessed with good role models, and they are looking to us for guidance and encouragement. Reproduce yourself in another. Listen to John Donne, the English poet laureate:

> No man is an island; no man stands alone.
> If one clod of earth falls off Britain, Europe is the less.

Are you a Titus 2 man or woman?

Do-gooders.com

The Internet is here to stay: indeed, it is the most powerful tool in our modern technological arsenal. As huge as radio became during the '20s and '30s, and as overwhelming as television has been since the '50s, the Internet is bigger than the combination of them both. It's truly mind-boggling. No one or no place on earth is remote any longer. I can sit in the quiet of my home and "instant message" a person in the jungles of New Guinea as rapidly as I can talk to the neighbor next door. What a tool.

Just like any other tool, the Internet has the potential for good while simultaneously having the capability for astounding evil. We know this, and it stuns us. How could an entity so potentially good become so very lethal so very quickly? Paul gives the church some helpful "reminders:" *Remind the people to be subject to rulers and authorities, to be obedient, to be ready to do whatever is good, to slander no one, to be peaceable and considerate, and to show true humility toward all men* (Titus 3:1-2). One phrase really jumps out from Paul's list of reminders: "do whatever is good."

I know what; let's set up a website. We'll call it: do-gooders.com. In view of the incalculable influence of the Internet, can you imagine the force of our new website? When someone is home bound, we could take them food or clean their house. When a friend is discouraged, we could give them a call. When there's a natural disaster, we could be a volunteer. Instead of sitting around and talking about television sitcoms, we could go together to a homeless shelter and assist the exhausted workers. You've got the idea. It's bigger than the Internet. I want to subscribe to this website rather than the mindless chat rooms or cheap pornographic sites that are so abundant and destructive.

Do-gooders.com could change your world.

Lamentations 2:7-3:39
Philemon 1
Psalm 119:121-128

Spiritual Refreshers

People *love* refreshments. We demand them for everything: school class parties, birthday parties, ballgames, committee meetings, work sites, seminars and workshops, Bible studies, the break room, even for funerals. Food and drink are refreshing; we have that one down pat. Whenever we plan any event or get-together one of the major questions is always, "Who'll bring refreshments?" Times of physical refreshment compel us to stop whatever we're doing at the time, ingest some nourishment, and enjoy the company of others. It feels good to be refreshed, both in body and relationally.

Physical nourishment is refreshing, and it's beneficial to spend times with others; however, there is another critical dimension that we can't afford to overlook in the "refreshment category." Our souls need refreshment. Do they ever! Life is busy and disappointing and overwhelming; it's easy to lose focus and become discouraged. God had a great idea about spiritual refreshment; He called it Sunday. Observing Sunday worship and times of reflection and Bible study are great starting places; actually, they're imperative to a refreshed spiritual life. And then, there's more.

One of the biggest joys of the refreshed spiritual life is the privilege we have of passing on our joy and thus "refreshing" someone else. Listen to Paul as he writes Philemon: *Your love has given me great joy and encouragement. Because you, brother, have refreshed the hearts of the saints* (Philemon 1:7). What a commendation. It's bigger than the *Good Housekeeping* award-winning recipe you brought to the church picnic; bigger than *Krispie Kremes*; bigger than the latest designer coffee. Your *love* can be a refresher to a parched and weary fellow traveler.

Bring on the refreshers.

The Face in the Mirror

It's a daily reality check—that first look in the mirror. We can put makeup on it, clean it up, brush its teeth, and apply all the cosmetic applications available, but the basic face remains the same. Even plastic surgery doesn't change the face entirely; it merely improves it—and even that's debatable. What we see reflected in the mirror is pretty much what we get. Mirrors sometimes distort; they can be too convex or too concave, but they never lie. Tomorrow morning you can't wake up and mentally "wish" to be the reflection of someone else—you're you, and that's that.

Or is it, really? Humanly, we see great resemblances between fathers and sons. One of my brothers, for instance, is a "carbon copy" of my father. We take pride in birthing a "chip off the old block." It bolsters our ego to know that a child resembles us so much that people can see us in them. Christ is the epitome in reflection of the Father: *The Son is the radiance of God's glory and the exact representation of his being…* (Heb. 1:3). Let's follow the train of thought laid down in John 14 as it relates to this passage: If the Son is in the Father, and if we are in the Son, and if the Holy Spirit is in the Father, and if the Spirit is in us, then is it logical to deduce that we, too, can radiate God's glory and be His exact representation? Pretty heady, isn't it? But, it makes sense. Not a distortion—an exact representation.

The Psalmist expressed it years before the writer to the Hebrews: *Make your face shine upon your servant and teach me your decrees* (Psa. 119:135). His face is the reflection of God's glory in our lives. When his glory is "all over us," we will reflect Him to our world.

I have one deep, supreme desire; that I may be like Jesus.
To this I fervently aspire; that I may be like Jesus.

What reflection is in your spiritual mirror?

All Saints Day

Halloween is a part of our American culture. Initially, it was a celebration of all the saints of the church, but it has evolved into a day of evil. My brothers and I knew it as innocent fun; we dressed in costume as a princess, cartoon character, ghost, or witch and went door-to-door begging candy. We weren't afraid of anything or anyone on Halloween; it was just a magical day where we had freedom to solicit candy from neighbors. The concept was simple: "You give us a treat, and we're good to go. You don't; and we play a little trick on you." Unfortunately, that innocence has been distorted. Thank goodness many churches have recognized the need for an alternative, creating "The Pumpkin Patch Bash," and other such events for our communities.

Recompense is the Lord's, and He has used it unsparingly throughout history. If you sow good deeds, you will reap good deeds; if you sow evil; you will be paid accordingly. There is a day of reckoning for mankind; we're not going to get away with evil forever, and good will ultimately be repaid. We love to read and study about the repayment that God has prepared for the righteous, but listen to the prophet, Obadiah: *The day of the Lord is near for all nations, as you have done, it will be done to you; your deeds will return upon your own head* (Oba. 1:15).

God's not playing games with man—games that provide little sweet rewards. This isn't about candy or soap on windows if we don't get candy. This isn't a game of any kind; it's reality, and God is serious. Obadiah was warning the people in his day, and wise citizens will heed his warning as though it were in today's newspaper. Your deeds and mine and the deeds of all nations will come back to haunt or to bless. It's a law of God.

Trick-or-treat

Reflections on the Word...

_____

_____

_____

_____

_____

_____

_____

_____

_____

_____

_____

_____

_____

_____

_____

_____

_____

_____

_____

November

Joel, Ezekiel, and Daniel 1-6
Hebrews 3-13, James, I and II Peter, and I John 1-2
Psalm 119-136 and Proverbs 26-29

My Prayer Time for November...

T hanksgiving_____
_____
_____
_____

I ntercession_____
_____
_____

M inistry_____
_____
_____
_____

E ncouragement_____
_____
_____
_____
_____

God, the Builder

Construction is one of the physical evidences of man's creativity. Those of us who are not gifted in these areas are astounded by the ease with which architects and contractors can vision and dream and then bring into reality buildings and bridges and monuments of grace and usefulness. Whatever is finally constructed would never have come to pass without the initial genius of its creator.

The writer to the Hebrews compares Moses with Christ; *Jesus has been found worthy of greater honor than Moses, just as the builder of the house has greater honor than the house itself* (Heb. 3:3). Many identify Moses as an Old Testament personification of the coming Christ. Moses was faithful as God's servant, but Christ was faithful as God's son. Each had a task to do in the divine scheme of things. Moses was obedient under pressure, and Christ was obedient unto death. As huge as Moses' obedience was for the Israelites, Christ's obedience was much, much more for mankind: *For every house is built by someone, but God is the builder of everything* (Heb. 3:4).

Little children love to emulate. One of the latest children's crazes is "Bob, the Builder." It's cute to see little tots toting toy tools and creating make-believe buildings of all descriptions. Tim Taylor, the television *Tool Time* mogul, is as popular with adults as Bob, the Builder is with children. We see Bob and Tim everywhere. God is everywhere also, and He's building people of grace and usefulness to His kingdom. Christ, the great architect, has many different tools with which to build you. Your life and mine are merely the buildings that He builds to house His blessed Holy Spirit: *But Christ is faithful as a son over God's house; if we hold on to our courage and the hope of which we boast* (Heb. 3:6b). He's still working on His house—that's you and me. Get ready.

It's tool time.

God's Repayment Plan

The biggest consumer concern when we purchase a car or a house or any big ticket item is, "How will I pay for this?" Once purchased, we have an obligation to repay borrowed funds. There are a lot of "creative financing" techniques: wrap-around loans, 10/10/80 loans, twice a month instead of monthly loans, and more. Each of these methods is a short cut of one kind or another to get the loan paid in time—maybe even early.

We wouldn't ask "How will I pay?" so often if we first asked, "Can I afford it?" Many Americans—sadly many Christians—find themselves over their heads financially because they purchased items they could not afford. Once an individual is in a debt cycle, he or she must continually "rob Peter to pay Paul" until the situation seems bleak and impassible. We regret the day we bought our boat or the big screen TV or a number of other gadgets that we could have lived a lifetime without. It doesn't seem so shiny and necessary at the end of the month when the bills pile up. We literally rob ourselves of the joy of life because of a heavy burden of debt.

Spiritually, many of us feel robbed—not because God let us down. No, not at all. If there has been any robbery; ironically, we've done it to ourselves by neglecting the means of grace and over investing in worldly philosophies. The Israelites were in a parallel predicament; they made one mistake after another, until metaphorically, the locusts ate away their joy. Enter the prophet Joel with this reassuring promise: *I will repay you for the years the locusts have eaten* (Joel 2:25a). What a relevant promise for today. When we contritely return to Him, He will replenish all the years of loss. And there's more: *I will pour out my Spirit on all people. Your sons and daughters will prophesy...* (Joel 2:28). What more can we ask from a loving God?

You can be debt free.

John-John, Caroline, & Amy

Twice in my life time we've had a president with young children. We all have prized mental pictures of little John-John Kennedy playing hide-and-go-seek in the Oval Office with his father, the President of the United States. Another mental image recalls Caroline and John-John, running into the arms of President Kennedy as he stepped off a helicopter onto the White House lawn. A few years after President Kennedy, President Carter entered the White House with his little daughter, Amy. She was often seen in his company, and it was very obvious how much he adored his little girl.

These little children didn't know how "privileged" they were to have ready access to such a powerful person. Of course they didn't. He wasn't a powerful person; he was their dad. And with that intimate relationship they were afforded all the privileges and benefits of presidents and world dignitaries. No special announcement or clearance, it seemed, was ever necessary for them to enter the Oval Office. They were the President's beloved kids; the time they spent together was precious to them all.

Regardless of your history with your earthly father, you have a heavenly father who loves you dearly. Special announcement or clearance for your arrival is never necessary. Listen to this: *Let us then approach the throne of grace with confidence, so that we may receive mercy and find grace to help us in our time of need* (Heb. 4:16). There is no need for feelings of intimidation or qualification with the Father. He loves you. Even more than that, Christ experienced the same temptations as you and I, and He was victorious. With that victory, He intercedes on our behalf. God loves it when you come into His presence boldly and with confidence. You can run into His arms, for His mercy and grace are extended to you.

You're in the "First Family."

`Special Education`

Education is driven by special needs. It seems that every child has a disability requiring accommodation. There are BD kids, ADHA kids, ADD kids, the hearing impaired, the speech impaired, the emotionally impaired, the physically challenged, the mentally gifted, to name just a few. Very soon each student will have his own IEP (individual educational plan). Law mandates parents and teachers to adhere to an IEP.

This is certainly not a treatise against serving children's specific educational challenges; and yet, many frustrated teachers are asking, "Where are the 'normal' kids? Are there any left who learn what they should learn when they should learn it?" More teachers are spending more time in remedial teaching than in implementing new concepts. While it is critical to teach kids where they are, educators still are wondering how so many kids have missed so much.

Spiritually, there are more and more remedial learners who demand accommodation. This isn't new. Hebrews addresses the lack of spiritual maturity: *We have much to say about this, but it is hard to explain because you are slow to learn...by this time you ought to be teachers, you need someone to teach you the elementary truths of God's word over again. You need milk, not solid food. Solid food is for the mature...*(Heb. 5:11-14).

Do you find yourself gumming the same spiritual food year after year? Your pastor cannot lead you into the deeper things of God, for instance, because his time is dominated by so many spiritual disabilities. If you have been "around the church" for very long, you should be teaching and discipling new Christians—not demanding baby food yourself. Every Christian has his own spiritual "IEP" that employs growth in the Word and spiritual multiplication.

Are you following your spiritual IEP?

The Anchorman

Although there were radio forerunners of the modern anchorman, Huntley and Brinkley and Walter Cronkite are the three men who catapulted television news into the "anchorman" era. In the '60s these men became a part of our national fabric. For years Walter Cronkite, for example, was considered the most trusted man in America. Today, the favorite national news anchorman has been augmented to include a favorite local newscaster as well. These are people who we trust, follow, and believe.

God's promises are certain. That's apparent throughout the entire Old Testament and into the New Testament as well. Whenever He speaks—good news or bad—it is believable. Those of us who remember the day Kennedy was shot recollect seeing and hearing America's most trusted man, Mr. Cronkite, break down on the air. When Cronkite wept, the country wept with him. That day and that announcement are intrinsically ingrained on our national psyche. God's announcements are even more indelible on the Christian heart. Sometimes His heart must break when man's evil and sinful nature compels Him to pronounce destruction on the world.

We're comforted nightly by the appearance of our favorite anchorman. Regardless of the news, when he or she tells it firmly and assuredly, we can bear it. It gives us hope to see a familiar face on the tube dispensing the news. God is the anchorman of the soul: *We have this hope as an anchor for the soul, firm and sure* (Heb. 6:19). He is firm; He is sure; He is believable, and He can be trusted. Put your trust in the heavenly anchorman who will be there night after night.

He is "the" most trusted anchorman ever.

Divine Heart Surgery

By-pass surgery, heart stints, and even heart transplants are common occurrences. Just a few years ago, though, by-pass surgery was considered high risk. One of my best friends lost her father in by-pass surgery in the late '60s. His physical condition was dire, and this experimental operation was his only hope; alas, he bled to death. That same operation is so routine today that it only requires a minimal hospital stay, followed by a brief convalescent period.

Ezekiel is one of the most fascinating of all the prophets. He saw far-fetched visions—wheels inside wheels, cherubims with four different faces, chariots that hovered and flew—just to name a few of the weird things he wrote about. At first glance it's all very confusing; Ezekiel seems to be hallucinating—a good candidate for a mental institution. On second blush, though, the majority of the book is allegorical and extremely relevant when studied. By way of allegories, visions, and dreams, Ezekiel persistently warns Israel—and us—to abandon our wicked ways and return to God.

In the middle of Ezekiel's convoluted visions, he gives Israel—and the church—a blessed promise: *I will give them an undivided heart and put a new spirit in them; I will remove from them their heart of stone and give then a heart of flesh* (Eze. 11:19). What a beautiful promise of a "new" heart—but it's conditional. We must abandon our wicked ways and return to God's initial plan of a relationship with Him—one based on total dependence and obedience. Do you long for your church or family to be united in purpose and heart? Do you yearn to have that "moving of the spirit" once again on your cold, indifferent heart? Return to Him; tear down the detestable images and every idol that you've built into your life. He can do amazing surgery on your heart and the heart of your church.

God's heart surgeries are successful.

Prophetic Imaginations

He was a dear friend, but he was a liar. "How can you say such a thing about a dear friend?" you're asking. It's sad, but true. He and I did a lot of worthy projects together for the church. I could count on him. One day, though, he didn't finish a task, and rather than say so, he fabricated the most creative explanation imaginable. It was plausible; I believed him. Ultimately, he was revealed. My friend's entire life was a lie—a lie that culminated in his death. He was so accustomed to lying and was so believable that he lied when the truth was more beneficial—even *he* believed his lies. We all felt betrayed when the "real" person was finally exposed.

Betrayers aren't new. People have manipulated others with convincing lies since the Garden. Hear Ezekiel: *Say to those who prophecy out of their own imagination…Woe to foolish prophets who follow their own spirit and have seen nothing…Their visions are false and their divinations a lie. They say, 'The Lord declares' when the Lord has not sent them; yet they expect their words to be fulfilled* (Eze. 13:2-6). These men "whitewash" their lies and make them seem appealing, but underneath there is a weak, crumbling foundation: *when a flimsy wall is built, they cover it with whitewash* (Eze. 13:10b).

What an alert sign to the serious Christian. Everywhere we turn someone is purporting their personal premise. Don't permit yourself or your church or your family to be sucked in and deceived by false prophets with evil imaginations. They are not of God. When you test a man's words against "the" Word, *You will know that I am the Sovereign Lord* (Eze. 13:9b). When God is in an event, you won't have "funny feelings" or doubts about it; He will give you full assurance of His will and His way.

Beware of Elmer Gantry.

Overfed and Unconcerned

D o you know the difference between indifference and apathy? "I don't know, and I don't care." The church and its mechanics can become our Number One priority. We don't have time to help a neighbor, for instance, because we must attend Bible study. Many get so absorbed in busy "religious" lives that they fail to even notice the abundant needs in the world, much less stop and help. "I just don't have time," we say. Perhaps a more honest response would be, "I just don't care."

Ezekiel pictures Jerusalem in a captivating allegory. She is seen as a baby girl left on a trash heap. A benevolent man sees the baby, rescues her, lavishing her with love. She becomes a beautiful woman, but she trusts her beauty instead of the one who gave her a life. She becomes a prostitute, defiling her body, and leading her daughters astray along with her. The wicked people of Sodom and Samaria are called her sisters. Ezekiel describes Jerusalem's wicked sisters: *This was the sin of your sister, Sodom. She and her daughters were arrogant, overfed and unconcerned; they didn't help the poor and needy. They were haughty and did detestable things before me* (Eze. 16:49).

Here's the clincher: As wicked as Sodom and Samaria were, Jerusalem was worse: *Samaria did not commit half the sins you did. You have done more detestable things than they...Because your sins were more vile than theirs, they appear more righteous than you* (Eze. 16:51-52). This scripture doesn't make us want to shout, but it does gives serious pause for reflection. How convenient it is to point at another and accuse them of being overfed or unconcerned spiritually. In our "religiosity," we too, can become haughty and arrogant toward those in need. We have been rescued from the trash heap and raised as sons and daughters of the King. We have an obligation:

Share the wealth.

A Song of Ascents

Erupting from the Gastineau Channel in Juneau, Alaska are Mt. Roberts and Mt. Juneau. Our first home in Juneau was on 7th Street—halfway up Mt. Roberts. We could slip down the mountain one block to 6th Street and begin the ascent to the top. Or, we could walk up two blocks to 9th Street and follow Basin Rd. into the mountain beside Gold Creek. During the three years we lived in Juneau, my family did a lot of mountain climbing or hiking around Mendenhall Glacier. We didn't have money for anything else; hiking was free, yet it offered us a freedom that we never felt in the valley.

At the beginning of the journey upward to the top of a mountain or along either side of the famous Mendenhall it was difficult to see the peak; we were usually overwhelmed by rain and always had to fight brush and beat off ubiquitous mosquitoes. The closer we came to the top, the freer we felt—regardless of the weather or terrain. Our lungs were bursting with fresh oxygen; the air was crisp; a song swelled in our souls. Many times our family spontaneously broke into song as we climbed the mountain or glacier. It was exhilarating to near the top. We were closer to God then than any other time or place. The Psalmist describes our euphoric experience better than I:

> I lift up my eyes to the hills—where does my help come from?
> My help comes from the Lord, the Maker of heaven and earth.
> He will not let your foot slip—he who watches over you will not slumber:
> Indeed, he who watches over Israel will neither slumber nor sleep.
> The Lord watches over you—the Lord is your shade at your right hand;
> The sun will not harm you by day, nor the moon by night.
> The Lord will keep you from all harm—he will watch over your life;
> the Lord will watch over your coming and going both now and forevermore.

Lift your eyes—He's at the top of your mountain.

Mirages and Reality

Did you ever drive across the Southwest? I have. It's enchanting in an air-conditioned car, but the first several times I drove across the California desert, Arizona, and New Mexico we didn't have air-conditioning. The Southwest is a completely different experience without "air." The dry winds become stifling and your stomach sickens as mile after mile of endless highway stretches ahead to infinity. Then you see it—water. "If we can just get to the water, we'll drink and refresh." But there is no water—just a hollow reflection of nothing caused by atmospheric conditions casting illusionary reflections across the hot pavement. It's only a mirage—a trick of the mind.

Men have always tried to compensate for sin through sacrifice. Before Christ died for man's sin, sacrifice was God's method of allowing men to make recompense for sin. Sacrifice was His law. Christ's sacrificial death, though, was given "once and for all." He wasn't going to do this again; in fact, it wasn't necessary. Man has misunderstood the all-inclusive forgiveness of Christ's death: *The law is only a shadow of the good things that are coming—not the realities themselves* (Heb. 10:1). Oh, now I get it. Because of Christ's death, we don't even need the law anymore. Is that it?

Not at all. We still need boundaries and perimeters, but the law is never an end unto itself: *First he said, 'Sacrifices and offerings ...you did not desire, nor were you pleased with them.' Then he said, 'Here I am, I have come to do your will, we have been made holy through the sacrifice of the body of Jesus Christ once and for all* (Heb. 10:8-10). You know what? I think I see. The law has value, but in the end it is only a mirage. Christ and His death are the true reality. He is the water that we've searching on life's hot, dry desert.

He's no mirage.

Armistice Day

On the eleventh hour of the eleventh day of the eleventh month—Nov. 11, 1918—an armistice was signed in Rethondes, France to end World War I. This treaty was to end the war that would end all wars; it was intended to preserve peace forever. We are painfully aware that has never happened. Since Nov. 11, 1918, we've fought World War II, the Korean Police Action, the Cold War, the Vietnam War, Desert Storm, and the Iraqi War; plus, there have been constant conflicts and blood shed globally. War is a component of life—it's not going away until Christ returns—at least physical war, that is.

Spiritually, God has provided a sure-fire way to preserve the peace. We need not continually war with others or repeatedly fight the same battles in our souls. It's possible to be done with war: *Since we have a great priest over the house of God, let us draw near God with a sincere heart in full assurance of faith, having our hearts sprinkled to cleanse us from a guilty conscience ...for he who promised is faithful* (Heb. 10:21-22). He is the great high priest, and He's taken His place at the right hand of God. When we come near Him sincerely and with true faith, He cleanses us from the guilty conscience that spurs us into devious acts of war. He is faithful to His word on this. Aren't you glad for that? I sure am. No more war. Sounds like a great arrangement in a warring world.

Once we cease fighting with ourselves and others, we can refocus our energies on things that really count: *Let us consider how we may spur one another on toward love and good deeds* (Heb. 10:24). As long as a battle is raging in the soul, there will be war. You can't avoid it, but His blood applied to our lives gives us the assurance and confidence to lay down our arms and move ahead peacefully, willingly working side by side with our brothers.

He has won the war; it's Armistice Day.

Hans Brinker and Ezekiel

Many have read the children's classic, *Hans Brinker and the Silver Skates*. Written in 1865 by Mapes Dodge, it is the story of Hans and Gretel Brinker and how they helped restore their father to health through kindness and good deeds. Within the book is a famous Dutch legend: Young Hans saved the countries of Holland and Belgium from a potential flood by holding his finger in a hole in a dike. No one knows for certain if this legend is true. If it is, though, today fifteen million people in Holland and five million people in Belgium owe their existence to his heroic gesture.

God is always searching for men and women who are willing to step forward for His cause. At times men have answered: Abraham and Moses and the Apostles to mention a few. All these willingly laid down their futures to follow God and defend His name. At other times, God has called and no one has answered: *I looked for a man among them who would build up the wall and stand before me in the gap on behalf of the land so I would not have to destroy it, but I found none* (Eze. 22:30). Every leader knows the empty feeling of asking for help, but finding no one willing to answer. It's discouraging and debilitating to leadership.

Ezekiel advised the people repeatedly about pending doom, but they refused to listen—much less heed his warnings. God was looking for "one" willing man to stand against the rampant wickedness of the day and "put his finger in the dike." No one was forthcoming. The world is as wicked and evil today as it was hundreds of years ago. God is still looking for men and women who will take a stand and bridge the gap between evil and righteousness. You can be that person. Like the people of Holland and Belgium today have a young boy to thank for their existence, future generations will bless you.

Take a stand; put your finger in the dike.

The Word in Real Time

NOVEMBER
13

Ezekiel 24-25
Hebrews 11:17-40
Psalm 124

The Wall of Faith

My friends thought I was nuts, but yearly I led a group of middle schoolers to Washington DC during spring break. "DC" is one of our nation's most beautiful cities, and it was my joy to see Midwestern pre-teens light up at the sight of the big city. Washington has so many highlights: the Capitol, the White House, Ford's Theater, Arlington Cemetery, Mt. Vernon, the Holocaust Museum, the Smithsonian, and on and on. It is also replete with monuments; the Lincoln Memorial, the Washington Monument, the Iwo Jima Memorial, the Jefferson Monument, the Korean Memorial, and the Vietnam Wall.

The kids enjoyed every place we visited; yet, their behavior was typically adolescent. There was one spot, though, where I could count on my "pre-human friends" becoming serious, somber, and full of questions. That was the Vietnam Memorial. The moment we stepped from the bus and began our long quiet walk along the face of the "wall," they became quieter and quieter. Many stopped to respectfully trace a name to take back home. Back on the bus, the kids were a flood of questions and comments: "Mrs. Slamp, why did so many have to die? This war wasn't fair; what did it prove?"

The "wall" is our national keepsake; it is a national reminder that these men and women will not be forgotten—regardless of our opinions on Vietnam. Hebrews Chapter 11 has a wall of its own, and what a wall it is: Thirteen are named and hundreds more are referenced—men and women who could not be bought and were willing to stand against opposition and persecution for the sake of the gospel. They were jeered, flogged, chained, stoned, imprisoned, sawed in two, stabbed, destitute, alone—*the world was not worthy of them* (Heb. 11:38). *These were all commended for their faith...* (Heb. 11:39).

Is your name on God's wall of faith?

The Thrill of Victory

Recently, my husband and I attended a game between the *Chiefs* and the *Rams*. I really don't understand football very well, but it was still a great evening. Simply driving onto the stadium property was exhilarating; everyone was dressed in KC red; tailgate parties were abundant; flags were flying; obviously, the fans were there to have a good time and support the home team. Inside the stadium the excitement heightened. Thousands were there to cheer their team on to victory, and win they did. I watched as a player took the ball, set his eye on the goal post, and ran for a TD. The crowd went wild; bands played; lights flashed; the home team was winning.

All teams have loyal fans. Our son, for example, is the world's most avid *Cowboys* fan. He is loyal to the "boys," regardless. Winning or losing, if their players are in jail, or if they've recently fired the coach, they are his team. Fans help revive a team that's in a slump and lift a winning team to greater heights. Not even the Olympics, though, can hold a candle, to the game of life. Paul equates our Christian life to a race in which each one of us can be a winner.

Pretend you're running your final lap of life. Let's put music behind this scenario and allow it to crescendo as you approach the finish line: *Since we are surrounded by such a great cloud of witnesses, let us throw off everything that hinders and the sin that so easily entangles, and let us run with perseverance the race marked out for us. Let us fix our eyes on Jesus…* (Heb. 12:1-2). Can you hear the crowd? Loved ones and friends who have successfully run the race are in that cloud of witnesses. As you make your final turn, you shed the burdens of life—sadness, sickness, loss. Thousands attend major league games; millions are in this cloud. They're all there, cheering for you. Choirs are singing; the Son is gleaming.

You've won the crown of life.

Mountain Climbing

I've lived many places—the Midwest, the West Coast, the Southwest, the Northwest, the Arctic, the South. All of these areas have their own corner on beauty, and I've enjoyed each one. But, I must admit, some places are just a bit more stunning than others. As a child our family lived within driving distance of Mt. McKinley—Denali—the "great one," the tallest mountain in North America. It's unspeakably breathtaking. I've also lived along the Columbia River where on a clear day I could see Mt. Hood from my front door and Mt. St. Helen's and Mt. Adams from my back door.

Mountains are invigorating; they challenge us. We want to conquer them, hike above the timber line and to their very peak. From the top of a mountain the view is fantastic. On a clear day everything comes into perspective from the mountain top. We can see the trail we've climbed and we can survey the horizon in all directions. Do you want to clear your mind and get a better perspective on life—then climb a mountain? It'll do it every time.

There are many scriptural references to heaven, and although we aren't certain what it will be, we have hints here and there, and we know it will be terrific. The view will be great; our perspective will be clear; we'll be able to see the path we've taken. Sometimes heaven is called a city; sometimes it's called a mountain; sometimes both: *You have come to Mount Zion, to the heavenly Jerusalem, the city of the living God. You have come to thousands upon thousands of angels in joyful assembly, to the church of the firstborn, whose names are written in heaven. You have come to God, the judge of all men, to the spirits of righteous men made perfect, to Jesus the mediator of a new covenant...* (Heb. 12:22-24). Keep climbing the mountain; my friend, heaven awaits, and the view is terrific.

Keep Climbing; the view is terrific!

Don't Forget

We've heard those two little words all our lives. When we were small, they might have been our parents last words as we left the house, "Don't forget…" When we're dating, we don't want to forget anything. After we marry, our spouse may send us on an errand with the injunction, "Don't forget…" On the job we can't afford to forget, for forgetting is hazardous to job security. When we grow older we hope we don't suffer a senior moment and forget. We have a lot of little tools to help us remember; we keep calendars and manage palm pilots; we write lists, and we have bells to remind us when to do something or when to stop doing something else. Forgetting is simply too dangerous; we do everything possible to "remember not to forget."

"Don't forget" stated positively is "remember." The writer to the Hebrews gives us an exhaustive list of things to remember:

- Remember to entertain strangers; they're angels in disguise.
- Remember those in prison; but for the grace of God, you could be there, too.
- Remember those who are mistreated; feel their pain.
- Remember to keep your marriage pure and above reproach.
- Remember to be content with what you have; don't lust.
- Remember; God will never leave you or forsake you.
- Remember where your confidence is—in Him alone.
- Remember your leaders and pray for them.
- Remember: Jesus is the same—yesterday, today, and forever.

"Forgetting" is no excuse—Remember!

Location; Location; Location

When we lived in San Diego, my husband and I enjoyed driving along the Pacific Coast to view the magnificent and resplendent homes suspended above the sea. Many of these multi-million dollar palaces were "securely" anchored into the hillsides by giant stilts that held them above Highway 101, augmenting their breathtaking view of the beach and ocean beyond. From lofty perches, the "lucky" home owners were lifted above the mundane life below. Relaxing on their decks, they could watch migrating whales, experience dazzling sunsets, and enjoy pleasant ocean breezes.

Ever so often, though, Southern California experiences relentless rain. It's amazing; the rains fail to discern the splendor of these proud homes. When they aren't firmly anchored, they slide into the ocean just like anything else on the hillside. The rain is no respecter of home or person. This brings to mind an old Sunday school chorus:

> The wise man built his house upon a rock
> The foolish man built his house upon the sand.

You remember it, don't you? The wise man's house withstood the floods, but the foolish man lost his home. The Psalmist reminds us of the significance of a sure foundation to our homes—not our houses—our homes: *Unless the Lord builds the house, its builders labor in vain* (Psa. 127:1). Many things are essential in building a "home." Unless He is in its center, your home won't be able to withstand life's storms. Is your home so securely anchored that it can survive the storms of life? Storms will come with predictable surety. What a shame it would be to view the destruction of a home that could have been secure if He had been its center.

How's your home building project going?

That's My Seat

Once my husband was the guest speaker in a neighboring town for Sunday morning worship. Together we arrived at the church early—too late for Sunday school, but with plenty of time yet before the morning service. My husband went to the pastor's study to prepare, leaving me alone in the empty sanctuary. Quietly, I took a seat and began to read. When Sunday school was dismissed, people began to filter into the sanctuary for worship.

My time of reflection was broken by a couple speaking to me; how nice. It took a second for their words to sink in. They weren't greeting me—hardly. In a curt, agitated voice, the woman spoke, "Excuse me maam; do you mind? This is *my* seat." Did I mind? I would have left if that were possible. If a bad situation ever got worse, it did that day. During church I was introduced as the speaker's wife. When service was over, the same people came to me with feigned sincerity and told me how glad they were that I was there. What pretense!

James has piercing words about this duplicity: *Don't show favoritism. Suppose a man comes into your meeting wearing fine clothes, and a poor man in shabby clothes also comes in. If you show special attention to the man wearing fine clothes and say 'Here is a good seat for you,' but say to the poor man, 'You stand there,'…have you not discriminated…* (James 2:2-3). Possibly the people who spoke to me thought their church was friendly. They weren't intentionally rude, but they sure didn't think. It appeared that I only counted when they knew "who" I was. Every person should matter to us and our churches because they matter to God. *God, help me to see everyone as through your eyes. This "stranger" beside me could be one who has ventured into church for the first time in years. Help me to make my church welcoming and friendly to anyone, anytime. Amen.*

Welcome! I'm so glad you're here.

The Word in Real Time

Misty Fjord

My summer job is to comment about Alaska from a cruise ship bridge. One of the most spine-tingling events of each cruise is a visit to Misty Fjord. Once we sail down Revillagigedo Channel from Ketchikan, turn north into Behm Canal, pass Eddy Stone Rock, we're there. Words fail this glacially sculpted wonder. Massive bare rock mountains extend skyward five thousand feet and more, while the water beneath is nearly as deep. The fjord is incredibly narrow; yet its depth and sheer walls make it navigable. Finally, we turn into Rudyerd Bay, and then take one last turn into the Punch Bowl, where we turn around. What an event—especially from the bridge.

The ship's center beam thrusters make it possible for a giant ship to "turn on a dime." I've had the unspeakable thrill of watching the captain maneuver and turn a massive ship—more than three football fields long—in a complete circle, with only about one hundred feet of clearance on both the bow and the stern. The captains are amazing and oh, so capable. Once this past summer after a flawless turn in the Punch Bowl, I addressed the passengers below: "If you can hear my voice, applaud our captain." The entire ship burst forth with applause. He had used his skills wisely and safely for them.

The tongue is even more powerful than the thrusters of a cruise ship: *Take ships as an example. Although they are so large and are driven by strong winds, they are steered by a very small rudder, wherever the pilot wants to go. Likewise the tongue is a small part of the body, but it makes great boasts* (James 3:4-5). The tongue is a powerful tool—it can be constructive and it can be dreadfully destructive. It all depends on the "captain" of the tongue. *With the tongue we praise our Lord, and with it we curse men… Out of the same mouth come praise and cursing. My brothers, this should not be* (James 3:10).

Be a good captain; curb your tongue.

Push Back

Good parents walk a fine line in teaching self-defense. We want our children to get along and not be bullied, but we also want them to learn to settle conflicts without fighting. I've taught enough classes and been with enough kids to know that there's a bully in every bunch who will continually intimidate other children until he or she is dealt with "up close and personal." It's always amusing to see a quiet, seemingly timid child, set the class bully straight—either with well-chosen words, or sometimes with a punch!

Adults can be bullied, too. A friend of mine was constantly bothered by a classmate who pestered and needled him continually. This man had an annoying habit of walking up to my friend, punching him, and then following the punch with a verbal barb. Day after day my friend steamed over this but never said or did anything to stop it. Finally, he had enough; he sustained one punch too many. Before he realized it one day, my friend turned to the man, punched *him* and said, "Don't ever do that again. You don't know me that well." Guess what? They've been on mutually respectful terms ever since.

The devil is the biggest bully on the playground. He will needle, cajole, pester, and irritate as long and as persistently as you allow him to get by with it. Like my friend; when confronted, he will run: *Resist the devil, and he will flee from you* (James 4:7). The next time the devil slips in beside you and tempts you or tries to destroy your self-confidence, don't let him get away with it; push back. He's not really a bully; he's a big baby. You'll have him on the run so fast that your head will spin. When you push the devil back, you're moving closer to the Lord: *Come near to God and he will come near to you* (James 4:8). What a trade off. When you take a step away from Satan, you're moving toward God.

Pushing back is really drawing close.

A Farmer's Patience

We live in Central Kansas where they grow wheat and maize and corn, and we've lived in West Texas among the cattle ranches. What I know about farming and ranching wouldn't fill a primer, but I respect and esteem these amazing individuals. Farmers must indeed be the biggest risk takers out there. Every single year demands a staggering financial outlay. They must own or lease vast sections of land to produce a crop big enough to justify the astronomical expense of their equipment alone. Seed, fertilizer, and water must be purchased and paid for, and fields need constant tending.

All this effort and expense culminates in one thing only—a successful and profitable harvest. Right up until harvest week, everything can be lost in one fell swoop: too much rain, not enough rain, hot dry winds, tornados, plagues of insects—one or all of these can destroy an entire year's work and send the optimistic farmer back to the bank for a loan to start anew. Talk about patience. My hat is off to the farmers—they are truly phenomenal. And they have patience.

Lack of patience terrorizes our lives. We grow weary of the evil, the wickedness, and the duplicity that we see daily; we just want it to be over—now! James addresses this: *Be patient...until the Lord's coming* (James 5:7a). "What are you talking about, James? Until the Lord's coming? That's far too long; that means I might have to wait until eternity. I want this situation resolved today." James goes on with a humbling example: *See how the farmer waits for the land to yield its valuable crop and how patient he is for the autumn and spring rains. You too, be patient and stand firm...* (James 5:7b) When there's too much or not enough rain, and hot dry winds or tornados blow across your life and you want a situation resolved today, take a lesson from the farmer.

Wait, I say, on the Lord.

Because I Said So!

Most of the time "because I said so," is not a good explanation when dealing with kids. They want to know "why," and in all fairness, they deserve to know—some of the time, that is. When a small child is dashing after a ball into the middle of a busy street is NOT the time to stop and explain to him the dangers of running in traffic. When you shout "stop," he needs to obey— pronto; otherwise, it could be dangerous to his health.

Peter instructs us to be holy. "How in the world is that possible? We're human; that's asking too much." I know what you're thinking. News flash: It *is* possible to be holy—not perfect—but holy in motives and actions. Listen to the Word: *As obedient children, do not conform to the evil desires you had when you lived in ignorance. But just as he who called you is holy, so be holy in all you do, for it is written: "Be holy, because I am holy."* (I Peter 1:15). The first time a small child runs into the street, he's ignorant to its latent dangers. Once informed, though, he knows— because Mom or Dad told him so. Obedience could be his salvation. It's that basic.

We're God's children, and He tells us that we can be holy. How in the world does this flesh out, especially in light of our humanity? It's all about obedience: *Now that you have purified yourselves by obeying the truth so that you have sincere love for your brothers, love one another deeply, from the heart. For you have been born again...* (I Peter 1:22-23). Purification is representative of God's holiness. Once He cleanses and purifies our hearts, we are responsible to obey. Everything is new when we're "born again." We sing and say that we "want to be like Jesus." Here's how: "be holy as I am holy." According to Peter, our holiness is revealed by our unfailing, sincere love for one another. Why should we obey God and be holy?

Because God says so.

The Master and "the David"

Augustino di Antonio, a little-known Italian sculptor, chiseled for years on a nineteen foot slab of lifeless marble. After repeated attempts to bring something to life out of the stone, in despair he abandoned it. Within this discarded marble, Michelangelo discovered his most famous masterpiece—*the David*. It took him three full years to unlock the seventeen foot statue from its marble tomb, but when *the David* was at last completed and placed on public exhibition, all of Florence stood in wonder. Since 1504 the world has continued to marvel at the intricacies of *the David*—the veins of the stone that flow through his arms and the lifelike look of determination in his eyes.

Many objects of great value are often overlooked. Even Jesus was rejected: *As you come to him, the living Stone—rejected by men but chosen by God and precious to him—you also, like living stones, are being built into a spiritual house…* (I Peter 2:4-5). The stone that gave birth to *the David* was rejected as worthless, yet it became a timeless work of genius. Many people of Jesus' day—especially the supercilious religious leaders—considered Him unworthy. Their opinion mattered none. God chose Christ from the beginning of the world to be the Savior of mankind—the living Stone.

You, too, are "elected" by God. Something worthwhile is hidden in your life; you are chosen and precious to Him. Let Him chisel and refashion your stony heart. Within you is something priceless, timeless, and beautiful. It just may be that God will chisel and carve on you for years just like Michelangelo worked on *the David*. But, oh the beauty that He can ultimately reveal. His beauty has been latent within you since your conception. Let Him work on you, and create something beautiful out of your life.

You are God's masterpiece.

Want a Blessing?

My mother-in-law is remarkable. She gave her heart to the Lord a few months before my husband was born. Because she was a Christian, her husband abandoned her and his infant son. Ever since that day, life has been hard, but you wouldn't know it if you spoke with her. When she became a Christian, she inherited eternal life, eternal optimism, and contagious joy. She's uplifting. Her trailer is modest and worth little; she has no insurance; and her pension is just enough to get her by each month. Despite it all, she is leaving a tremendous inheritance of joy and laughter and hope to her children.

It's Thanksgiving—our collective time to reflect on all our abundant blessings. And how blessed we are! Even the poorest of us has been so indulged that we have no conceivable comprehension of the magnitude of the blessing of just being an American. But, do you want to be *really* blessed? Here's how: *Do not repay evil with evil or insult with insult, but with blessing, because to this you were called so that you may inherit a blessing* (I Peter 3:9).

My husband and his siblings are so blessed in the inheritance category; there will be nothing of value to argue about when Mom is gone. There will, however, definitely be an inheritance. Years ago when she was left alone and penniless, David's mother could have grown bitter, angry, and revengeful. Many would even say that she had a "right" to these attitudes. The inheritance this amazing woman is leaving to her children isn't one of stocks and bonds or land or bank accounts. She has lived forgiveness all their lives. Her life is real. She chose not to repay evil for evil or insult for insult. She chose the high road—the Christian road. Her children have quite an inheritance—great blessings that can't be bought, sold, or bartered, or fought over—a life of forgiveness and love.

What blessing are you leaving?

He's in the Building

To be with someone famous or important gives us a thrill and vicariously gives meaning to our humdrum lives. We spend exorbitant amounts to purchase tickets to see a musician or attend a play that features a renowned thespian. Or we drive great distances to attend a ball game where an athlete may break a record. As a crowd gathers, there is an air of calculable expectancy; someone important is coming. And then we hear the announcement: "Ladies and gentlemen, *So and So* is in the building." In one body, the crowd rises to its feet and cheers. They're in the presence of greatness.

Ezekiel is a captivating book; it's a disturbing book; it's difficult to understand. In the first several chapters it appears like Ezekiel is having hallucinations—at least weird visions. In the middle of the book, he talks about dry bones that come back to life, and we begin to see the allegory. Eventually, if you stay with him, Ezekiel makes sense. He pronounces multiple prophecies against Israel's neighbors, and continually warns Israel and Jerusalem of their wicked ways. In closing, Ezekiel discuses the land divisions and delineates specifically the care for the temple and the priests.

And then, seemingly out of nowhere, the book ends abruptly: *The Lord is there* (Eze. 48:35b). Just like that, Ezekiel is finished. There's a HUGE message in his final four words. Our churches have so many plans and programs, and they can be as exact as those Ezekiel gave. We know that wickedness will come against God's people, and that can frighten us. But our churches, like the temple Ezekiel described, are to be houses of prayer and cities of refuge. The Lord should be there. What's going on in your church? Is the Lord there? Do you make room for Him? He wants to come, but He will only come to a people and to a church whose hearts and motives are pure.

Ladies and gentlemen: Is the Lord here?

Resolve

Determination and resolve are essential in any endeavor. We can witness resolve in "successful people" of all ages. A little child may resolve to conquer the bicycle. He or she may fall and tumble and get scratched up, but if he's determined, he will learn. He knew what he wanted and he was single-minded about learning until he had the skill down pat. Once learned, bike riding is his forever.

King Nebuchadnezzar chose to tone up and educate some of the keener exiles and make them Babylonians. Daniel was chosen, yet he was the epitome of resolve. He was far from home; no one was watching. Survival should have been his focus. The king even gave him a new name. Daniel didn't care what they called him; he cared about his belief: *Daniel resolved not to defile himself...* (Dan 1:8). Daniel and his pals made a pact with the official: Allow us to follow our Hebrew diet for ten days; then test us to see how we fare. Fearfully, the official conceded. If Daniel were wrong, it would cost him his head. Daniel wasn't wrong: *At the end of the ten days they looked healthier and better nourished than any of the young men who ate the royal food* (Dan. 1:15). Daniel's entire life was a testimony of his resolve and determination against unbeatable odds.

Are you resolved to know the ways of God, regardless? Once learned, anything in life is "as simple as riding a bicycle;" the journey is the difficulty. A victorious Christian life demands determination and unwavering resolution. We must first know what we believe before we can defend it. Paul "determined that neither death nor life nor principalities nor things present nor things to come" would separate him from the love of Jesus Christ. Go, Paul! Paul knew what he believed; nothing would deter him from his goal—eternal life.

Resolve is like riding a bike—once you get it.

Spiritual Nearsightedness

I remember the day my husband got his first pair of glasses. As we drove down I-10 in El Paso, Texas, he turned to the kids and me, "Look, I can see leaves on the trees." And, "When did they put that road sign there?" We were dumbfounded. No one knew until he had his eyes tested how nearsighted he was. He still takes *off* his glasses to read. Anything that's up close he understands, but if it's at a distance, he needs help—prescription glasses.

We need spiritual glasses: *His divine power has given us everything we need for life and godliness through our knowledge of him…* (II Peter 1:3). What's the prescription? Here goes: faith, goodness, knowledge, self-control, perseverance, godliness, brotherly kindness, love. That's a big prescription, but if we don't fill it, there's danger: *If anyone does not have them, he is nearsighted and blind, and has forgotten that he has been cleansed from his past sins* (II Peter 1:9).

This prescription has an awesome guarantee: *If you possess these qualities in increasing measure, they will keep you from being ineffective and unproductive…* (II Peter: 1:8). There is no way that we can keep all of these gifts alive in our lives unless we are alive in the Spirit. Take note: these gifts multiply. For example, as muscle produces muscle, so self-control produces more self-control, and kindness produces more kindness.

My kids and I were frightened to realize that their Dad had gone for years not seeing clearly; he was a potential road hazard. In addition, he was unknowingly missing out on so much. Spiritual nearsightedness leads to spiritual blindness. When Peter's prescription is absent from our lives, we are a potential hazard to the body. Neglecting to have your eyes checked may make you the biggest casualty of all.

Do you need to visit the optometrist?

Out of the Fire

At the sound of the royal band, every Babylonian was mandated to bow to King Nebuchadnezzar's gold image. The Bible fails to mention any reward for this idolatry, but it does mention a consequence for those not complying: Death in heat seven times hotter than hot. When the band struck up, the Babylonians bowed to the idol and kowtowed to the king. Three of the Israeli captives—Shadrach, Meshach, and Abednego—paid no attention.

The king's sniveling officials became royal tattle-tales: *They neither serve your gods nor worship the image of gold you have set up* (Dan. 3:12b). That did it; the king would show the whole country, and especially these ungrateful captives: "Tie them up, leave them fully clothed, and throw them into the fire. That will show the captives and everyone else, that *I* am king, and what I say goes." The king was flabbergasted, though, when he checked the furnace. Something was wrong; he saw four men, not three: *and the fourth looks like a son of the gods* (Dan. 3:25b). Out of the furnace they came; unscathed, unsinged, and cool as cucumbers. These men weren't willing to sacrifice a thing that meant going against their god: *They...were willing to give up their lives rather than serve or worship any god except their own god* (Dan. 3:28b).

Have you been in the furnace? I imagine so. Has a powerful tyrant in your life tied you up and thoughtlessly thrown you in the fire, intending to use your demise as an example of his or her power and authority? When you're true to God and His word, people will come against you; it's a fact. Bring it on—hotter than hot. You'll discover His spirit in the fire; He will be there when no one else is. Don't fear the heat; you'll discover something unique about the fire:

It's cool in the furnace.

The Writing on the Wall

At the feast of Belshazzar and a thousand of his lords,
As they drank from golden vessels as the Book of Truth records.
In the night as they reveled in the royal palace hall,
They were seized with consternation at the hand upon the wall.

Can you imagine? I've been to an assortment of dinners and banquets. I've seen a variety of entertainment, but never anything like "the hand." This banquet of Belshazzar's had become an orgy. After much drinking, Belshazzar called for the stolen gold goblets that Dear Old Dad (Nebuchadnezzar) had taken from the temple in Jerusalem. These articles intended for use in worship to God were being desecrated, ridiculed, and blasphemed. God doesn't like that.

More than a little inebriated, Belshazzar was shaken. His face turned red and his knees knocked. Frightened beyond words, he called all his sorcerers and soothsayers. They were as speechless and baffled as the king. "Hands on the wall" were out of their realm of capability. In their drunkenness, someone remembered Daniel, the Israeli captive. He had wisdom; maybe he could interpret "the hand." Daniel's report wasn't good. They had tampered too long with the sacred; God would destroy them for their sacrilegious behaviors.

Stop what you're doing and swallow what you're chewing. Some scriptures become such an everyday part of our colloquial expressions that we forget their origin. Take heed: Occasionally, God writes a message on the wall of our life with His own hand. It's plain, and it's staggering: "Don't mess around with the sacred." God won't tolerate disrespect forever. By the time Belshazzar saw "the hand," his party was out of control. Pay attention to His warnings before He writes on your wall because, "When the hand writing is on the wall, it's too late."

God's penmanship is legible.

The Word "is" Real Time

R*eal time* is our way of explaining that something is happening in the present. We aren't predicting when we talk about *real time*; we're reporting. We aren't reporting about someone else. *Real time* reports are personal and up-to-date. A *real time* event didn't happen in the past; it isn't predicted to happen in the future; we haven't heard a rumor that it "might" happen. No, when we speak of *real time,* we are certain of our references and our citations are accurate.

Since the dawning of civilization, man has searched for the creator of His soul. He has explored many avenues to find an answer and a reason for his existence. Surely, this isn't all there is? There must be more. Hear John's melodic verbal tune: *That which was from the beginning, which we have heard, which we have seen with our eyes, which we have looked at and our hands have touched—this we proclaim concerning the Word of life. The life appeared; we have seen it and testify to it, and we proclaim to you the eternal life, which was with the Father and has appeared to us* (I John 1:1-3).

Many things that appear *real* turn out to be hollow disappointments. Christ is *real*; He's relevant; and He's up-to-date. The "Word," both written and living, can become *real* life. John witnessed "the Word," (Christ) first hand; he saw Him; he touched Him; he listened to Him teach. Christ isn't a theory; He's ever so relevant. All the things you amass won't bring your real happiness; your achievements won't deliver pure joy. When life crashes around you with a sudden surety, when friends abandon, and organizations disappoint, you will discover that Christ, and Christ alone is *real*—the living Word of God. You can know Him in all His *reality*: *Our fellowship is with the Father and with his Son, Jesus Christ. We write this to make our joy complete* (I John 1: 3b-4).

The "Word" is the real deal.

Reflections on the Word...

Reflections on the Word...

_____

_____

_____

_____

_____

_____

_____

_____

_____

_____

_____

_____

_____

_____

_____

_____

December

Daniel 7-12, Zechariah, Esther, Ezra, Nehemiah, and Malachi
I John 2-4, II and III John, Jude, and Revelation
Psalms 137-150 and Proverbs 29-31

My Prayer Time for December...

Thanksgiving _____

_____

_____

_____

Intercession _____

_____

_____

_____

Ministry _____

_____

_____

_____

Encouragement _____

_____

_____

_____

_____

Daniel 7-8
I John 2:12-27
Psalm 136:13-26

Love and Fidelity

Weddings are happy occasions that we enjoy. Young people sit in awe, wondering when they will meet their Prince Charming or Lady Love. That will, they think, be a glorious day. Those who have been married a long time look at the young bride and groom through eyes of experience, knowing that it won't all be flowers and soft candlelight. Life can be stark at times, but true love will endure. Wedding vows are serious. The young couple is pledging their lives, their love, and their fidelity "'til death do they part."

Not once in all the vow exchanges I've witnessed have I heard this: Pastor: "Do you take this woman as your wedded wife?" Groom: "Yes, I do—364 days a year. But, pastor, I'm sure my new wife will understand. You see, I've had a lot of girl friends before her, and one day and night a year, I really need to spend with one of them. It's just one day; that shouldn't make any difference." How preposterous is that? That groom's wife-to-be would run from the altar faster than a speeding bullet. Love is jealous and expects the other's devotion— every iota of it—with no reservations.

It's impossible to love God and continue loving worldly things: *Do not love the world or anything in the world. If anyone loves the world, the love of the Father is not in him* (I John 1:15). Attempting to love God and the world simultaneously is as crazy as our wedding illustration. Two loves can't coexist. The groom must make a decision, and we must also. I can see the terrified bride turning to her fickle groom: "She or I; who will it be? You must be mine all the time, or none of the time; another woman can't even have one day." When we truly love God, He has our complete love, our undivided attention, our unwavering loyalty, and our abiding fidelity. We refuse to even look at another. There are no two ways about it.

It's either all or not at all.

Masters of Intrigue

Scheming leaders deceive and manipulate reality to such a degree that it appears right. Their half-truths cause intriguing issues to capture our minds and occupy our thoughts. D'Argagnan, the hero in Dumas' novel, *The Three Musketeers*, says it well:

> Oh, what a tangled web we weave
> When first we practice to deceive.

Daniel, the Jewish exile in Babylonia was far from his home, yet God knew where he was, and He knew whose he was. God trusted Daniel with visions and messages for His people that are still relevant. Reminiscent of today, the people were being manipulated by evil leaders: *...a master of intrigue will arise. He will become very strong, but by his own power... He will... succeed in whatever he does... He will cause deceit to prosper; he will consider himself superior. When they feel secure, he will destroy many and take a stand against the Prince of princes. Yet he will be destroyed, but not by human power* (Dan. 8:23b-25).

Daniel's ancient words are germane and contemporary. I John 4 teaches that we can test the spirits; either they are from God, or a "master of intrigue" is maneuvering others like pawns for his bene-fit. Charismatic leaders generate appealing agendas, but they're only weaving a tangled web that will ultimately destroy thousands. No matter how powerful a leader appears, God is still in control. We can freely call on Him: *We do not make requests of you because we are righteous, but because of your great mercy* (Dan. 9:18b). Despite the manipulations of deceitful leaders, His mercy is extended to those who call on His name. *He* will bring down the wicked.

Refuse to be a pawn; test the spirits.

He's the Greatest

In 1964 the world was awed when a brash young man from Louisville beat Sonny Liston and won the Heavyweight Championship of the World. As surprising as this upset was, the world was stunned to hear the braggadocios Clay proclaim, "I am the greatest." Ali went on to successfully defend his title nineteen times *and* win an Olympic gold medal; for a while, he truly was the greatest boxer. Clay, Alexander the Great, Kathryn the Great, Ivan the Great; all are mere blips on history's radar screen. Self-proclamations of greatness vanish. Sometimes we refer to celebrities as "the great," as the great Winston Churchill. However outstanding his accomplishments, a man has only a short time span to enjoy celebrity; then he is history. Sooner or later, all the greats will become "the late great."

Daniel and John lived about six hundred years apart, yet they both wrote about the damage fabricated by false prophets. Daniel put man on alert about his imminent destruction unless he returns to God. John gives a comforting promise: *The one who is in you is greater than the one who is in the world* (I John 4:4). False voices constantly bid for our attention and allegiance. Many sound plausible; and as John commands, we must test the spirits. He is greater than any spirit of any false prophet, any false religion, or any false doctrine.

When confronted, test the spirit of darkness against the Word. His word will always reveal truth. With the confidence of the indwelling Spirit, you can confront any opposition squarely and confidently. *He* is truly the greatest of the great. His Kingdom will endure after all nations and principalities and ideologies and isms have blipped off the screen of history. He has no equal. All the greats who have ever lived, ruled, invented, created, or led can't even begin to equal His power, His wisdom, and His ultimate supremacy.

He wins the gold medal.

What is Love?

Since time began, children have confronted adults with questions. When kids are little, we get of lot of "Why?" and "How come?" As kids grow, the questions become more serious: "What is truth?" "Why do bad things happen to good people?" These questions and ones like them tax parents' wisdom as they seek to answer the seeking mind of a child. Perhaps the deepest question for which everyone is seeking an answer is, "What is love?"

What *is* love? We certainly recognize its absence, but do we know love when we see it? Donating a kidney for a family member is an indisputable act of love. If a parent or spouse makes huge sacrifices so that a partner or a child can achieve his or her educational dream, we might call that an act of love. This love thing, though, is all so very nebulous. People do lovely deeds with unlovely motives. When motives are wrong, it will ultimately become evident when anger or resentment erupts. How, then, can we ever define love?

John defines love brilliantly: *This is love; not that we loved God, but that he loved us and sent his Son as an atoning sacrifice for our sins* (I John 4:10). True love demands no "by-lines;" it's satisfied with anonymity. There is nothing that man can do that is worthy of His love; yet He continues reaching out to man in loving kindness. We resent it when love isn't returned; that's human. Breaking news. It's not Christian to resent: *...since God loved us, we also ought to love one another ...if we love one another, God lives in us and his love is made complete in us* (I John 4:11-12). Christ, the sinless Son of God, continues loving man even after His brutal treatment at the hands of man. It's a piece of cake to love when love is returned. With God's love in us, He enables us to love the unlovely and give—especially when love is *not* returned. That is true evidence of love.

Love is a HUGE four letter word.

The Word in Real Time

Spiritual Pulse Taking

Every time I visit the doctor, they take my pulse. This seems a bit odd to me. Isn't pulse an indicator of life? Since I'm there, I must be alive. So, why do they always have to do this? Medically, I'm sure there's a good explanation. Spiritually, though, many people are continually and forever taking their pulse. "Am I still okay with God?" "Did I do or say something that made God unhappy?" This spiritual "pulse-taking" is exhausting and unnecessary.

Spiritual pulse-taking isn't new; it goes back generations. John gives a straightforward explanation: *He who has the Son has life, he who does not have the Son of God does not have life* (I John 5:12). What is he saying? God gave man His testimony through Christ. If you are in Him, then you are alive in Him, and that life is evidenced through your words, deeds, and thoughts. Just as you know each and every day when you awaken that you're alive, so you can know that you are *in* Him: *I write these things to you who believe... so that you may know that you have eternal life* (I John 5:13).

We're human—prone to wander and err. When He is truly in us, we have the will to confess any sin. The liberating truth is not so much that we can go to Him; it's much more than that. We can *know* that we are *in* Him. That knowledge sets the Christian free to cease the constant pulse-taking and get on with the business of living for God. Listen to David: *O Lord, you have searched me, and you know me. You know when I sit and when I rise; you perceive my thoughts from afar... you are familiar with all my ways* (Ps. 139:1-2). God knows your heart and its motives. If there is any necessity for pulse-taking, He will notify your heart. We visit the doctor when we're sick; the rest of the time, we enjoy living. You can be assured in His love. Stop beating yourself up spiritually; enjoy living for Him.

You can know that you know.

I'm So Busy

There's no question; these are busy times. Recently, I've been startled by the unfailing similarity and almost rote response from *everyone* I meet. Almost to a person, when I greet someone, this is their response, "I'm so busy." That continual comeback is haunting me. In our day-to-day encounters, do we ever express the "joy of the Lord?" In the middle of our "busyness," God continually gives us occasions to witness about Him. We are so remiss; our confessions aren't about Him, but rather they are about our busy lives.

The prophet Haggai faced this dilemma. The people were as busy as we seem to be today. They were overwhelmed by life: planting, harvesting, eating, and drinking. But they ignored God's house. God told them to rebuild His house, but they were too busy. He caused winds to deplete their harvests, and yet they didn't catch on. Month after month they labored just to get by. Haggai warned them: *the Almighty declares, 'Because of my house, which remains a ruin, while each of you is busy with his own house"* (Hag. 1:9b). The warning continued; things would only get worse until they paid attention and took care of God's house.

Twice, Haggai reminded them: *"I am with you," declares the Lord* (Hag. 1:13b & 2:4b). "So, what does this ancient history have to do with me?" you ask. A lot. We always seem to be busy, but Christmas is the busiest season of the year. Christ *is* the reason for the season; He *should be* the vertex of everything that happens. Take a lesson from the ancient Hebrews. Everyone is busy; that's a given. Here's what I'm purporting for the rest of the month: Make a conscience effort to eliminate, "I'm so busy" from your conversation. The Christmas season is an open door to testify about Him. In your own unique way let people know that "God is with you."

Never be too busy to acknowledge Him.

Not by Might or by Power

During the Korean War, I enjoyed and appreciated and even felt comfort from displays of might and power. Every Memorial Day and Fourth of July regardless of the weather, soldiers from Ladd Air Force Base came into Fairbanks accompanied by tanks and trucks and large guns and brass bands. The entire town it seemed lined the streets three to four deep as we corporately witnessed and enjoyed their display of strength. In the winter when we experienced black outs and air raids, an entire army was prepared to protect us against a pending invasion of Communists from the West.

Military protection is vital, but the spiritual world is not one of might and power: *"Not by might nor by power, but by my Spirit," says the Lord Almighty* (Zec. 4:6b). True, God is mighty and powerful; but without His spirit, His army is impotent. It is His spirit—His essence—that separates the spiritual world from nations and work places and arenas of human struggle for supremacy. I've heard it said, and I believe it's true: "God's army goes forward on its knees." We can have big buildings with gorgeously groomed campuses. We can have eloquent speakers. We can have commendable social programs that benefit the needy. We can send missionaries to distant lands. But, if we don't have His spirit with us and in the middle of everything, we are doomed to fail.

In greeting Gaius, John refers to God's spirit: *I pray that you may enjoy good health and that all may go well with you, even as your soul is getting along well* (III John 1:2). What a prayer! Good health and comfortable conditions are terrific, but the most important thing is man's soul. That's what John is referencing. It is the Spirit of God living in you that will be victorious—not the might or power of man.

How's your Spirit getting along?

Peace in Abundance

Webster defines *abundance* as "more than enough and amply sufficient." He defines *peace* as "a state of calm and quiet, freedom from disturbing thoughts and emotions, or a state of concord between persons or governments." What if it were possible to combine those two words into one thought: *abundant peace*? How cool would that be? Pretty neat, I would say—but impossible. Your first reaction, I'm sure, is the same as mine: "There's no way in this world environment or in my life that there will ever be peace in abundance. That's a contradiction of terms if I ever heard one."

In a sense, you're correct. Until Jesus returns, the world will be lacking in outward symbols of peace. We'll continually struggle for quiet time; our thoughts and/or our emotions will be disturbed either by our own actions or because of the deeds of others. Conflict between governments is biblical: "there will be wars and rumors of wars." Yet, we can have inward peace in abundance. Jude reminds us, *Mercy, peace and love be yours in abundance* (Jude 1: 2). In light of world conditions, where is Jude coming from? That's easy. Jude is talking about our spirit—the condition of our soul. You can have peace in the middle of a storm tossed life; you can love those who don't love you; and you can have mercy on those who deserve retribution. How? Through the indwelling power of the Holy Spirit.

Jude's closing prayer is one of the most beautiful ever written and so very apropos for today: *To him who is able to keep you from falling and to present you before his glorious presence without fault and with great joy— to the only God our Savior be glory, majesty, power, and authority, through Jesus Christ our Lord, before all ages, now and forevermore!* Abundant peace and everlasting joy.

Amen, Jude!

The Alpha and the Omega

Common terminology sometimes expresses totality: the *alpha* and the *omega*, the first and the last, "a" through "z." Biblically we go from Adam to John, from the start to the stop, the beginning and the end. All these expressions indicate a quality of "all inclusiveness." Nothing is omitted and everything is included. When it's all said and done, it's over. There is nothing to be added, nothing to be subtracted; it's complete.

Prophets predicted the coming Messiah, the Savior of the world: *See, your king comes to you, righteous and having salvation, gentle and riding on a donkey...* (Zec. 9:9b). We know through study of the Word that Zechariah's prophesy and dozens of similar ones came to pass. When Jesus came, He at last became the all inclusive sacrifice for man's sin. No sin and no one were omitted; everyone was included. Through Him, we all have free access to salvation and everlasting life. Years after the prophet Zechariah, John talks about God's all inclusive nature in the introduction to the revelation: *"I am the Alpha and the Omega," says the Lord God, "who is, and who was, and who is to come, the Almighty,"* (Rev. 1:9). Study closely: It's a quote. God, Himself, is describing His all inclusive nature. John isn't saying it; he's only reporting.

It's the Christmas season—the busiest and the most enjoyable time of the entire year. Here's a test: Can you put Him first and last during this season? In the middle of the shopping and the decorating and the parties and the cooking and the traveling, is it possible to stop and remember what this season is all about? He has always been, is today, and will always be the author and finisher of this world and of our salvation. Throughout this season, I challenge you to put first things first. He is still the *Alpha* and the *Omega*.

He's the reason for the season.

A Word with a Bark on It

Mother raised my brothers and me on numerous terse and pithy colloquial sayings. Regularly, we heard that "people who live in glass houses shouldn't throw stones;" "the kettle shouldn't call the pot black;" and "pretty is as pretty does." I got those, but Mother had one saying that I never fully comprehended, yet I understood her. When she grew utterly exasperated and wanted to make herself emphatically understood, Mother would say, "That's a word with a bark on it." I never knew if she was talking about a dog or a tree, but whenever she said those words, I knew she meant business. There was no room for compromise or negotiation; Mother was finished with the discussion. Obedience was prudent.

John's letters to the seven churches are exceedingly relevant today. Each letter was targeted to the uniqueness of the church, either to warnings about congregational needs or commendation on a job well done. He commended the Ephesians on their hard work and perseverance, yet he admonished them for forsaking their 'first love." To the Smyrnans he acknowledged their earthly poverty and affliction, yet he called them rich. He encouraged them not to fear future suffering; for in the divine scheme of things, it would only last ten days—a short time. He reminded the Pergamum Church that he was aware of the wicked area where they lived. Yet, he encouraged them to stay true to God. Some were still worshipping Balaam, and John reprimanded them for this idolatrous compromise with the world.

In closing each of his letters to these churches, John reiterates the same colloquial saying: *He who has an ear, let him hear what the Spirit says to the churches* (Rev. 2:7, 11, & 17). Reminiscent of my childhood, I think John is saying, "That's a word with a bark on it." We get it, and it's relevant today.

Heed the word; He's serious.

Alive, but Dying

Visiting *Disneyland* or *Disney World* is an American experience. Most of us have been there several times; we have favorite attractions: perhaps, *It's a Small World* or *Pirates of the Caribbean*, for example. The *Hall of Presidents* in Florida is one of my favorites. From one side of the stage to the other, presidents appear—each of them as realistic as the last. They stand, gesture, and speak. In another era, people might have thought them to be alive. Not today. They are merely aberrations and animated characters created purely for our entertainment. They appear alive, but they're dead.

Dead things—even people—are useless. Sure, a person's reputation and contributions can live after him or her, but there's nothing new that one can contribute beyond death. At death, we enter a completely different world. Life, then, is for the living and demands the living to sustain it. John addresses churches that "appear alive" but are actually dead—or nearly so: *I know your deeds; you have a reputation of being alive, but you are dead. Wake up! Strengthen what remains and is about to die* (Rev. 3:1b).

Have you seen a church that has a resemblance to life, but is rapidly dying? They have programs, promotions, and services, but there's a death knell in it all. Vitality and energy and passion have vanished; people endure habitual motions and rituals—almost as if the Church were attached to a spiritual ventilator. Nothing winsome or attractive is remaining. People have an aversion to death, even dying churches. The spirit of death renders them uninviting. People can't put a finger on it; but they don't want to be a part of it either. To paraphrase John, "Wake up, Church, before you gasp your last breath."

Is your church alive, or just an animated replica?

Who Knows?

There's much conjecture regarding the demise of Czar Nicholas Romanoff. We know that the czar and his wife and daughters and their son, Alexander, were executed in the Revolution—or at least that's what we think we know. Since the end of World War II, though, there have been rumors that one daughter—Anastasia— survived the brutal slaughter. Several have claimed to be she, and many believe these claims. Regardless, the entire family with its influence and wealth were obliterated. The fact that the children were with the czar the day he was executed insured their death.

Esther was in a similar situation. Uncle Mordecai introduced her to King Xerxes; she caught the king's eye and ultimately became his queen. Enter Haman. His story of jealously and resentment is reminiscent of so many stories; he wanted Mordecai dead. "Why settle for just *one* Jew," he reasoned, "when I can negotiate the death of *all* the Jews at once." And so, Haman set in motion his own ultimate demise. He contrived a plan whereby all Jews would be mandated to bow and worship the King—including Queen Esther.

Mordecai appealed to Esther's national pride; her people were more important that her personal comfort: *Do not think that because you are in the king's house you alone of all the Jews will escape... Who knows but that you have come to royal position for such a time as this* (Est. 4: 12 & 14). She understood her place in this divine tragedy; first and foremost, Esther was a Jew. In world class fashion she promised to appeal to the king: *And if I perish, I perish.* Esther recognized her insignificance in light of the potential destruction of her people, and she loyally took a stand when it could have cost her life. Each day provides this same possibility. Will you speak up regardless of potential personal danger or will you keep silent?

Are you prepared for "such a time as this?"

13

High Noon

Gary Cooper and Grace Kelly's classic rendezvous with destiny in the award winning film, *High Noon*, is etched in the memories of movie buffs. Even today, on any given Saturday afternoon, you might stumble across Cooper strolling down the streets of town to the ticking of the clock. Some things, it seems, are destined to happen—it's just a matter of time as to when they will occur.

Haman's crafty scheme to destroy the Jews was foiled, and he was hanged at high noon on the gallows he himself erected to hang Mordecai. The Jewish population was spared. Because of his love for Queen Esther, King Xerxes presented her all of Haman's estate. Esther wanted more; she implored the king to strike all of Haman's wicked decrees against the Jews and free them from the tyranny he set in motion. Mordecai wrote the ruling. With the seal of the king's ring, word was dispatched to all Jewish cities, far and wide: They had the right to assemble, defend themselves, and annihilate any forces coming against them. Certainly reason to rejoice!

A *pur*, or a lot, was cast to decide the day of the proclamation: *The day appointed for the Jews to do this... was the thirteenth day of the twelfth month* (Est. 8:12). Ever since, *Purim* has been celebrated by Jews each Dec. 13—today! *For the Jews it was a time of happiness and joy, gladness, and honor* (Est. 8:16). Because a young Hebrew woman had the courage to take a stand, a potentially catastrophic situation became a yearly day of joy and gladness for all the Jews.

Has God delivered you or your family from inevitable destruction when you took a stand against overwhelming odds? Your experience demands a *Purim* remembrance. Like Cooper in the classic movie, you can celebrate your spiritual rendezvous with destiny.

Celebrate your own "Purim."

Handel and the Lamb

The Christmas season is never complete for me without at least one opportunity to experience Handel's magnificent oratorio, *The Messiah*. Whether I participate by singing in it, attend a performance given by a choir, or merely hear the *Hallelujah Chorus*, *The Messiah* always completes and crowns the season. Handel's majestic and stirring rendition of the prophetic scripture lends dignity to all the tinsel and glitz and noise of the year's busiest season. One of my favorite numbers is *Worthy is the Lamb*. Taken directly from scripture, its words, coupled with Handel's music, waft the rapt listener to heavenly realms of splendor.

John's vision revealed a great sealed scroll descending from heaven, but no one in heaven or earth was "worthy" to unseal the scroll and reveal it to man. The vision continued: *Then I saw a Lamb, looking as if it had been slain, standing in the center of the throne...* (Rev. 5:6). The Lamb took the scroll from *him who sat on the throne*. When the Lamb held the scroll, all the creatures and elders bowed down before it. In an instant, they recognized "the Lamb" as the Son of God—the *only* one "worthy" to unseal and read the scroll. In harmonious chorus, they loudly sang:

> *Worthy is the Lamb, who was slain,*
> *To receive power and wealth and wisdom and strength.*
> *And honor and glory and praise!* (Rev. 5:12).

Led by this heavenly chorus, all the creatures in heaven and earth swelled their voices in praise. Sing a Christmas carol to Him:

> *To him who sits on the throne and to the Lamb be praise*
> *and honor and glory and power, for ever and ever!* (Rev. 5:13b).

Worthy is the Lamb!

White Elephants for God

White elephants are useless items that one person pawns off on another; they aren't purchased at luxury stores. Holiday white elephant exchanges can be a hoot. Several times I've been involved with a group in which year after year a specific white elephant gift appears and reappears at gift exchanges. What fun we have camouflaging a useless trinket in beautiful wrapping and presenting it as though it were something special. The entire group guffaws when the unknowing culprit opens a worthless box of nut shells, or a natty old crocheted toilet paper wrapper. "Ha, ha," the joke's on you.

Giving gifts of substandard quality are not a joke to God; in fact, He would rather not have them at all. When His people were trying to pawn off on God blind and crippled animals as sacrifices, Malachi warned against these "blemished sacrifices." He used the knowledge that God recognizes taxes as well as tithes and offerings to scold the people: *Try offering them* (blemished sacrifices) *to your governor! Would he be pleased with you? Would he accept you (Mal. 1:8b)*? That's as ludicrous as an American, for example, sending the government an old broken down car on April 15. Not only would it be rejected, but taxes would still be due—along with a sizable fine.

Malachi called this behavior robbery: *How do we rob you? In tithes and offerings… Bring the whole tithe into the storehouse, that there may be food in my house. Test me in this…* (Mal. 3:10). This is the *only* Bible directive to "test Him." And what is the result of this testing? It's a pretty neat promise: *See if I will not throw open the floodgates of heaven and pour out so much blessing that you will not have room enough for it* (Mal. 3:11). We are ending another calendar year. Are you planning for next year to be better than this last one? Here's a helpful hint: Leave your white elephants at the Christmas party.

…and "test" the Lord!

Artaban and Malachi

Henry van Dyke's book, *The Other Wise Man*, is a prerequisite for my holiday season. Since I was eleven, I have read it in its entirety each December, and often I've presented it publicly. During a hectic season, its stirring message redirects me to the "reason for the season." Artaban, the hapless hero, makes many attempts to meet the Magi, but with repeated distraction. He *never* finds them—or the baby Jesus. On the desert, compassion overtakes him when he aids a beggar. In Bethlehem, he's hindered when he protects a baby from execution at the hands of Herod. His gifts for God were all forced into the service of man. Continual delays short-circuited his search of the King: "though he found none to worship, he found many to help." One gift—a pearl—he steadfastly saved for the King.

Malachi continues his discourse about our gifts to God. He compares God to a refiner's fire and a launderer's soap; in other words, our gifts to Him must come from "pure and clean" hearts: *Then the Lord will have men who will bring offerings in righteousness and the offerings… will be acceptable to the Lord* (Mal. 3:4). Artaban longed for his gifts to be accepted, yet he *never* found the King.

At Passover, Artaban wearily came to Jerusalem. A commotion and cries attracted him: *"The King of the Jews."* How strangely those words fell on his tired heart. A young girl being sold as a slave was forced in front of him. On an impulse, Artaban paid her ransom with his pearl. He had no more gifts to offer the king. Then it occurred; a brick fell from nearby, wounding him. As Artaban lay dying, a man carrying a cross was shoved past him. This man was uniquely different from anyone Artaban had ever met. His eyes reflected pain, innocence, and abuse. Their eyes met; Artaban knew Him. His life was pure; his gifts were accepted. Artaban had found the King.

Will your gifts be accepted this season?

A New Christmas Carol

Each year someone reinvents the Christmas carol or the holiday tune. In 1949 it was *All I Want for Christmas is My Two Front Teeth.* I remember that specifically because I was minus my two front teeth that year; everyone thought it was real cute to sing that song to me. Over the years, "new" tunes have become a part of each new season: *White Christmas, Frosty the Snowman, Silver Bells, a Tennessee Christmas.* It's really the old Christmas carols, though, that unite our hearts: *Silent Night, O Come All Ye Faithful, Joy to the World, O Little Town of Bethlehem.* Since they are consistently the same year after year, these carols conjure memories of people and Christmases long gone. In a word, they've become sentimental.

Sometimes, a "new" Christmas song is refreshing. Yes, we love the old tunes—but give us something new. The Psalmist David was deeply stirred by God's protection and magnificence: *I will sing a new song to you, O God; ...I will make music to you* (Psa. 144:9). He sang to God for victory and relief. His song appeals for deliverance from his enemies and the deceitful people in his life. The answer to his prayer is revealed in a portion of the verse of his song:

Then our sons in their youth will be like well-nurtured plants, and our daughters will be like pillars carved to adorn a palace.
Our barns will be filled with every kind of provision (Psa. 144:12-13).

It is Christmas again, and we're busy shopping for gifts for our sons and daughters; we look for items that will "adorn" our homes; our cupboards overflow with provisions for the season. What about a new song? During this season, do you have a carol in your heart that's aching to be set free? Christmas isn't all about gifts and it's not all about decorations; and it's not all about fancy food.

Sing a new song about Jesus.

Want Butter? Churn the Milk!

A farm girl I'm not. My "big" farm experience consists of two weeks at Aunt Roxie's ranch in West Texas. We were home from Alaska, and Mother and Dad left us kids there while they attended business. What a contrast to Alaska. In Alaska a horse or a cow was a rarity. At the ranch there were many animals—horses, cows, pigs, and chickens. There was a horse trough with horseflies and cow licks; there was an out house and a storm cellar; there was a large barn and acres of land. The ranch was as primitive in its way as Alaska was in its. They had no running water, electricity was intermittent. It was remote—miles from Wheeler, a town of 1,200.

I have many memories of my farm experience; one of the most indelible was the churn. I had never seen anything like it. Aunt Roxie poured warm, whole milk into the separator. After the thick cream came to the top, she transferred it to the churn. I watched with eyes of wonder as she diligently turned and cranked the handle of that old churn. Given enough time, a miracle occurred; white milk "suddenly" became rich yellow butter.

Solomon wisely taught in short little parables. Here's a dilly: *If you have played the fool and exalted yourself, or if you have planned evil, clap your hand over your mouth! For as churning the milk produces butter, and as twisting the nose produces blood, so stirring up anger produces strife* (Pro. 30:32-33). It's as clear as churning white milk into yellow butter. It may take some time, but sooner or later your actions and your words will return to haunt or bless you. Solomon's warning is implied; stop doing wrong before it's too late. If not, there will come a time when it will be too late, and the inevitable will happen. You choose.

You produce what you set in motion.

Seventh Chair Trumpet

Our son is a good trumpeter. We bought a horn at a garage sale just to see if he'd like it. Did he *like* it? He had a natural talent; he *loved* it. His initial horn was exchanged for a beginner's trumpet, which was ultimately replaced by an expensive silver trumpet. He was good; he deserved the best. Since he was good, every band or orchestra he was in awarded him the first chair position. First chair is a place of honor and respect; you don't get it or keep it unless you are good. But first chair has responsibilities; others are always "challenging" to get it. You must sustain excellence to keep first chair.

Everyone loves a good trumpeter; there's something regal and commanding about the trumpet. In his Revelation, John sees seven different trumpeters—each with a message of warning about end times. Some of the visions appear convoluted and complicated, but there's a message in each of them. And then, the seventh trumpet blasts through clearly and understandably:

> The kingdom of the world has become
> The kingdom of our Lord and of his Christ,
> And he will reign for ever and ever (Rev. 11:15b).

Do you hear the clear tones of the message? Ultimately, everything we think we control will be out of our hands. He'll be in charge. Do you hear it now? *He will reign for ever and ever.* There are no time restraints; John is foretelling eternity. One of these days, He will "challenge" all the authorities of the world—and win. He will be *the* First Chair. This world will be over, and He'll be in charge for ever and ever. And He is so worthy. The Psalmist summarizes all our hearts in this song; *Great is the Lord and most worthy of praise, his greatness no one can fathom* (Psa. 145: 3).

He's the ultimate "First Chair."

Set Free by a Banker

Our church in San Diego was a little building on a corner. When we arrived in 1971, my husband found three sets of blue prints. Three previous pastors had visions of building, but no one got the job done. Quickly, attendance grew; unless we built, growth would be stymied. The answer was simple: Build. Everyone was for it; the congregation was excited; my young husband was eager to begin.

Starting wasn't as easy at it sounded. We needed funds. "I'll get a loan, and then we'll build," David thought. He had a lot to learn. Bank after bank turned him down—flat. Some even chuckled at this naïve young man asking for a large amount of money with no provable evidence of ability to repay. Finally, a banker in one of the large San Diego banks said, "Bring me a prospectus, and then we'll talk." A prospectus? David didn't have a clue. The bank wanted a dossier detailing net worth, annual giving, denominational backing and debtor track record; in other words, could we repay the loan? David put together a very nice prospectus—and we got the loan.

God instructed Ezra to rebuild the temple. That was clear, yet kings and circumstances opposed him. Obstacles appeared repeatedly. Just when he thought he was set to begin, there was another "review" of records. It seemed like the job would never get started—much less finished. At last, King Darius reviewed all the records. These were God's people, and he had a lot to fear by continuing to block this divine project: *I Darius have decreed it. Let it be carried out with diligence* (Ezra 6:12b). The temple rebuilding began: *The king had granted him everything he asked, for the hand of the Lord his God was on him* (Ezra 7:6). Once you have your "ducks in a row," there is nothing that can impede God's progress. People in authority will come to your defense in a way that will surprise you and honor God.

Listen to your banker's advice.

Letters to Santa

Children love Santa, the benevolent man in red who knows when they're "naughty and nice." In December kids of all ages put on their best behavior. If they behave well, Santa will come. Everything focuses on one day—December 25—when kids rush to the tree to see if Santa came. Parents—the real Santa Clauses—do anything in their power to delight and please their kids. Christmas is a time for children and joy and laughter. It goes both ways; kids are delighted, but parents are equally elated to see the kids happy.

God is certainly not our heavenly Santa Claus, but He sure does delight in making his children happy. In Psalm 145 the psalmist defines God in terms befitting the most gracious and loving parents:

The Lord is faithful to all his promises and loving to all he has made.
If a parent promises; he does everything he can to fulfill his word.
So it is with God.
The Lord is righteous in all his ways and loving toward all he has made.
Loving parents make every effort to be fair with their kids.
So it is with God.
He fulfills the desires of those who fear him.
Loving parents *want* to fill their kids' Christmas wish list.
So it is with God.
The Lord watches over all who love him.
Parents innately want to protect kids from harm and danger.
So it is with God.

If the kids haven't written Santa yet, now's the day. There aren't many days left. If you haven't told God lately what you need or how much you love Him, now's the day. There aren't many days left.

Post a letter to God

Three Magi and Three Angels

Y ou know the story of the magi from the East—how they followed the Super Nova from afar, bringing lavish gifts to the baby King. Herod, himself, invited them to be his palace guests; then he wined, dined, and plied them with questions about this baby. They exhibited superior wisdom when they secretly left Jerusalem without forwarding information to Herod. They worshipped the baby, presented their gifts, and slipped silently into the pages of history.

John's Revelation is intriguing and mind-boggling predictions of last days and end times. For generations theologians and eschatologists have postulated about the meaning of it; hundreds of books have been written about it; thousands of sermons have been given. There's nothing new that anyone—especially me—would hope or even try to add to these volumes. And yet... well, here goes...

In Revelation 14, John saw three angels: The first angel invokes man and nature to worship God, their creator. The second angel heralds the news that Babylon has fallen. The third angel warns against participation *in* and worship *of* the beast—the representation of Satan's presence on the earth. Then, a voice heralds from heaven: *Blessed are the dead who die in the Lord from now on. ...they will rest from their labor, for their deeds will follow them* (Rev. 14:13).

At Christmas we remember the "deeds" of the Magi—great men who truly worshipped from their hearts. The three angels remind us that the end times will be dire—and soon. Yet, there is hope for those who "die in the Lord." When a Christian "dies in the Lord," his sincere wish is that his gifts will be accepted. The example of the Magi gives us hope and comfort during this season of giving. Giving isn't about a season; it's about a life style.

Your gifts can be acceptable.

Thank You Notes to God

During this season, we give gifts to nearly everyone in our lives: family, neighbors, friends, beauticians, in-laws, our pastor; the list goes on an on. Yearly, the list grows interminably longer. When we receive a gift, we feel obligated to emulate the kindness and give a gift in return. "Tag gift giving" can be frustrating; just when we think our Christmas shopping is completed, someone else gives us a gift, and we're at "it" again. Back to the mall one more time.

One of the more vanishing gentilities is that of sending thank you notes. People just don't write notes like they did years ago, but thank yous are still important. Not just at Christmas, but anytime anyone gives you a gift, hosts you for a meal, or extends an act of kindness, a thank you note is so appreciated. The small amount of time spent is multiplied numerous times over by the grateful heart of the receiver. "What I did mattered," they reason; "it was appreciated."

Have you ever received a gift that "blew you away?" You didn't deserve it; you didn't earn it. Someone loved you enough to sacrifice and give you an amazing and awesome gift. You're speechless. God's gifts are far greater and more overwhelming than any gift that any man ever gave to another. Have you sent a thank you note to God for His continual and abundant blessings, gifts, and kindnesses?

The Psalmist begins and ends his beautiful "thank you" with identical words: *I will praise the Lord all my life; I will sing praise to my God as long as I live. He upholds the cause of the oppressed and gives food to the hungry. The Lord sets prisoners free, the Lord gives sight to the blind, the Lord lifts up those who are bowed down, the Lord loves the righteous. The Lord watches over the alien and sustains the fatherless and the widow... Praise the Lord* (Psa. 146).

Send a Christmas "thank you" note to God.

Santa is Coming to Town

When our children were small and we lived in San Diego, one Christmas Eve a friend surprised us. He dressed up like Santa Claus and dropped by to see if the kids had been "naughty or nice." Our son was about seven and playfully went along with the ruse; something was in it for him. Our daughter was a different story; she believed! After all, if Santa came to your front door early in the evening to see if you had been good, it was "a given" that he would return before the night was over. A very excited little girl slept fitfully, listening for reindeer hoof sounds on the roof.

During that year we moved to El Paso. It was Christmas again; no one thought much about Santa's California visit. But, surprise of all surprises, a new friend who knew nothing about the Christmas Eve events the year prior, dropped by—in full Santa Claus regalia. That did it. Our daughter was a card-carrying Santa Claus believer almost until she was a teenager. He found her in San Diego, and he found her in El Paso. Santa was real! There was no denying it.

In his Revelation John predicts about Christ's return: *Behold, I come like a thief! Blessed is he who stays awake...* (Rev. 16:15). We don't know *when*, and we aren't certain *how*, but one of these days, this world will be finished. The trumpet will sound, the skies will split, and the Son of Man will return to "catch His bride away." Children don't know what time during Christmas Eve that Santa will come, but they know he's coming. Shoes are kept by the bed so they can run to the tree at the first sounds of his reindeer on the roof. Sleep is fitful because they don't want to miss the big arrival. We, too, are to always be ready for His return. We don't know *when*, and we aren't sure *how*, but we know that He's coming—and it could be anytime soon. Be prepared and watchful.

Jesus is returning to town.

The Word in Real Time

A Christmas Cease-Fire

Warring and fighting have been a part of world history since biblical days. Man simply must fight his battles with fists and weapons. There is, though, an uncanny aberration that happens during wars: On Christmas days, opposing sides call a twenty-four hour "Christmas Cease-Fire." Weapons are laid down; makeshift feasts are prepared; enemies cross "no man's land" and share jokes and laughter. Even in the midst of heated world conflict, enemies stop on Christmas and acknowledge the "Prince of Peace."

One day is all too brief, and soon the clock strikes twelve, concluding this magical day dropped into the middle of horror and bloodshed. Weapons are re-shouldered; enemies glare across battlefields at one another once again; the battle commences where it left off just a brief twenty-four hours earlier. There is a huge difference, though, between a cease-fire and a truce. A cease-fire is temporary; a truce is final—at least for *that* war. When a truce is signed, enemies lay down their weapons and shake hands, reparations are made, and opposing sides attempt to heal their differences with civility. The psalmist speaks of a truce: *He grants peace to your borders and satisfies you with the finest wheat* (Psa. 147: 14).

Today is Christmas; the most beautiful day in the year. Nearly everyone declares a "relational cease fire" on Christmas day. We make conscious efforts to express love; it is abundant. For one day, we drop petty differences. We avoid family arguments and concentrate on children and shared memories. What about today? Is a cease-fire good enough? I suggest not. You can make this Christmas different in your family and relationships: Declare a truce. "Let there be peace on earth, and let it begin with me."

Dona Nobis Pachem

Strengthen My Hands

Despite the continual intimidation of Sanballet, Tobiah, and their cronies, Nehemiah successfully completed repairing the wall. He didn't do this alone—not at all. The men of Israel rallied, and each one completed the part nearest his own home. It was an ingenious construction tactic that worked regardless of all the efforts made to interrupt or stop it. Sanballet and his men wouldn't let up: *They were trying to frighten us thinking, "Their hands will get too weak for the work, and it will not be completed." I prayed, "Now strengthen my hands* (Neh. 6: 9).*"* It's predictable: When you begin a task for God—either alone or corporately—the enemy will try anything and everything to stop you. When legal maneuvers fail, they will resort to intimidation. *He had been hired to intimidate me… and then they would give me a bad name to discredit me* (Neh 6:13).

If the task is from the Lord, He will make a way for its completion; nothing will ultimately stand in the way. Nehemiah's "strengthen my hands" prayer was answered in a remarkable way, and the wall was repaired in record time—fifty two days—a phenomenal feat. Everyone was forced to acknowledge it; the completed wall was its own testimony: *All the surrounding nations were afraid and lost their self-confidence, because they realized that this work had been done with the help of our God* (Neh. 6:16).

What job has God asked you to do? What has He asked you to repair? You can bet your bottom dollar (Oops!) that when you begin a project that's directed by God, opposition and intimidation will come your way with ever increasing intensity. Remember Nehemiah. Refuse to be intimidated; God can strengthen your hands. With His help, you can accomplish any task that He divines.

Where you're weak; He is strong.

Hallelujah! Amen!

Sometimes one word says it all: Eureka! Terrific! Amazing! Awesome! Hallelujah! Amen! You can talk until your blue in the face, but from time to time, one word is sufficient. Throughout John's revelation, he predicts the end times and Christ's return. A lot of the revelation is confusing, but if you labor through it, it is fascinating—and it makes some sense. In conclusion, John talks about the twenty-four elders and the living creatures that fall down and worship God. In one voice they cried, "Amen, Hallelujah!" (Rev. 19:4b). After the tribulation and destruction of the world, that seems to say it all. Yet, John has more:

"Hallelujah! For our Lord God Almighty reigns
Let us rejoice and be glad and give him glory!
For the wedding of the Lamb has come,
And his bride has made herself ready (Rev. 19:6b-8)."

One day this life and the world will be finished. No one knows when but John explicitly tells us how. Those who survive and those who have died in Christ will have reason to rejoice, *Blessed are those who are invited to the wedding supper of the Lamb... These are the true words of God* (Rev. 19:9). A wedding is a time for celebration in which we eat together and rejoice in the splendor of the day and the newly established union. No earthly experience can compare to the wedding supper of the Lamb or the amazing union of God with His chosen few—those that have been washed in the blood of the Lamb. My heart swells with the classic anthem:

**How 'oft in holy converse with Christ the Lord, alone
I seem to hear the millions that sing around the song.
Hallelujah, Amen! Hallelujah, Amen!**

Amen! Amen!

Nehemiah 9:1-37
Revelation 19:11-21
Psalm 148:7-14

He is Just!

There is something inherent in each of us that can bear anything if we think it is fair or just. Unfortunately, much in life isn't fair or just. We suffer through events and circumstances over which we have no control. A drunk driver crosses a median and crashes head-on into us or a loved one, and we suffer because of someone else's sin. Terrorists crash a plane into the World Trade Center, and the world suffers because of a senseless inexplicable deed. Thorns in the flesh cause us to suffer, yet they keep us humbly dependent on Him.

These things and many more like them all seem so unfair and uninvited. What in the world is God trying to teach us? Is He truly a just God? The truth, my Christian friend, is that unless we experience suffering, we have no testimony. There is no "invisible shield" that protects us against harm and danger just because we claim His name and faithfully serve Him. Suffering provides us impetus for self-review and opportunities to totally rely and depend on Him.

What about the things that cause us to suffer over which we *do* have control? We make errors in judgment; we refuse to regard the filters of the past that define our mistakes; we suffer from disciplines that God enacts upon us in His endeavors to get us to return to Him. So, the question remains, "Is God just?" Nehemiah has a great answer to this question: *In all that has happened to us, you have been just; you have acted faithfully, while we did wrong* (Neh. 9:33). Wrong or right, God is just. Just as a good earthly parent disciplines a recalcitrant child, God disciplines those He loves when they do wrong. Yet, He is always fair, always forgiving, always faithful, and always loving. As painful as it may seem to you and me at times, the truth remains…

He is always just.

Nehemiah 9:38-11:21
Revelation 20
Psalm 149:1-9

It's in the Book

Igloos are an anomaly. As glamorous as they appear in books, Eskimos don't live in ice houses. Hunters and fisherman use them as temporary shelters, but they are not permanent dwellings. When our family returned from Alaska, we traveled from place to place talking about our far north territory. At one presentation a man asked my father about igloos. When Dad gave the correct explanation, the inquirer challenged his authority: "I *know* that Eskimos live in igloos; it's in my son's textbook." My father's response was classic: "Sir, it's in my son's textbook in Alaska also, but it still isn't true." Somehow if it's in writing, we tend to believe it's true.

God has a book called the Book of Life. In it He has kept record of man's deeds. Every word of it is true. It's His biography of each man's life. One of the best sources of documentation is "first hand" accounts. We call this eye-witness testimony. God has been around since creation and nothing has missed His omniscient eye. He has seen and observed every deed—good or bad—perpetrated by every person ever born. When we confess our sins, He writes that in the book and erases the record of our evil past. One day the Book of Life will be opened, and everyone will be judged: *Another book was opened, which is the book of life. The dead were judged according to what they had done as recorded in the book* (Rev. 20:12b).

This declaration doesn't frighten the true believer. I John 1:9 is still in "the book," *If we confess our sins, he is faithful and just and will forgive us our sins and purify us from all unrighteousness.* To opt to disregard this verse is to propagate a theological error. We cannot suffer over confessed sins that God has forgiven and forgotten. When you confess your sins, He blots out your wicked past; He turns a page in the Book of Life, and "all things become new."

Is your name in "the book?"

Everything New—Again

There's something exhilarating about "new." Little children love a new pair of shoes—they can run faster and jump higher. We *all* love new things: A shiny new car is something to strut about as we demonstrate its "bells and whistles" to friends. A new house lends occasion to discard old furniture and redecorate with all new accompaniments. And, of course, a new baby is the best of all. He or she is a brand new life with all the promise of a bright future.

A year ago, we began this book with a devotional titled "Everything New!" Another year has come and gone; we're at the threshold of a new year. Perhaps this year brought joy and accomplishment beyond your wildest imagination. Maybe you bought a new car or a new house or had a new baby or grand child. Possibly, you completed an advanced degree and began a long sought career path. Maybe you received a promotion or a new job or an unexpected recognition. This has been a good year for you.

Some of you are reading this right now and thinking, "That surely doesn't define my year. This year has been more than difficult for me and my family; we've nearly gone under several times. There were disappointments, natural disasters, death visited our family unexpectedly, and I lost my job." Regardless of which of these explanations defines your year, God has been in them both.

This past year isn't the end! One of these days, He is going to make everything new—forever! *"Now the dwelling of God is with men, and he will live with them. He will wipe every tear from their eyes. There will be no more death or mourning or crying or pain, for the old order of things has passed away." He who was seated on the throne said, "I am making everything new!"* (Rev. 21:3b-5)

That's the best "news" ever.

Anticipation

Expectation charges us with excitement. Just a week ago kids were anxiously anticipating the arrival of Santa. Adults anticipate a phone call that will confirm a new job or the approval of a long awaited home loan. When our kids were still home, they were always anticipating the next holiday. As soon as Christmas was over, for example, they wanted to know what we were doing for President's day. Expecting and anticipating the future gives us a goal—something to live for. It's healthy to have expectations and anticipations; they make the mundane daily events bearable.

Christians have a hope of a home with Him forever. Heaven isn't "wishful" thinking; it's real. The longer we endure life's trials and tribulations, the more we anticipate heaven and long for it to come soon. John paints beautiful word pictures about heaven: *Then the angel showed me the river of the water of life, as clear as crystal, flowing from the throne of God and of the Lamb* ... (Rev. 22:1). In addition to his word pictures, John offers some incredible promises: *There will be no more night… for the Lord Give will give them light* (Rev. 22:5). Listen to the Apostle Paul: *The city does not need the sun or the moon to shine on it, for the glory of God gives it light, and the Lamb is its lamp* (Rom. 21:23).

Anticipation? I should say; I'm making plans for heaven, and I'm making every possible effort to take one or two along with me. I hope to see you there. *The Spirit and the bride say, "Come! Whoever is thirsty, let him come; and whoever wishes, let him take the free gift of the water of life* (Rev. 22: 17). A new year begins tonight. Each New Year presents renewed hopes and anticipations. *"Behold, I am coming soon! My reward is with me, and I will give to everyone according to what he has done* (Rev. 22:12).

Anticipate heaven—it's worth the wait!

Reflections on the Word...

Vessel Ministries II Corinthians 4:7

☐ Please send me additional information about
Kathy Slamp's speaking and tape ministry.

My name is _____

Address _____

City/State/Zip _____

Phone _____

Email _____

• • • • • • • • • •

☐ I am interested in information about Kathy's other
publications. Please send me information regarding:

 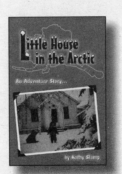 

Walking Through Life...

You Might Be A Pastor's Wife If...

Little House in the Arctic

Reflection Profiles (a Bible study series)

Mastering Women's Ministries (women's ministry manual/audio tapes)

Kathy Slamp – *Vessel Ministries*
% 1900 N. 175th St. • Shoreline, WA 98133
(206) 542-2111 • Web site: vesselministries.com

Quotations and References...

Henrietta Blair, p. 391
Richard Carpenter, p. 268
Mapes Dodge, p. 344
John Donne, p. 325
William A. Dromgoole, p. 223
Alexander Dumas, p. 250 & p. 386
Nelson Eddy, p 308
Robert Frost, p 219
Bill Gaither, p.32
William Golding, p. 73
Oscar Hammerstein II, p. 112
George Handel, p. 378
Brewster Higley, p. 252
Oliver Wendell Holmes, p. 205 & p. 168
Virginia Hudson, p. 222
Victor Hugo, p. 116
Earl Lee, p. 92
Robert Louis May, p. 172
McGuffey Reader, p. 19
Rich Mullins, p. 106
Edna St. Vincent Millay, p. 298
Ira Sankey, p. 286
Robert Service, p. 92
Henry Van Dyke, p. 27 & p. 380
Rick Warren, p. 203

Acknowledgments...

Michael Coldren, back cover photo
Lynn Baskerville, cover design and technical support